Bernard Boyd

# THE CRISIS

# IN THE

# UNIVERSITY

SIR WALTER MOBERLY

# THE
# CRISIS
## IN THE
# UNIVERSITY

SCM PRESS LTD
56 BLOOMSBURY STREET LONDON

PUBLISHED FOR THE
CHRISTIAN FRONTIER COUNCIL

First published April 1949
Second Impression June 1949
Third Impression November 1949

Distributed in Canada by our exclusive agents
The Macmillan Company of Canada Ltd.,
70 Bond Street, Toronto.

Printed in Great Britain by Bristol Typesetting Company
Bristol and London

# PREFACE

'No one,' wrote Thomas Arnold, 'ought to meddle with the universities, who does not know them well and love them well.' This principle should be regarded as axiomatic. But academic patriotism, however devoted and well-informed, does not exclude, but rather impels, a clear recognition and searching diagnosis of ailments. This book is the product of a conviction that much ails universities to-day, that what is wrong with them is closely connected with what is wrong with the whole world; and that the chief seat of the malady is to be found in the underlying assumptions, largely unconscious, by which their life and work are determined. The older universities grew up in a world very unlike our own. Their traditional assumptions are, to some extent, outdated and, in practice, discarded. But there is no agreed answer to the question how far this process should go and what alternative assumptions should take the place of the old. Concerning the *raison d'être* of universities, and the standards to which they should pay allegiance and by which their policies must ultimately be judged, there is some discord and a great deal of vagueness.

Yet, during the last ten years, these questions have been discussed in a number of books and from a number of angles. 'Mr. Bruce Truscot,' in particular, has vigorously stimulated thought by his lively *Redbrick University* and its sequel. His special concern is to recall universities to one strain in academic tradition, that which lays its main emphasis on investigation and the advancement of scholarship. Another strain is emphasized by the admirable Harvard Report, *General Education in a Free Society*. Here the most urgent question is, How are universities in a democratic and industrial society to implant a wide culture, such as the older among them once imparted through the medium of the Classics? Yet a third section, probably the most forceful and influential, is frankly modernist. For it, the sensational triumph of applied

7

science in the last two or three centuries, bringing with it a quite new power of transforming the conditions of life, is one of the great turning-points of history. It is effecting a 'Copernican change' in human affairs and human culture, and the governing ideas of twentieth-century universities ought to be derived from the new, and not from any earlier, dispensation. This outlook, combined with an impetus to social revolution, is found in such a representative work as Professor Bernal's *The Social Function of Science* and it has captured very many of the younger men. But, with the solitary exception of Mr. Arnold Nash's deliberately provocative and challenging *The University and the Modern World,* I know of no substantial recent work which deals with the university to-day from a Christian standpoint.

*The Crisis in the University* is written from a Christian standpoint, though not all its emphases are identical with those of Mr. Nash. It is an attempt to crystallize the interim results of discussions among a few Christian university teachers which have been going on for some time. The initiative in these discussions has come from two bodies, the Student Christian Movement and the Christian Frontier Council. In pursuing their immediate concerns, the officers of the S.C.M. found themselves driven to take account of the structure and character of the university itself as it impinges upon student life. They invited a few professors and lecturers, 'senior friends' of the S.C.M., to confer with them. Informal meetings were held and some of the results were embodied in one or two preliminary papers. About the same time but independently, the Christian Frontier Council was discussing some of the same questions from a similar point of view. (This is a body of Christian laymen who endeavour to work out together the bearing of their faith on secular life to-day, particularly in the spheres of their own professional responsibilities; some of its members are themselves university teachers or administrators.) Contact was made between the two and further steps followed.

First, the S.C.M. Press published a series of 'University Pamphlets,' many of which dealt incisively with questions of fundamental principle.

1. *The Mind of the Modern University* by John Baillie.

2. *Objectivity and Impartiality* by H. A. Hodges.

3. *The Christian in the Modern University* by H. A. Hodges.

8

4. *The Foundations of a Free University* by Dorothy M. Emmet.

5. *Christianity's Need of a Free University* by A. R. Vidler.

6. *Universities Under Fire* by Colin Forrester-Paton.

7. *Calling All Freshmen* by Paul White.

8. *The Place of a Faculty of Theology in the University of To-day* by Daniel T. Jenkins.

9. *Religion in the University* by David M. Paton.

10. *Work and Vocation* by W. G. Symons.

11. *Vocational and Humane Education in the University* by L. A. Reid.

12. *Halls of Residence in Modern Universities.* A Group Report.

In my judgment these were all of high, and some of them of outstanding, quality. Several of the writers had taken part in the preliminary discussions, and the Pamphlets showed a striking measure of agreement.

Secondly, the S.C.M. and the C.F.C. combined to convene a conference of between thirty and forty university teachers of Christian outlook, who met for several days in Cambridge in September, 1946. They were drawn from a wide variety of universities, faculties and age-groups. The Pamphlets, which had been circulated in advance, provided much but not all of the material for discussion. Here again there proved to be wide agreement. In general the diagnosis and the policies of the Pamphlets were endorsed and a strong sense of urgency was manifested. It was felt that, owing to the confusion of purpose which they share with the modern world, universities are at present crippled in performing their most important function; that Christians have a vital contribution to make, though much work remains to be done by them before that can be clearly formulated or become effective; and that, if it is to be made at all, there is no time to be lost.

Clearly any real advance can only come from groups of Christian teachers inside each university or college, thinking and working together continuously. The chief function of an occasional inter-university conference is to stimulate such local groups to get together and to get to work. But a need was felt also for some compendious statement of principle to which we could point as representing our general position. Twelve separate pamphlets, however excellent, cannot meet this demand. 'We must put the Pamphlets into book-form,' it was said; and, before dispersing, the conference appointed a small committee to carry this out.

But, in the nature of the case, the actual writing of a book cannot be done by a committee. It must be deputed to some individual, and, in this case, the committee deputed it to me. The committee approved my synopsis, saw the book in draft, and made useful criticisms and suggestions. But the whole, as it stands, is my composition and responsibility for its shortcomings is mine alone. My original intention was to draft something which might be issued as the collective statement of a group and not of an individual; and traces of this still appear in the text. But when I set out to give in a single whole the gist of the Pamphlets and of the Cambridge discussions, I found it impracticable, either to incorporate everything or to restrict myself to reproduction. So, in the end, it has seemed more honest to publish under my own name. But I must, in fairness, explain that my work has been little original. Form and content have been largely determined by the material available, and, in many respects, I have been redactor rather than author. For instance I have shamelessly appropriated the ideas, and occasionally even the phrases, of the Pamphlets without specific acknowledgment, though I fear much of their original force and pungency has evaporated in the re-cooking. Unless I had been assured of the writers' willing consent to this proceeding, I should have been guilty of gross plagiarism. Any value the book may have will be due to its expressing the converging thought of many minds.

The writing has had to be done in the spare moments of a busy, administrative life, and I am painfully aware of the discrepancy between the greatness of the theme and the crudity of the execution. No doubt a writer's apologies for imperfections in a book he is not obliged to publish are apt to ring hollow. But all our discussions have been carried on under a strong sense of urgency; and it has seemed better to complete a statement, however rough, in 1948 than to purchase the opportunity of removing some blemishes at the cost of further delay.

Since I am at present chairman of the University Grants Committee, I ought to make it clear beyond doubt that I am now writing in a personal, and not in an official, capacity and without any consultation with my colleagues on that Committee. They have no responsibility, direct or indirect, for the views here expressed. Indeed the only forecast of their reaction to them which I can make with confidence is that it will not be uniform. The considered opinions of the Committee, in which I share in full degree, are to be found only in the Report, *University Development* 1935-1947, which will have appeared before this book is published. But that hardly touches on the issues to which I have here devoted most attention.

There remains only the pleasant duty of thanking those who have helped me. Apart from the writers of the Pamphlets to whom my obligations are overwhelming, Sir Hector Hetherington and Professor W. R. Niblett have read the whole book in typescript and have made a number of pertinent comments by which I have profited. The Christian Frontier Council have undertaken all the mechanical work involved in preparation and have made the arrangements for publication; and I am particularly indebted to the Rev. Daniel Jenkins of their staff for invaluable editorial help.

W. H. M.

*August,* 1948.

# CONTENTS

# I

# INTRODUCTION

## I THE WORLD TO-DAY

The crisis in the university reflects the crisis in the world and its pervading sense of insecurity. Two world-wars have culminated in the threat to civilization of the atom-bomb. The background of all that is planned or done in the years immediately ahead will be the imminent peril of world-wide disaster. We are living ' in the midst of uncertainties and on the edge of an abyss.'

This physical insecurity is matched by a moral and spiritual insecurity and indeed largely results from it. The menace to civilization consists, not in the discovery of atomic energy and the invention of the bomb, but in the presumed will to use it. It lies in the fact that the generation which has acquired these stupendous powers of destruction is full of fear and suspicion and that these notoriously govern the relation to each other of rival groups of the Great Powers. A state of war, says Hobbes truly, consists not only in actual fighting but in ' the known disposition thereto.' Coupled with this is the terrifying emergence of the underground man. To an extent which even fifteen years ago we should have thought incredible we have witnessed bestial cruelty, lust and lawlessness, not only as an occasional morbid aberration, but rampant and in power. The veneer of civilization has proved to be amazingly thin. Beneath it has been revealed, not only the ape and the tiger, but what is far worse—perverted and satanic man.

But the real trouble lies deeper still. It is true that the heart of man is deceitful and desperately wicked; to ascribe that view to the vain invention of ' unpleasing priests ' is much less plausible than it was. But our predicament is beyond cure by exhortations to individuals to a change of will and to ' moral rearmament,' needful as those may be. Our situation is due to the interaction of myriads of wills, each pursuing its own limited purposes, but for their accomplishment combining in larger and larger units, and finally producing a total state of things which no one foresaw and no one wanted, and in which the individual feels himself powerless because of the colossal scale of the influences which actually govern his life. Maine laid it down that the progress of society is from Status to Contract. It is ironical that the operation of Contract should have brought the great majority back again to Status; that the road should be so short from over-weening optimism to cynical despair; and that, when the range of *Man's* choice is indefinitely extended, the range of *men's* choice should often be so painfully restricted.

This was William Temple's reading of the signs of the times, when in one of his latest utterances he said that the crisis of our time is not moral but cultural.[1] 'Mores,' ways of life, the recognition of binding obligations are bound up with some accepted view of the nature of man and of the world, though this may take the form less of a doctrine embraced by the mind than of a picture dominating the imagination. But it is just this common picture or framework that has now so largely disappeared. For instance, it is notorious that the impact of western civilization on primitive communities, e.g. in Africa, has been disintegrating. Apart from any conscious intention or propaganda, it destroys the foundation of belief, custom and sentiment on which primitive life is built. Unless it also brings some new world picture and way of life to replace that which is in ruins, it leaves behind it devastation. But nemesis has followed. To-day the 'civilized' communities are suffering from a similar devastation. Over a large part of Europe and Asia binding convictions are lacking and there is confusion, bewilderment and discord. The whole complex of traditional belief, habit and sentiment, on which convictions are founded, has collapsed. All over the world indeed the cake of custom is broken, the old gods are dethroned and none have taken their places. Mentally and spiritually, most persons to-day are 'displaced persons.'

## 2 THE POSITION OF THE UNIVERSITIES

The influence of the universities has been, and may again be, immense. Rashdall begins his authoritative book, *The Universities of Europe in the Middle Ages*, with a quotation from a medieval writer, who links the Universities with the Papacy and the Empire as being the outstanding representatives of the three parallel powers

[1] *Christian News-Letter,* 198, Supplement.

or 'virtues,' *Sacerdotium, Imperium, Studium,* by whose harmonious co-operation the life and health of Christendom are sustained. It might not occur to a modern writer to put their claim quite so high. But he would agree that they are power-houses for the production of intellectual leaders in many fields and centres of thought, where the ideas which transform the world may be elicited, developed, tested and diffused. Yet they grew up, took their shape and formed their mental habits and their working assumptions in a world widely different from the present. By comparison with our own time it was a world of security, mental if not physical. Its standards of judgment were firm and acknowledged. However violent the storms, the charts were undisputed. The reprobate no more than the saint ever seriously doubted that he lived in a world of which God had 'cast the dark foundations deep.'

The question now arises, Can the universities adapt themselves to a world of insecurity? Have they anything creative to contribute to it or are they themselves immersed, or about to be immersed, in the maelstrom? Can they 'rise to the height of the times'? All the familiar questions of university policy—questions of clientèle, of curricula, of ways of living, of forms of government, of relation with the outside world—require to be rethought in the new perspective. This need is put at its most challenging by Dr. Hutchins, the Chancellor of the University of Chicago : ' Civilization can be saved only by a moral, intellectual and spiritual revolution to match the scientific, technological and economic revolution in which we are now living. If education can contribute to a moral, intellectual and spiritual revolution, then it offers a real hope of salvation to suffering humanity everywhere. If it cannot, or will not, contribute to this revolution, then it is irrelevant and its fate is immaterial.'[1] To the majority of people perhaps, inside as well as outside universities, such language may seem somewhat strained, hysterical, and at bottom insincere. ' Whatever you say,' they will ask, ' do you not in fact go about your daily business and recreation in the unquestioning assurance that " as things have been they remain "?' No doubt we do; and so, presumably, did the intelligentsia of Herculaneum and Pompeii in the summer of the year A.D. 79. But that is only because our imaginations have not kept pace with our reason.

[1] *The Listener,* Vol. xxxvi, No. 934.

# 3  THE SPECIAL ROLE OF GREAT BRITAIN

In material resources, for the first time for some centuries, Great Britain is no longer quite in the front rank. So far as leadership and initiative depend on such resources, they are passing into the hands of others, but a full share of leadership in the realm of ideas is still open to us. There has been much less disintegration here than in Europe generally. Nearly all foreign observers who visit us seem to be struck by the greater stability and continuity of ethos which Great Britain has maintained. Again, as compared with Europe, and even with the United States, it is fairly widely recognized that Great Britain has a greater political maturity, and an experience in combining law and liberty and in avoiding Thucydidean 'Stasis' that is unique. Here is a possible basis for a mission.

But if there has been admiration, there has also been mordant criticism; and we have learned in modern times to criticize ourselves. Have we really, it is asked, any positive gospel to offer the world? Is not such a belief an illusion, due to the fact that in Great Britain our insular position has retarded the pace of dissolution, while our intellectual timidity and slovenliness have enabled us to postpone putting to ourselves crucial questions which we, like the rest of the world, must now face? We may still be shocked by the barbaric gospels of others; but is not all that is positive in our way of life and our moral codes simply a relic of an old hierarchical order in which we have ourselves ceased effectively to believe? For ceremonial occasions, no doubt, we still have a Church as we still have a King; but neither has much to do with the realities of power. Even the notorious British 'hypocrisy' is on the wane. It has never deceived other people and it is now ceasing to deceive ourselves. Our young men do not see visions, but they dream troubled dreams. We have been fumbling, unsure of ourselves and of our standards, and we have largely lost any sense of mission.

But 'Dunkirk and all that' showed that there was life in the old dog yet. That 'life' was not merely a tough will for physical survival. It was also moral and spiritual, a sense of standing as a nation, even alone, for something of vital moment to the whole world, of bringing forth from our national treasure things new as well as old and of whole-hearted, all-out, response to a call which enabled our people to rise to their 'finest hour.' We have not kept to that level. Then the issue was simple and clear-cut, and the alternative was unmistakable destruction. Now the situation is far more tangled, and yet it is no less critical. Much of the world is looking to this country for moral leadership with an expectancy which we have disappointed, but have not yet forfeited. It does not seem fantastic to suggest that the fate of civilization in the next period may hang on the question whether this country can rise to its moral opportunity. In the fulfilment of God's will for the world a special mission may be assigned to Great Britain. Unfortunately, whatever truth such a statement contains, if it be true at all, it can hardly be put into words without at once being cheapened and falsified. On the natural plane such a task makes demands far beyond our nation's powers, and the prospects of success are infinitesimal. Hope is only possible because the British tradition includes an element which transcends the natural plane and which looks to the plenteous operation of divine grace. On that level all complacency is merely silly and absurd. Indeed it is dizzying to picture what a heightening of spiritual resources the fulfilment of such a mission would require.

## 4 THE BRITISH UNIVERSITIES

It is in this perspective that the present university scene in this country must be surveyed. First, there are Oxford and Cambridge whose prestige is deservedly equal to that of any university in the world. Through 'the attractive, magnetic power of their sweetness and splendour' they have come to embody 'the idea of the university' in the eyes of the nation. They have had their bad days, as in the eighteenth century; but during the last hundred years they have been at the height of their fame. Next, the Scottish universities have also an ancient tradition. With less of grace and poetry than Oxford and Cambridge, and with far more slender material resources, they embody the distinctive excellences of their national character, an insistent hunger for learning and a dour, and often sacrificial, determination to achieve it. But even before the last war, the majority of students were to be found at a third type of university, that represented by the Universities of London and Wales and those of the great provincial English cities, to which a recent writer has given the convenient, generic, name of 'Redbrick.' These have been much less in the public eye than Oxford and Cambridge. London, the oldest of them, has existed for little more than a century, and in the main they are the creation of the last fifty years. But already they contain more than half, and before long they are likely to contain three-quarters, of the total student population of Great Britain. Originally these had to encounter in many quarters a certain patrician contempt and scepticism. ('Can any good thing come out of Nazareth?'; 'We are not cotton-spinners all.') They are still often looked on as 'poor relations.' But their inception was due to public-spirited and far-sighted citizens in each area, and it is well to recall the high hopes with which it was accompanied. They were not designed to be inferior imitations of Oxford and Cambridge. They were to excel them in seriousness of purpose, in range of studies, and, as befitted 'a nation of shopkeepers,' in intimacy of relation to a commercial community. That those hopes have not as yet been fully realized, has been due, in the main, to causes outside their own control. Their chief handicap has been their relative poverty and, for some time, the backwardness of secondary education in their areas.

A big stride forward is now being taken. War experience has produced in the public mind a more lively and sympathetic interest in the universities and a new sense of their value to the nation. This is due to realization of the essential part played by university scientists in winning the war, of the backwardness of our industry in the use of experts as compared with that of several other countries, and of the national need, at point after point, of 'fundamental brainwork.' It is due also to the intensified demand for social justice to the individual. On that basis, if a university education is an advantage to the student, it ought to be brought as effectively within the reach of the son of a working man as of the son of a squire. There is now a disposition to do much more for universities and to expect much more of them. Within the universities too there is a new sense of expectancy, a belief that the lean years are over, the public no longer indifferent and the Treasury no longer niggardly, that the universities are to have 'a new deal' and that large developments are, for the first time, possible. In spite of temporary shortages and disappointments, it seems that the universities are to have their opportunity. Can they use it? Can they 'rise to the height of the times?'

The present ferment is promising and good, as far as it goes. But, mostly, it does not yet go far enough or deep enough. This book is the product of a twofold conviction. The group of university men and women out of whose discussions it has emerged are convinced of the greatness of the present call to universities and of the possibility of their rising to it through the enabling grace of God. But they are also convinced that, on the human side, this possibility depends on a more searching and realistic facing of our present shortcomings than is at all common in university circles. Here we are feeling after something which it is hard to express clearly. But the war, the resistance movements, and the political convulsions which have accompanied them in many countries have, as it were, revealed a new dimension of depth. Like a fierce blast they have passed over Europe, burning up what is second-hand and conventional. 'The only value that remains to us in the collapse of values is sincerity.' Against this background much existing discussion of what universities should be and do is unsatisfying, because it is superficial. That is, it does not take place at the level at which genuine convictions are formed and operate; it does not engage the whole self of the participant. But no half-belief in a casual creed can stand for a moment before the daemonic forces now abroad in the world. Any contribution from this country or its universities which was unequal to this test would be futile. In a confused and turbid fashion students are often more sensitive to this new dimension than are many of their seniors.

In this perspective, the questions normally discussed in Senate or Faculty, in Government Reports about various aspects of university life, in the pamphlets and magazine articles of reformers, are of secondary, rather than of quite primary, importance. When we turn to the primary questions, concerning the things that really make or mar a university, and ask—'What are universities for? What effect should they have on their alumni? What are their responsibilities to the outside world?', we are asking questions to which a minority of university teachers return discordant answers and the majority return no clear answers at all. Beneath the façade of development and hopefulness, the British universities to-day share with the universities of the world a peculiar malaise and impotence. They have little inner self-confidence, because they lack, and are increasingly aware that they lack, any clear, agreed sense of direction and purpose. At this moment they cannot give an effective lead because they themselves share, and have shown small sign of transcending, the spiritual confusion of the age. Hence for them the most urgent injunction is, 'Physician heal thyself.' To fit themselves for service, a rather drastic 'Metanoia' or mental remaking is required of them.

In particular, the universities are not now discharging their former cultural task. That task has been well described by Professor Dobrée as 'the creation, generation by generation in a continuous flow, of a body of men and women who share a sense of civilized values, who feel responsible for developing them, who are united by their culture, and who by the simple pressure of their existence and outlook will form and be enlightened public opinion.'[1] Few persons who are familiar with the inside of most universities to-day will contend that such a task is being successfully carried out. This is attested by Sir Richard Livingstone, speaking as Vice-Chancellor of Oxford at the 1946 Universities Conference, ' What the world most needs and most lacks to-day is a clear and worthy view of life. . . . What do we do to give the undergraduate such a view? I think we must reply, "Little or nothing." ' In modern conditions, perhaps, this is hardly surprising. But there are two further facts that are really significant and sinister. First, the task is no longer even being seriously attempted. Secondly, this abdication is due less to any deliberate and clear-cut decision than to a process of drift.

This process has been going on for a long time. But, in the last few years, it has been accentuated by the moral collapse of the German universities under the Nazi régime. Of no universities had the intellectual prestige been higher; during the last century they had been a model to the world. Yet when the stress came, with certain honourable exceptions among individuals, they showed little resistance, less indeed than the Churches. They failed to repel doctrines morally monstrous and intellectually despicable. Like the Press and the Wireless, they suffered themselves to become an instrument for manipulating public opinion in the hands of the powers that be. No doubt certain weaknesses in the German make-up contributed to this collapse, but to ascribe it solely to a double dose of original sin in the German people is unconvincing. It seems to have been due in large measure to the fact that the German universities had no independent standards of value of which they felt themselves the guardians and which they held with sufficient conviction and tenacity to stand up against the torrent. But, British teachers cannot help asking themselves, ' Is not this also our own case? If we were subjected to a like pressure, are we confident that our own standards of value are too coherent and assured to be obliterated? Are we sure that we too should not

[1] *Political Quarterly* XV, p. 343.

succumb?' They do not find it easy to answer with the ringing confidence they would wish.

The cultural failure of the universities is seen in the students. In recent years large numbers of these have been apathetic and have had neither wide interests nor compelling convictions.[1] The active-minded minority have often been in revolt. A few years ago a shrewd observer at one of our older universities said that he was struck by the rarity with which undergraduates expressed or felt any deep respect for, or debt to, dons as having opened up for them a whole attitude to life; though unless all the biographies are untrustworthy, such discipleship was not uncommon in earlier generations. This estrangement between the generations has come about largely because students feel themselvs to be living in a different world from their teachers, a world which is grimmer and less secure economically, politically and morally. 'The young are met by teachers whom they do not understand and who do not understand them. They are hungering for leadership and there is hardly a man to lead them; they long for certainty and there is no idea that can grip them.'[2] If they find prophets at all, it is outside the universities; a few years ago perhaps Shaw or Wells, to-day more probably a voice from Moscow. Their teachers' philosophy of life, if any is discernible, strikes them as academic and unreal. 'Out there in the street is something new in the making, which will shatter all the syllogisms and formulae of the schools.'

But the most cogent evidence of this ' sickness ' is the gulf between appearance and reality, between the ideals to which the university traditionally professes allegiance, and for which it mostly still supposes itself to stand, and the springs of action by which it is really moved. Here the warning of a Spanish thinker is most relevant. ' It is vicious to pretend to be what we are not, and to delude ourselves by growing habituated to a radically false idea of what we are . . . An institution which feigns to give and require what it cannot is false and demoralized.'[3] Many who are intimately concerned with universities to-day are hampered by an uneasy sense of the discrepancy between profession and actuality in such respects as the following :

---

[1] This generalization is probably less true of the ex-service students than of others. But it remains to be seen how far these will set the standard for the future.

[2] Kotschnig, *The University in a Changing World*, p. 11.

[3] Ortega y Gasset *Mission of the University*, p. 50.

First, the university professes to turn out ' rounded persons ' with an understanding of themselves and of their place in the cosmos. But, in fact, a very large proportion both of students and of their teachers are narrow specialists with extremely limited horizons.

Secondly, the university professes to stimulate a liberal and disinterested attitude to study. In the words of a recent, admirable address to Freshmen, ' anyone who regards his studies as a means of personal advancement just doesn't belong here.' But, in fact, the common attitude is self-centred and utilitarian, and the common motto is ' The shorter learning, the sooner earning!' Study is a means to success in examinations, and success in examinations is the most practicable avenue to economic and social advancement.

Thirdly, the university professes to cultivate objectivity and impartiality. In fact university teachers and their pupils, like other people, are commonly swayed by unexamined assumptions or by ' archetypes,' that is by deep-seated, emotionally coloured and only partially conscious, mental attitudes. It is such assumptions and attitudes that really determine the convictions even of the so-called ' intellectuals.' Reason affects to sit in judgment on them, when it is really briefed, like counsel, in their service.

Lastly, the university professes to be a community and to derive from this fact much of its educational power. It has, traditionally, claimed to exercise a transforming influence on its members, and to awaken in them the sense of wonder through contact with inspiring persons. In the words of the address quoted above, ' When you have been a member of a university in a true sense for any length of time you will be thenceforward and for ever a different person.' In the case of Oxford and Cambridge, such a claim has had some substance. But for the majority of students in the non-residential universities at least, their university has been less an *Alma Mater* than a bargain-counter, at which certain specific articles they require are purveyed. There is little vital communication between different Faculties or even between different Departments, and there is no profound mental effect on the average student.

Is this picture exaggerated and misleading? If we insist on these failings of the contemporary university, it is not because we hold that ' where all is rotten it is a man's work to cry stinking fish.' It is because, in a time that calls for greatness, the universities can only rise to their task if they experience a shaking and a coming together again which is fundamental. If the present ferment remains on the surface, they will only re-enact 'the treason of the clerks.' We conceive that the present situation of the British universities resembles that of the British nation depicted above. Both have a distinctive tradition, in embodying which they have a sense of standing for something of high value. In this tradition there is a strong Christian ingredient; the Bible has entered deeply into the British mind and into the accepted values and attitudes of the older British universities. In modern times both have fallen away from this tradition. The 'Redbrick' universities at least cater predominantly for a clientèle which is 'suburban,' without roots and without standards; and they have too much taken their colour from their environment. But like the nation in 1940, they are capable of a great revival, which will in part take the form of a recovery of antique virtue, overlaid but not perished. But no more than in the nation can it be simply a restoration. More is required than to go back to Queen Victoria, Queen Anne or Queen Elizabeth. Our people could only have 'their finest hour' through the pulling out in them of some new stops. 'Archaism'[1] is impracticable; what is revived is never more than a *simulacrum*. It is also undesirable, since the past always has grave faults, the revival of which would be unpardonable. Within the last year or two there have been some first, faint, encouraging signs of a new spirit. For instance the ex-service men among the students, though touched by the prevailing disillusion, have commonly more purpose, energy and sincerity than their immediate predecessors. Much will depend on whether such sparks flicker out or whether they can be fanned into flame. It is our conviction that this, in turn, will largely depend on how far our universities and their members are confronted by the authentic Christian challenge and respond to it.

## 5  A CHRISTIAN CONTRIBUTION

In such a situation have Christians anything vital to say? This book is written from a definitely Christian standpoint, but in the last few years the most significant contribution has come from another quarter. It is the work of a number of like-minded thinkers who call themselves 'scientific humanists.'[2] In some, though not in

---

[1] See Toynbee's *Study of History*.

[2] See, for example, J. D. Bernal, *The Social Function of Science*; L. Hogben, *Dangerous Thoughts*, and, from a student angle, B. Simon, *A Student's View of the Universities*.

all, respects our standpoint is sharply opposed to theirs. But they have done a great service in forcing into the open issues to which most people are still blind; and it is to our discredit, as Christians, that we have produced so little constructive work on universities to match theirs.[1] The following chapters are an attempt to express the mind of a group of Christian teachers and administrators who, after a good deal of preliminary thought and discussion, believe that they have something to say. In the first instance it is addressed to our fellow-Christians within the universities. But we hope it may be overheard by others, for much of it is relevant to others.

Our difficulty is that we look back, half-ashamed, to the centuries when the Church dominated the universities, and to a later time, in the nineteenth century, when churchmen in retreat fought an obstinate but unsuccessful rearguard action to retain old privileges and restrictions. Those battles seem to have been decided once and for all. The defeat was sweeping, and few people to-day, secularist or Christian, would defend the restrictions for which Christian leaders of a previous generation so stubbornly fought. More lately any corporate action of Christians in university affairs has tended to be sectional. It has been concerned with retaining or with winning a small 'place in the sun' for specifically 'religious' interests. Thus Christians have striven to make good a claim for the creation of a Faculty of Theology or for the inclusion of some form of religious teaching among the options for a general degree, or to set up here and there a Hall of Residence under religious auspices as a small enclave in the middle of a secular university. Certainly such things have their value. (See Chapter X below). But the main issue which concerns us is quite different. It is this: 'What can Christian insight contribute to enable the university *to be the university?*' It is here that we have hitherto been so culpably lacking. The vital question is not whether the university does or does not include certain directly religious activities. It is concerned with the university's *raison d'être* and with the whole of its life and work.

To-day many university teachers and administrators are Christians. But few, if any, of us are *Christian teachers* or *Christian administrators*. That is, we have failed so far to bring any distinctive Christian insight to the problems of university training and governance with which, in our professional capacity, we are constantly concerned. On such issues as those of freedom

[1] But see Arnold Nash, *The University and the Modern World.*

and planning, scholarship and citizenship, a carefully balanced and predetermined curriculum or a free choice of subjects by the individual student, an austere scholastic standard or the throwing open of university training to the widest possible number, the respective claims of teaching and research, and a hundred others— on all these the Christian professor or lecturer may well have a personal view. But he probably holds it on grounds which would be exactly the same if he did not happen to be a Christian, and his fellow-Christians on the staff are as likely as anyone else to be at variance with him. On the main questions of university policy, Christian teachers or students, as such, are not aligned in any particular way.

But such a disjunction is no longer defensible. For the questions in debate are no longer, if they ever were, merely technical. They involve fundamental values and a basic philosophy of life. A religion which had no light to throw on them would be self-confessed bankrupt. A Christian who draws no guidance for academic policy from his faith is failing in his duty as a member of the university community; he is also failing in his integrity as a Christian. For one thing, as yet too little realized, is now becoming clear. In the assumptions governing syllabus and academic method, the universities to-day are, implicitly, if unintentionally, hostile to the Christian faith and even to a liberal humanism. As Christians therefore we are in a radically false position. ' We are trying to live at this moment in two worlds, in the world of our work occupying most of our time which assumes that the Christian faith is untrue and the world of our spare-time Christian activity or prayer or praise which assumes it is true.' If this startling judgment is itself true, as in the main we believe it is (see Chapter III below), we are bogged in a moral morass, and it is imperative to get out of it.

But even if Christians should have something to say in this field, can they expect a hearing? Will not their colleagues retort somewhat as follows? 'You have had your chance and misused it; never again shall we be caught that way. For centuries you controlled the universities with the result that, in effect, they were merely ecclesiastical seminaries. The clergy monopolized the teaching posts. Thought was canalized within the narrow limits sanctioned by the Church. Nothing was legitimate but what could be squared with the Bible, as interpreted by the Fathers and the Schoolmen. It is only by throwing off this yoke and secularizing the universities that the revival of learning and the triumphs of science have been made possible. However uncertain the future, at least we shall give ear to no senile Pétain and restore no ecclesiastical Bourbons. Nowadays, no doubt, you are relatively harmless. But that—forgive us!—is only because you " cut so little ice." For what you are worth, you are still an alien element within the academic body. However high-minded your intentions, you are like government servants who use their position to further the interests of a foreign power. When you lay your plans to bring in quietly a few theological teachers here, a chapel or a chaplain there, you are not serving the university but are seeking to use it as an instrument for purposes which are not its own.'

We must recognize frankly that such a reaction is not wholly unnatural or unprovoked. In their day of power Christians did misuse it. In most of the contests which ensued truth was divided, and often the balance was on the side of the rebels. The history of the last two hundred years is not simply the story of a fall from grace, nor is what is required to-day the reinstatement of any régime which once existed. On the other hand, the prophecies of woe with which such men as Pusey and Burgon greeted any loosening of the bonds between the universities and the Christian religion do not appear to-day so simply wrong-headed as they used to do. They foretold that such a loosening would ultimately result, by a series of inevitable steps, in moral anarchy and the obliteration of all landmarks. To all but diehards such forecasts once seemed fantastic and hysterical, but their thesis has at least become more plausible than it seemed. *Post hoc,* if not *propter hoc,* some part of the prediction has been realized. Whatever the cause, the university to-day lives and moves and has its being in a moral and cultural fog.

But a Christian policy for the present age will be very unlike what it has generally been in the past. There are two reasons for this. First, the world-situation, as we have seen, is totally different. Secondly, apart from any consideration of tactics, on some points of principle a change is imperative. Much as we have to learn from our Christian predecessors, we have some things also to unlearn.

A policy is not a programme, and to speak at this stage of a Christian programme, would be misleading. Certainly we ourselves can offer no slick solutions to the problems we raise. The situation is still too confused for that and most of the requisite thinking and experimenting has still to be done. Yet the first and crucial step in any enquiry is to ask the right questions, and, as Christians, we do claim to have some distinctive insight into what is wrong with the universities to-day. In part, as will appear, our diagnosis agrees with that of others. But our perspective is different and, at a number of points, we believe that our criticism cuts deeper. Further, though we have no detailed scheme of reform to propose, certain general lines of policy are beginning to stand out. We offer no Christian programme, but certain suggestions for guidance in the preparation of a programme and a preliminary statement of the principles to which it should conform.

It is characteristic of the Christian gospel that it contains both bad and good news; it discloses otherwise unsuspected depths and heights. On the one hand, the obstacles to progress in human nature itself are more formidable than the secularist allows. It is not so much the villainy of villains as the canker in the righteous, not the satanism of the Hitlers and the Mussolinis but the flaws in the Wilsons and the Roosevelts, that cause shipwreck. So universities have to fear the subtle self-deception and self-glorification of reformers as well as the more blatant stupidity and selfishness of the obstructionists. On the other hand, Christianity discloses unexpected resources of grace for the empowering of human feebleness; it recounts the achievements of those who 'out of weakness were made strong.' The university reformer who is a Christian should be at once more modest than others in his expectations and more bold.

# II

# CHANGING CONCEPTIONS OF THE UNIVERSITY'S TASK

How has the university arrived where it is? Within the last century there has been more than one revolution in the conception commonly held of its fundamental aim and methods. But perhaps ' conception ' is hardly the right word, since our concern is rather with underlying assumptions, largely unconscious. What really counts is, less opinions consciously adopted and maintained than, what is silently and unreflectingly taken for granted. As T. E. Hulme pointed out, there are certain doctrines which have become so much a part of men's minds that they are never really conscious of them. 'They do not see them but other things *through* them.' Any change in such a body of basic acceptances tends to be slow and imperceptible; it easily escapes notice like the setting of the tide. Yet it is that, rather than the swimmer's own efforts or the waves he breasts, which determines his progress. So we have to recognize that, by the very fact that they are articulate and self-conscious, the representative thinkers from whom we must draw our illustrations are not quite representative.

## I CHRISTIAN-HELLENIC

For the greater part of the nineteenth century Oxford and Cambridge exemplified a highly distinctive type of university, based on Christian and Græco-Roman traditions. In various respects this type has become inadequate to the modern world. But it represents the most characteristic English contribution to ' the idea of the university,' and it is of the first importance to understand and appreciate it. Its classical statement occurs in Newman's *Idea of a University* and is inimitable. But, in substance, it is by no means peculiar to Newman, and there is nothing about it that is specifically Catholic. He is drawing on his recollections of Oxford and is painting its characteristic excellences. What he depicts, is Jowett's ideal of Oxford quite as much as it is his own.

A somewhat more pedestrian exposition of a view substantially the same had been given fifteen years earlier by Whewell in the sister university, and some of its most important features are to be found fifteen years later in J. S. Mill's Rectorial address to the students of St. Andrew's.

On this view the chief duty of the university is to produce good citizens. It should train an élite who are to be the future leaders in affairs and in the learned professions. Thus it differs from a seminary, a technical college, or a research institute. For neither training in the technique of particular callings, whether ecclesiastical or secular, nor the advancement of knowledge is its primary function, though it may contribute to each. The training it gives is an initiation of select young people into their cultural inheritance. In Matthew Arnold's words it seeks to familiarize them, with ' the best that has been thought and said in the world ' and so to bind together the generations through their sharing in a common intellectual estate.[1]

Such education has the following characteristics. First, it is ' liberal ' as opposed to ' servile.' That is, it aims at mental development for its own sake and not for any ulterior end. It seeks, not to make the student an effective tool to serve someone else's purpose or to give him power to make tools of others to serve his own purpose, but to train him to recognize, to respect and to delight in, what is intrinsically true, good and beautiful. It does so simply because this is a want of man's nature and in its satisfaction he fulfils himself. It encourages the student to master the Greek language, not because ' it not infrequently leads to positions of considerable emolument,' nor even because familiarity with Thucydides may make him a more capable statesman in after-life, but in order that he may appreciate and enjoy Homer or Plato for their own sake. By exposing young men to the acknowledged masterpieces of human thought and knowledge, it evokes a culture which is valuable for what it is rather than for what it does, and which is inseparable from mental health in all who are capable of it, since without it they would be less than fully human. Thus refinement rather than effectiveness is its direct aim; and yet, in a large view, it is just the people who have achieved refinement who are also the most effective and excel in practical judgment and knowledge of life. ' A cultivated intellect, because it is good in itself, brings

[1] Whewell, *On The Principles of English University Education*, p. 34.

with it a power and a grace to every work and occupation which it undertakes.'[1]

Secondly, this education is general as opposed to specialized. ' The man who has been trained to think on one subject only will never be a good judge even in that one '[2]; while if he ventures to express opinions outside his own narrow field, he will be like a schoolboy or a ploughman presuming to judge a prime minister. The student needs to gain a synoptic view, like a man who possesses a map of the country or one who gets up on to high ground to see the panorama. Henceforward he will have some catholicity of outlook and sense of proportion; however intensively he studies any particular subject he will see it in its relation to the whole scheme. ' Not to know the relative disposition of things is the state of slaves or of children.'[3] But he does not necessarily acquire this sense through having a very wide curriculum. That in itself may be a snare. The dilettante is no better than the narrow specialist; a smattering in a dozen branches of study is not enlargement but shallowness. True enlargement is got rather from the fact that the student is a member of a community in which the whole range of knowledge is being studied and is in intimate association with those whose speciality differs from his own. Thus ' he apprehends the great outlines of knowledge, the principles on which it rests, the scale of its parts, its lights and its shades, its great points and its little, as he otherwise cannot apprehend them.'[4] In this way he avoids provincialism.

Thirdly, this education is systematic. There must be no stuffing with knowledge, no passive reception of scraps, no ' unmeaning profusion of subjects.' What is important is, not the amassing of facts but their grasp, not cramming but mental digestion. Hence a habit of method must be formed. The student must learn to start from fixed points, to make good his ground as he goes, to distinguish clearly what he knows from what he does not know, to relate what he learns to what he knows already. Further he is being made acquainted with a world of intellectual order and not of intellectual anarchy and with a hierarchy of intellectual values in which some are fundamental and others subsidiary. He is intro-duced to laws and principles which are objective and independent of fashion or individual caprice. ' Universities ' says Whewell, ' so

[1] Newman, op. cit. p. 167.
[2] ibid, p. 173.
[3] ibid, p. 113.
[4] ibid, p. 101.

far as they are schools of *general* cultivation, represent the permanent, not the fluctuating elements of human knowledge . . . They have to transmit the civilization of past generations to future ones, not to share and show forth all the changing fashions of intellectual caprice and subtlety.'[1] Or, to adapt an aphorism of Burke's, one object of a university education is to make the student independent of his own private stock of reason which, in the nature of the case, is small and to make available to him ' the general bank and capital of nations and of ages.'

So much for the traditional aims of our older universities, but what of the methods by which they have sought to achieve them? These are based on the fundamental principle that the university, as a community of teachers and learners, is to be regarded as a family. Or, in words whose felicity has caused them to become a familiar possession, ' a university is . . . an Alma Mater, knowing her children one by one, not a foundry, or a mint, or a treadmill.'[2] In accordance with this principle, the bulk of the teaching has been tutorial or catechetical and has involved the direct impact of person on person. The student is required to answer questions, to write compositions or essays, or to engage in disputations. He is to be, not only a passive recipient of instruction, but an active co-operator in the process. His mental enlargement entails ' the mind's energetic and simultaneous action upon and towards and among those new ideas which are rushing in upon it.'[3]

In conformity with the family analogy, the relation between staff and students is regarded as being paternal on the one side and filial on the other. The student is under authority. He is subjected to rules and regulations, not many or burdensome but inescapable. He lives in a world of definite duties requiring of him some degree of self-restraint and self-regulation[4]; and this is part of his preparation for life. On the other side the teacher's is, to some extent, a pastoral office. He has a responsibility towards his pupils as human beings which extends far beyond his formal obligations as an instructor.

But the most potent educational influence of Oxford and Cambridge has been found outside lecture room or laboratory and even outside the private hour with the tutor. It arises, indirectly, from the character of the community life. No passage in Newman is

[1] *Op. cit.*, pp. 127-8.
[2] Newman, *op. cit.*, p. 145.
[3] *ibid.*, p. 135.
[4] Whewell, *op. cit.*, p. 79.

C

better remembered or more frequently quoted than that in which
he depicts and extols the influence of students on one another and
asserts that, if he had to choose between one system in which
students lived a corporate life but received no formal teaching and
were submitted to no examination and another in which they were
rigorously examined but lived no corporate life, he would un-
hesitatingly prefer the former. It is in this perhaps that Oxford
and Cambridge have differed most decisively from Berlin or
Tübingen. To live in college and so to be thrown together with
others who come from different regions and different types of
home, with different temperaments and interests and subjects of
study, is a continuous exercise in mutual understanding and adjustment. Meeting one another in Hall, in Chapel, in Common or
Combination Room, on the river or playing fields, and most of all
in their own rooms, they acquire insensibly some appreciation of
points of view other than their own, and some power of living and
dealing with other people. The outside world has dimly sensed
this. It has not enquired minutely what course the Oxford or
Cambridge graduate has taken or even what class in an Honour
School he has gained. It has been content to feel that, by the very
fact of his residence in the university during his undergraduate
years, he has undergone a peculiarly enriching type of experience.

Of course it is not simply by being communities that Oxford and
Cambridge have exercised their educative influence. It is because
they are communities which possess an extremely distinctive and
inspiring, historic tradition. Their ' atmosphere ' is the result of
many centuries of corporate life. To wander among green lawns
and stately buildings of crumbling grey stone or mellow red brick—
such as the garden front of St. John's College, Oxford or the street
front of St. John's College, Cambridge—to dine in Hall with its
walls lined with the portraits of great men and its tables loaded
with old silver, and to take part in the time-honoured ritual of
university ceremonies—all these have made the undergraduate
feel himself the citizen of no mean city and the inheritor of an
illustrious tradition. They have conduced to expansion and eleva-
tion of mind and to that ' energy of the soul ' in which Aristotle
found the essence of true well-being.

In this tradition one of the most pervasive and characteristic
ingredients has been religion. For far the greater part of their
history, Oxford and Cambridge have deliberately set themselves
to be ' places of religious and useful learning.' The two universities

and their colleges were originally religious foundations and mani-
fold traces of this origin still persist. Every college has its chapel,
in which in term time there are daily and weekly services. The
universities have their 'University Churches,' to which the
dignitaries go weekly in state. But behind these expressly religious
activities, the whole genius of the place and the view of man and
of the world which it has, half-unconsciously, disseminated have
been Christian. Even small things like the formula for the conferment of degrees or the saying of grace in Hall have borne witness
to this. Much of it, no doubt, is conventional and very unlike the
New Testament. Signs of any strong wind of the spirit have been
rare. The Christianity which the ordinary undergraduate drank
in was extremely diluted. Yet, such as it was, the atmosphere of
the place was impregnated with it. Anyone going from Oxford
or Cambridge to a modern and thoroughly secularized university
must at once be conscious of the difference. Till quite lately the
ancient universities have in this respect been in tune with the
temper of our national life. Less than a hundred years ago it was
possible for Newman to appeal confidently to the self-evident fact
that belief in God was 'the secret assumption, too axiomatic to be
distinctly professed, of all our writers.'[1] Only too obviously that
situation has changed. But, until comparatively recent times, the
work and recreation and common life of Oxford and Cambridge,
however little directly religious, have been carried on within the
setting of an ultimate Christian commitment.

At their best the older English universities have admittedly had
success in turning out men fit to exercise responsibility, and this is
no easy task. Some years ago one who carried large responsibilities
in connection with appointments in the public service said, ' I can
get any number of men with " First Classes," but what I want
and find it hard to get, is " round " men.' To produce ' round '
men, in his sense of the word, is exactly what the older universities,
through their traditional mental discipline, based on classics and
mathematics, set themselves to do. What they have cultivated and
valued most highly is neither technical expertise nor prodigious
learning but, as Newman puts it, the quality of judgment or the
power to grapple with any subject and to seize the strong point in
it. This, he says, is ' the education which gives a man a clear,
conscious view of his own opinions and judgments, a truth in
developing them, an eloquence in expressing them, and a force in

[1] *Op. cit.*, p. 68.

urging them. It teaches him to see things as they are, to go right to the point, to disentangle a skein of thought, to detect what is sophistical, and to discard what is irrelevant. It prepares him to fill any post with credit, and to master any subject with facility. It shows him how to accommodate himself to others, how to throw himself into their state of mind, how to bring before them his own, how to come to an understanding with them, how to bear with them.'[1] In the same vein the authors of the recent Harvard Report on *General Education in a Free Society* define ' the abilities to be sought above all others in a general education,' as being ' to think effectively, to communicate thought, to make relevant judgments, to discriminate among values.'[2] In so doing, they echo Newman and imply that the qualities at which Oxford and Cambridge aimed in the middle of the nineteenth century are still of major importance in the middle of the twentieth. The fine flower of such training has been seen in men such as Balfour and Baldwin, Asquith and Milner, Curzon and Lang; and perhaps most of all in Gladstone, of whom it was truly said in a recent broadcast that he ' habitually lived from day to day in communion with the highest peaks of the human spirit ' and, from that, derived much of his strength. Naturally the average product fell far behind such outstanding figures. But this is the type which Oxford and Cambridge endeavoured to foster and, with the better of their alumni, did in some measure achieve.

## 2    LIBERAL

Even in Oxford and Cambridge the traditional ideal has been largely displaced by a newer one. In the other universities of this country, as in Scotland, Germany and the United States, the triumph of the new ideal has been complete. It has been reached by giving a still stronger emphasis to some features in the Christian-Hellenic conception and by the total omission of others. Its own most salient traits are the following.

First, investigation matters more than instruction. The advancement rather than the communication—or, as some critics unkindly put it, the embalmment—of knowledge is the primary business of the university. The former is essential, the latter only incidental. It has been well said that Socrates, Plato and Aristotle were resorted to, not because they had made teaching their business, but

---

[1] *Op. cit.*, p. 168.
[2] *Op. cit.*, p 65.

because they were believed to have made philosophy their business. It is indeed a reproach to the British universities that, till comparatively recently, the great figures in our intellectual history have worked outside and not within them. This is true among philosophers of Hume, Bentham, Mill and Spencer; among historians of Gibbon, Hallam, Grote and Macaulay; and among scientists of Dalton, Davy, Faraday and Darwin. In Germany, on the other hand, Kant and Hegel, Niebuhr, Ranke and Mommsen, Jhering and Savigny, Liebig, Helmholtz and Virchow were all university professors; and so they incurred less danger of a certain amateurishness, wastefulness and freakishness, which is liable to come from isolation. Moreover the quality of the education itself is greatly heightened by its linkage with the great masters. From such a man, ' if he have also in any measure the special gifts of a teacher, all will come forth with a life and love, a power, fullness and freshness, which you will look for in vain from the man whose main business is to communicate, and not to possess something worth communicating.'[1]

Secondly, learning for learning's sake is the proper business of the university. This is a worthy, satisfying, and wholly self-justifying activity. As President Eliot of Harvard put it at the outset of his forty years' reign, the dominating idea should be ' the enthusiastic study of subjects for the love of them and without any ulterior motive.'[2] The savant's is a high calling. Like the poet,

> He lives detachèd days
> He serveth not for praise
> For gold
> He is not sold.

Alike in Germany and in Scotland this is recognized and he receives something of the esteem which the Indian villagers felt for Kipling's *Lama*. Here is implied an austere ideal of knowledge and a new type of scholar. In one of his books E. F. Benson, writing of Cambridge as it was sixty years ago, draws a vivid contrast between Walter Headlam and the ordinary college tutor. The ordinary classical tutor was widely read and an accomplished writer of elegant compositions; but his knowledge, though more extensive, was essentially of the same order as that of the better among his

[1] Scott, *Introductory Lecture on the opening of Owen's College, Manchester,* p. 22.
[2] Morison, *Three Centuries of Harvard,* p. 328.

pupils. But ' Walter Headlam's knowledge of Greek began where theirs left off.' Now such mastery involves concentration and specialization. ' A man who is not capable of, so to speak, putting on blinkers, and of working himself up into the idea that the fate of his soul depends on whether, shall we say, his conjecture about this particular passage in a manuscript is correct—then that man had better keep away from scholarship.'[1]

Thirdly the function of the University as a community of science and learning is quite distinct from that of Church or State or of commerce and industry, and it should never be subservient to them. It has its own business which it understands better than any outsider can do. Its proper task is to promote neither money-making, nor good citizenship nor holiness, but simply sound learning. So, Dr. Doerne argues,[2] the duty of the university is not to make but to interpret history, not to produce leaders of Germany but to be the guardians of pure knowledge in a time of fanaticism. So far as training goes, it is the training of the graduate rather than of the undergraduate that is the university's primary concern. A master and his disciples were the nucleus out of which the earliest universities grew. So Socrates trained Plato and Plato trained Aristotle; the training of Alcibiades or Critias for public life was, by comparison, incidental and secondary. In terms of American organization, the ' college ' is only a kind of junior department; the ' university ' proper consists of its graduate schools. On this view Oxford and Cambridge in the nineteenth century contrasted unfavourably with the German universities, since a hundred years ago they trained graduates hardly at all, and fifty years ago only to a small extent. They might indeed be regarded as finishing schools rather than universities, and Paulsen's irony is thinly veiled when he writes of them, ' The general aim is to give a gentleman that broader and deeper culture with which custom demands that he should be equipped.'[3] Things are very different now. Even apart from the genuine researcher, the engineer or works manager who had come anywhere near Rutherford in Cambridge, the civil servant or business man who had come near Tout in Manchester, was often raised to a higher plane of intellectual life. As Paulsen wrote of the German situation at an earlier day, ' Though only

[1] Max Weber, quoted by Stirk in *German Universities through English Eyes*, p. 33.
[2] ' Problems of the German University ' in *The University in a Changing World*, 1932.
[3] *The German Universities and University Study*, E.T., p. 1.

a limited number of students succeed in doing original scientific work, yet the majority have at some time or other been seized with the impulse to seek after the truth. This longing remains in the souls of many, they become permanently interested in science and scientific life. Even in their callings they regard themselves as parts of the academic world; the teacher in the gymnasium, the clergyman, the physician, the judge, all seek to keep in touch with science, and not a few succeed not merely in following the standard of science as sympathisers and sharers in its glories, but in serving under it, here and there, as active co-workers.'[1]

Fourthly, the academic thinker must have a completely open field and he should approach it with a mind free from antecedent bias or presupposition. For him all questions are open, all assumptions tentative, all conclusions provisional. There is no fixed framework of thought within which he must operate, no authoritative premises which must be the starting point of his reasoning and which it would be impious to question. He may and must follow the argument whithersoever it leads. 'For the academic teacher and his hearers there can be no prescribed and no proscribed thoughts.'[2] Each science is autonomous. In particular it must be free from all religious supervision. Neither the historian nor the physicist need look nervously over his shoulder to see what the theologian has to say of his hypothesis. The Darwinian theory, or any suggested modification of it, must be discussed on the basis of the scientific evidence and judged by biological canons. The discussion must not be cramped or bedevilled by any pressure to accommodate it to the Book of Genesis. *Lehrfreiheit* is sacred and every kind of 'test' is inadmissible. In the words of President Eliot, 'The worthy fruit of academic culture is an open mind, trained to careful thinking, instructed in the methods of philosophic investigation, acquainted in a general way with the accumulated thought of past generations, and penetrated with humility.'[3]

Fifthly, the university must cultivate detachment. It must keep itself clear of matters of current practical controversy in fields, such as the political or the religious, which excite passion. The heat and turbidity and partisanship which these engender are incompatible with the objectivity and serenity inherent in a scientific attitude. A university is a 'thought-organization' not a 'will-organization,' and its aim is understanding rather than action. It is a society for

---

[1] *Op. cit.*, p. 169.
[2] Paulsen, *op. cit.*, p. 228.
[3] Morison, *op. cit.*, p. 330.

the pursuit of knowledge and not for the promotion of this cause or the prevention of that abuse. The only fanaticism permissible is ' the fanaticism of veracity.'

No doubt this emphasis is due to long experience of the distorting influence of the *odium theologicum* on the one hand and of ' reasons of state ' on the other. The moral has been drawn in two, slightly different, ways. Some modern universities have played for safety by excluding altogether from their purview the fields in which controversies are most liable to arise. Others, without such drastic self-mutilation, have insisted that their treatment, e.g., of religious or political issues, must be in quite a different temper and perspective from that of those engaged in the hurly-burly. This difference is very clearly expressed by Matthew Arnold in his essay on ' The Function of Criticism at the Present Time.' There he deprecates the tendency of the young and ardent to see everything in inseparable connection with politics and practical life, and he asserts the value of criticism which is disinterested in the sense that the critic has no axe to grind, however altruistic. True criticism, he says, requires a free play of mind, and writing eighty years ago, he found it existing in France, in the *Revue des Deux Mondes.* But by contrast in England—' we have the *Edinburgh Review,* existing as an organ of the old Whigs, and for as much play of mind as may suit its being that; we have the *Quarterly Review,* existing as an organ of the Tories, and for as much play of mind as may suit its being that; we have the *British Quarterly* existing as an organ of the political Dissenters and for as much play of mind as may suit its being that, we have the *Times,* existing as the organ of the common satisfied, well-to-do Englishman, and for as much play of mind as may suit its being that.'[1] The disinterestedness and free play of mind which Arnold here requires of the critic are precisely the characteristics which, on the Liberal conception, should mark contributions from the universities to the discussion of major issues.

This view is expressed very clearly by Paulsen writing at the turn of the century and by Dr. Flexner thirty years later. ' The scholars ' says Paulsen ' cannot and should not engage in politics.' This is because some of the qualities required in the thinker are the opposite of those which the practical politician should possess. The latter must be a man of resolute will and even a certain one-sidedness, who having chosen one path, follows it without *arrière pensée*. The thinker must look at a question from

[1] *Essays in Criticism,* p. 19.

all sides and must constantly return to his starting point to make sure that no error has crept into the argument though, in action, this would produce some indecisiveness.[1] Dr. Flexner makes the same point. It is for the university to apply 'free, resourceful, unhampered intelligence to the comprehension of problems,' but it must preserve its 'irresponsibility.' By this of course he does not mean that the university is irresponsible absolutely; any theoretical advance in the field of the social sciences is likely to have practical repercussions. But immediate short-term applications are not its business: to concern itself with these would deflect it from its proper work. The professor ' has no practical responsibility for the trouble he makes . . . But he must go on thinking.'[2]

Sixthly, the university should be highly selective and even fastidious in regard both to the subjects it treats and the methods it employs. It should abhor mediocrity: its business is with an intellectual aristocracy. Energy can too easily and insidiously be dissipated in a multiplicity of interests. The university should therefore look critically at all new claimants for the provision of professional training. (Here Dr. Flexner's devastating criticism of the lengths to which some American universities have allowed the ' service-station ' conception of their function to carry them is much in point.) The criterion to be employed is not the social importance of the proposed faculty or subject but its inherent and intellectual value. It is only the ' learned professions ' or those that have intellectual content in their own right[3] with which the universities should concern themselves. So also they should eschew all that is half-baked or concerned with the shop-window. The public opinion to which the professor is rightly sensitive is that of his peers,

> Like Verdi when, at his worst opera's end . . .
> He looks through all the roaring and the wreaths
> Where sits Rossini patient in his stall.

Seventhly, in the university there should be plenty of elbow-room. It should not be rigidly organized or regimented. Members of its staff should have the greatest possible freedom of choice in regard to what they are to teach, and how, and when. A great deal of

---

[1] *Op. cit.,* p. 55.
[2] *Universities, American, English, German,* p. 22.
[3] Hutchins, *The Higher Learning in America,* p. 56.

wastage can and should be tolerated, so long as a congenial atmo-sphere is provided for a Mommsen or a Rutherford.

Finally, the liberty, initiative and adult status of the student are strongly emphasized. To the *Lehrfreiheit* of the teacher corresponds the *Lernfreiheit* of the student. The extreme example of this is the 'elective system' as it has flourished in the United States. This represents a violent reaction against the rigid curricula of earlier days. It is based on the principle that at all points the decision what to study and how hard to study should be made by, and not for, the student himself. His menu is to be 'à la carte'; or, as Professor Morison says of President Eliot, 'he wished every man's curriculum to be tailor-made.'[1] The curriculum is to be fitted to the student and not the student to the curriculum. It matters little what you study, provided you are interested. So it is for the university to offer the widest possible variety of choice. At one time in Harvard, 'the Bachelor's degree could be earned by passing eighteen courses, no two of which need be related.'[2] Similarly it is the student's own affair whether he works or idles. No official pressure should be put on him; that is appropriate only at the schoolboy stage. The university is not a kindergarten. Admittedly such liberty may, and in some cases will, be abused, but that is part of the price of freedom. Again, if the student is to be regarded as an adult, his morals are his own affair. They are outside the cognizance and jurisdiction of the university. It is a part of his education that he should himself bear this responsibility. At the student stage it is true, as never before or after, that 'the student belongs to himself, he is responsible to nobody and for nobody but himself.'[3] As Dr. Flexner has it, 'one wonders, not whether character and manners are unimportant, but whether, like cleanli-ness or clear speech, they may not now more or less be taken for granted.'[4] Accordingly the traditional, pastoral function and obligations of the staff are repudiated. The professor has an objective responsibility for his subject but not a parental respon-sibility for his students. Such an office as that of a 'moral tutor' is misconceived.[5]

[1] *Op. cit.*, p. 343.
[2] *Op. cit.*, p. 346.
[3] Paulsen, *op. cit.*, p. 266.
[4] *ibid.*, p. 224.
[5] These principles have been carried to a much less extreme point in Great Britain than in the United States and in Germany. Certain combinations of subjects have generally been prescribed, and the idler who passes no examinations is not allowed to prolong his stay indefinitely. Even in the United States the elective system has been modified.

The original source of this ' Liberal ' conception was the French ' Enlightenment '; and, through such a man as Jefferson, this had some direct influence on the American universities. In Great Britain the change was somewhat delayed through antipathy to the Revolution. Here, as in America during most of the nineteenth century, the operative influence was the achievement and prestige of the German universities. This is seen in Sir William Hamilton's slashing *Edinburgh Review* attacks on Oxford in the early thirties and a generation later, in two almost simultaneous publications, Mark Pattison's *Suggestions for Academical Reorganization* and Matthew Arnold's *Schools and Universities on the Continent.* A generation later again it found a persuasive missionary in Lord Haldane. Even to-day this is probably ' the idea of the university ' to which most academic people would subscribe. It is true that, under the surface, it is in process of being eaten away by newer forces, and it is no longer even the avowed creed of many of the younger men. Here, as in so many other fields, the twilight of liberalism seems to have set in. But a spirited note of recall to its ideals is sounded in such books as Flexner's *Universities, American, English, German,* and the various writings of the author who styles himself ' Bruce Truscot.'

## 3   TECHNOLOGICAL AND DEMOCRATIC

Since the heyday of Liberalism new influences have been at work, and have acquired an enormous, and for many purposes a dominating, importance. These are the rise of applied science and technology and the growing democratization of the universities. For the moment it is the former with which we are concerned.

It is hard to exaggerate the significance for the universities of the growth and achievements of applied science. It is not merely that the balance of studies has been altered and that large sections of staff and students are now engaged in training as engineers or in the many large-scale applications of chemistry which in the old days hardly existed and certainly found no place in a university curriculum. Far more crucial is the fact that it is just in these fields that the universities are genuinely in touch with ' culture,' understood as the system of vital ideas of the age.[1] It is just here that they treat of what is of living interest to the world outside and to the mass of students themselves before they enter, and after they quit,

[1] See Ortega, *op. cit.,* p. 44.

the universities. It is this scientific culture that determines the categories in which people normally and naturally think. It determines also the issues which challenge their interest and attention, and to which they will really apply their minds because they readily see the point. For example the average schoolboy is familiar with, and keenly interested in, the mechanism of a motor bicycle, far more than in the story of human behaviour told in history or literature. It is such things as this which come alive to him and give him ' the pungent sense of effective reality.' It is by them that his mind is formed. In this way, within the universities as outside, the intellectual climate has been, insensibly but radically, altered.

Such studies are distinctive both in their aim and in their methods. Their aim is predominantly practical and utilitarian; it is conquest of nature for the satisfaction of human needs. The ends pursued are not mysterious, high-flown or elusive, but plain, practical, earthy and popular. It is these rather than theoretical curiosity which give the drive behind scientific discovery and invention. As Francis Bacon expressed it, its aim is ' fruit '; it abhors sterile argumentation. It endeavours, not to storm the sky but to minister to human convenience, or, in Macaulay's words, ' not to make men perfect but to make imperfect human beings comfortable.' It seeks to overcome admitted evils such as hunger and cold, disease and death. Its hero, or archetypal figure, is the man who makes two blades of grass grow where one grew before. Naturally this entails a sharp change in the valuation of handwork and bookwork. Traditionally handwork was looked down on as plebeian and ' banausic,' but now the technician is exalted and the mechanic becomes the truly representative man. Even the small change of the new culture consists of gadgets rather than of phrases.

But it is in its methods that the new culture is most distinctive, that is in the general lines on which problems are tackled. First it is empirical. It relies on observation and experiment rather than on general reasoning; it asks what actually is rather than what ought to be or what must be. The scientist is distrustful of authority and endeavours to put himself in the way of stubbing his toe on a fact. ' Hippocrates may say what he likes, but the coachman is dead.' He is chary of appealing to first principles or to intuition. He deals less in axioms than in provisional hypotheses, very tentatively held and readily modified or abandoned in face of new evidence. He lays immense stress on verification and reaches anything like firm conclusions only from thoroughly tested data. In the words of the Harvard Report, he is ' tough-minded, curious and ready for change.' Education on this pattern has a mental discipline of its own, different from that engendered by Latin prose or by Euclid but, in its way, quite as real. It enjoins submission to fact in despite of all preconceptions and predilections.

Secondly it is analytic. In order to bring things to the test of experiment, it endeavours to break up what is composite into its simple elements which can be isolated and controlled. A motor-bicycle which can be taken to pieces and put together again or a machine-gun which can be stripped and re-assembled are the kinds of entity with which it can deal most successfully. It requires clarity and precision, and it steers clear of all that is cloudy, grandiose and emotionally coloured.

Thirdly it is deliberately selective. It discriminates between those fields and methods which promise practical results and those which do not. The things with which it has learned that it can deal are those that admit of being measured and weighed and counted and where the results of enquiry can be represented in graphs and statistical tables. It is by such discrimination that it has progressed beyond the pretentious futilities of the alchemist and the astrologer. It turns its attention away from issues where enquiry is likely to be fruitless because the conditions of testing do not exist.

From such aims and methods there results a prevailing mental attitude which is at once activist and optimistic. The unparalleled increase in human power over environment, which the new know-ledge has produced, has stimulated a strong drive for the removal of preventible evils, coupled with a recognition that a large part of those evils hitherto regarded as inevitable is in fact preventible. Many years ago Sir Alfred Zimmern drew attention to this change.[1] He observed that the women of Galilee and of Attica continued as a matter of course, generation after generation, the old accus-tomed methods of ' grinding at the mill,' whereas no intelligent Lancashire mill-girl would tolerate them for many months without some attempt to find labour-saving devices. Resignation ceases to be a virtue and becomes a vice. One of Stevenson's fables, ' The Penitent,' well illustrates this change.

' A man met a lad weeping. " What do you weep for?" he asked.

[1] *The Greek Commonwealth*, p. 218.

" I am weeping for my sins," said the lad.

" You must have little to do," said the man.

The next day they met again. Once more the lad was weeping.

" Why do you weep now?" asked the man.

" I am weeping because I have nothing to eat," said the lad.

" I thought it would come to that," said the man.'

To a much larger extent than the subjects previously studied in universities, the applied sciences require large-scale organization, for they often depend on bulky and expensive equipment and involve the co-operation of large numbers of workers. There is less scope for the free-lance, going his own way at his own time and purely on his own initiative. At present the backwardness of the social sciences is in marked contrast with the triumphs of the natural sciences, and the demand is growing for the application to social problems of the methods which have succeeded so well in the other field.

Of course what here concerns us is to understand, not the aims and methods of scientists in themselves, but those elements in them which have entered deeply into contemporary culture and thus are affecting the minds of university teachers generally and still more of students. Three of these are particularly significant. The first is the concentration of interest. " To an amazing extent people's environment has come to consist of machines and man-made things."[1] Beside the invention of the combustion engine, the discovery of insulin or penicillin, the splitting of the atom, with their obvious and stupendous consequences for human welfare, such pursuits as literary criticism, philosophical speculation or historical research are apt to seem secondary, remote and ineffectual. Secondly there is a new, and almost intoxicating, sense of power.

> Why then? The world's mine oyster
> Which I with sword will open.

To many the Russian experiment is a symbol and a pledge of the possibilities of social engineering. To a wholly unprecedented degree, men can and will determine their own destiny. Thirdly the colossal achievements of applied science have engendered a strongly optimistic temper. Professor Bernal goes so far as to enumerate among the major tasks to be undertaken the ultimate

---

[1] *General Education in a Free Society*, p. 15.

conquest of space, of disease, and death. 'Salvation by the acquisition and application of knowledge' seems on the way to becoming the religion of modern man.

The stream of influence derived from technological preoccupations coalesces with another. This springs from the change in the clientèle from which students, and in a rather lesser degree staff, are drawn. In the nineteenth century Oxford and Cambridge were predominantly upper-class institutions. The great majority of undergraduates were sons, not indeed of noblemen or plutocrats but, of the better-to-do professional men, country parsons, etc. They and their teachers shared a common social and cultural background. In their homes were space, books, a certain modicum of leisure and of intellectual interest. Their destiny was politics, the higher ranks of the Civil Service, the Bar, the Church, or the life of a country gentleman and landowner. The students of German universities were commonly drawn from a somewhat lower social stratum. But, there too, hardly any were of working-class origin, and in a broad sense, they expected to enter the ruling class of society.[1] To-day a large proportion of the students at modern universities in this country, and a substantial proportion at Oxford and Cambridge, come from working and lower middle-class homes, and have begun their education in the public elementary schools. To-morrow this change is likely to be carried a good deal further still; for one of the chief motive-forces in education to-day is a determination, based on a new sense of social justice, to achieve a far greater measure of equality of opportunity.

For large numbers of students to-day, to get to the university at all is a hardly-won achievement and by no means a matter of course. They are therefore more highly selected than their predecessors in the sense that they have been subjected to more exacting tests. On the average they certainly know more and they probably have more intellectual ability. Potentially therefore they are better material. On the other hand they are apt to suffer from handicaps which we have not yet found the way fully to overcome. They have not the background of culture which could once be assumed and often lack interest outside their prescribed subject. They have, as it were, been conducted over a prescribed route by forced marches, which leave them tired and with small inclination or energy for exploring by-roads, and so too often

[1] cf. Paulsen, op. cit., pp. 126-7, 265.

they have little initiative or resilience. At the same time their aim is utilitarian. To them the university is, first and foremost, the avenue to a desirable job, that is to one which promises some measure of economic security and social consideration. Success in examinations is therefore of dominating importance. The gay and carefree atmosphere and the absence of pressing material pre-occupations which gave so much of its distinctive character to university life is disappearing. ' Redbrick ' University has always been, and ' Oxbridge ' is fast becoming, the university of the busy.

These changes in the provenance and character of their students naturally affect the universities' own aims and methods. They call in question older ideals, whether christian-hellenic or liberal. For instance the demands of equity challenge the cult of those particular excellences which have been associated either with Oxford or with Heidelberg, on the ground that they are essentially aristocratic and sacrifice the many to the few. Questions such as the following are asked. Should not universities cease to concentrate on the training of the ruling classes or of *Gelehrte,* i.e., either of a political or an intellectual aristocracy? Should they not think more of furnishing recruits for the middle-grades of business and industry? Does not the absence of regulation, the suffering the average student to be idle provided that the outstanding student gets the maximum stimulus, involve an unjustifiable sacrifice of the many to the few? However attractive the products, are they not hothouse plants? Does not the whole system presuppose in the student a background of culture such as is impossible without a high degree of economic privilege? Is not disdain for the bread-and-butter motive a luxury of the well-to-do? Formerly the universities were avowedly inten-ded to buttress the existing social order; but was not their error, not as liberals would hold in attachment to any particular social order, but simply in attachment to the wrong one? In a democratic age ought they not to be engines of a beneficent social revolution? Should they not help to effect the transfer of power and of the chief right to consideration from the classes to the masses? Is not this indeed what the abler and more altruistic students, those who are leaders in bodies such as the National Union of Students, do in fact demand? In the war the universities directed all their resources to furthering the national cause; and in an age which is setting itself to achieve a juster social order, should they not repudiate the cult of aloofness and neutrality, and deliberately adopt a democratic orientation?

Within the universities as without, these two influences, the technological and the proletarian, are in course of producing a new culture; and this differs sharply from that in which universities originally were nourished and took their shape. It condemns liberalism as being aristocratic and fastidious rather than equalitarian, detached rather than ' mucking in,' and as exalting a sterile scholarship rather than being frankly occupational and utilitarian. It regards ' learning for learning's sake ' as an idol to be demolished. In its light the Renaissance humanist is as little a model as the medieval schoolman, Dr. Gilbert Murray and Mr. ' Bruce Truscot ' are out of date equally with Cardinal Newman and Dr. Whewell. As yet this new culture is articulate only in some of the younger teachers (e.g. the Association of Scientific Workers) and of the leading students (e.g. the National Union of Students). But, under the surface and only half-consciously, it is widely diffused. There is thus a widening gulf between the official and traditional professions of the universities and what, for large and growing sections of them, are the actually operative motives and beliefs. And here time seems to be on the side of the rebels, for it is they who are in tune with the movement of ideas in the contemporary world. To adapt a simile used by Gierke in a different connection, we may say, ' Within the liberal husk we see a scientific-utilitarian kernel. Always waxing, it draws away all vital nutriment from the shell and in the end that shell is likely to be broken.'

# III

# SOME CAUSES OF OUR PRESENT DISCONTENT

We have had the Classical-Christian university, which was later displaced by the Liberal university. This in turn has been undermined, but not as yet superseded, by the combined influence of democratization and technical achievement. What we have, in fact, to-day is the chaotic university.

## I SHIRKING OF FUNDAMENTAL ISSUES

Broadly speaking, the university to-day is not asking the really fundamental questions. In particular there has been something like a taboo on the treatment of contentious issues of politics or religion. Sometimes this has been statutory, but more often it has rested on a generally accepted convention. It seems to have been due partly to historical causes and partly to a national idiosyncrasy. Thus the coolness and indifference of the eighteenth century were a natural reaction from the fanaticism of the seventeenth. In this country, the ethos of Walpole replaced the ethos of Cromwell and has maintained itself ever since. The wars of religion had been ferocious and divisive; they served as a warning. In retrospect they seemed to have produced much heat and little light. Civil peace was now preserved by a tacit agreement to differ on ultimate questions or rather by a prudential disposition to let sleeping dogs lie; and it was in this ethos that the modern universities grew up. They were also influenced by a reaction from the intrusion of ecclesiastical considerations into a field where they were felt to be not only embittering but irrelevant, and by a recollection of the days when winning or keeping a chair in any faculty was determined less by the candidate's learning and scholarship in his own field than by his soundness on the doctrines of the Trinity or of Baptismal Regeneration and by his adhesion to the Thirty Nine Articles or to the Westminster Confession.

50

The taboo is due also to a characteristic ingrained in our national temperament. We have a semi-instinctive disposition to shy away sharply like a nervous horse from any question arousing strong emotion or likely to involve commitment at a deep level. This has its creditable side, a loathing for a Tartuffe or a Pecksniff and a healthy sense of the inadequacy of definitions and formulae to do justice to living reality. But a praiseworthy reticence in the expression of one's innermost convictions is one thing: to have no such convictions to express is another. Yet the transition is easy. Nearly all foreign observers note in us a certain intellectual and emotional unadventurousness, a tendency to remain near the surface, an indisposition to dig deep. This is particularly marked where religion is in question. We like to think that ours is the religion of all sensible men and that sensible men do not ask themselves too closely what that may be. How much of the creed of a Church to which we may outwardly conform do we actually believe? Why that, as Newman says ironically, is a question delicate to ask and imprudent to answer. When pressed on such matters, we feel uncomfortable, embarrassed and resentful. In its extreme form at least, this is a form of infantilism; for it is a refusal to grow up and to come to grips with a reality which might make claims on us. But it is a trait which those who live the academic life share in full measure with their fellow-countrymen.

Whatever its causes or excuses, such a taboo is disastrous and indefensible. It confines university education to the use of means as opposed to the choice of ends, to training in the acquisition and handling of tools as opposed to appreciation and criticism of the larger purposes for which those tools are to be used. It abjures any contribution to answering the master-question—How shall a man live? For instance a university professor of French may say—'I have studied the French language and literature and institutions with some thoroughness and I can expound them with authority. But whether Voltaire or Pascal has the truer apprehension of reality, whether Talleyrand or Fénélon has better mastered the secret of living, I have no idea. There you enter a region not of knowledge but of private taste or guess-work. My guess is no better than the next man's and I have nothing to offer my pupils.' On that showing a university can train a student to be a chemist or a linguist. But what he should do with his chemistry or languages when he has acquired them, whether and why injustice and cruelty and fraud are bad and their opposites are good, whether faith in God is a snare and a delusion or is the only basis on which human life can be lived without disaster—all these things the student must find out for himself as best he may, for a university education can do nothing to help him. If you want a bomb the chemistry department will teach you how to make it, if you want a cathedral the department of architecture will teach you how to build it, if you want a healthy body the departments of physiology and medicine will teach you how to tend it. But when you ask whether and why you should want bombs or cathedrals or healthy bodies, the university, on this view, must be content to be dumb and impotent. It can give help and guidance in all things subsidiary but not in the attainment of the one thing needful. In living their lives the young are left ' the sport of every random gust.' But for the educator this is abdication.

Whatever plausibility such a self-denying ordinance once possessed, in the present state of the world it has it no longer. In the nineteenth century it seemed possible for a university training to omit all transmission of communal wisdom concerning the art of living, because that was attended to outside the university. Whatever the differences on religious and philosophical issues between Whewell and Mill, Gladstone and Huxley, Newman and Matthew Arnold, they had substantially the same standards of what was good and evil in conduct, they all attached supreme importance to the difference between right and wrong and they were in general agreement as to the kinds of conduct which were ' right ' or ' wrong.' They all believed firmly in a system of objective values. In many ways his contemporaries looked on Mill as an iconoclast. But it was Mill who said that it was better to be a human being dissatisfied than a pig satisfied, better to be Socrates dissatisfied than a fool satisfied; and who added that, if the fool or the pig were of a different opinion, it was because they only knew their own side of the question. So the early students at University College London, Owens College Manchester, or Mason College Birmingham could acquire this ethical culture elsewhere, in home, school or church. But no one questioned its necessity. The *Edinburgh Review* which approved the secular system of University College and the *Quarterly Review* which condemned it were alike clear on that point. But it is the validity of any moral order at all that is in question to-day. In Europe amoralism is widely prevalent; and our own abler young men will accept nothing from tradition without searching examination. We academic people are too little awake to this disintegration. The indictment against us is like that brought by Jesus against the Pharisees. We have concentrated on what is of secondary, and have neglected what is of primary, importance; we have paid tithe of mint and anise and cummin, and have omitted the weightier matters of the law, judgment, mercy and faith.

## 2   FALSE NEUTRALITY

For some time now many of the abler students and of the younger teachers have been in sharp reaction against the liberal ideal of academic detachment and its embodiment of university practice. That ideal is indicted on two main counts; first as frivolous and irresponsible, and secondly, as bogus and hypocritical.

First the traditional academic attitude is felt by many of the younger men to be too exclusively the attitude of a spectator. It is appropriate to one who has a theoretical problem to solve rather than a practical choice to make. It is like that of a gifted Foreign Secretary, of whom it is related that he would hold his colleagues entranced by a masterly exposition, well-informed, witty and eloquent, of the situation in some Balkan country. At the end the Prime Minister would lean forward and say 'Thank you Foreign Secretary, and what action do you recommend?'; and then, it became painfully clear that he had nothing to recommend. He had done with the subject; his interest in it was academic; he had lectured on it, and that was that. But thought divorced from responsible action is sterile, and a purely theoretical analysis is liable to lead to impotence. On practical affairs the academic mind is prone to reach a state of permanently suspended judgment, of conscientious indecision.[1] In the words of Professor Hogben, it 'prevents you from coming to definite conclusions by propounding unanswerable questions' and it produces 'a vague broad-mindedness about the burning questions of the day.' To students this seems a form of elegant trifling in which dons engage while Rome is burning without their realizing it. Also dons suffer sometimes from a dead weight of learning which inhibits decision. 'Some scholars' said Jowett 'in their dread of ignorance . . . lose their elasticity and freedom of thought, their sense of the proportion and value of facts.'[2] This is the attitude glorified in *The Grammarian's Funeral*, 'Before living he'd learn how to live'; and in this spirit many a scholar spends his life in accumulating data for some

---

[1] cf. Paulsen, *op. cit.*, p. 265.
[2] *Life*, p. 133.

*magnum opus* which he never writes; or, if he does write it, his book consists of prolegomena. But intellectual fastidiousness is a snare. It is futile to wait for a vantage point of perfection, intellectual or moral, from which to act. Probability is still the guide of life, and here ' the better is the enemy of the good.'

In any case such detachment is antipathetic to the younger generation. Before, during, and since the war, they have lived in a habitual consciousness of a world which seems about to fall in on them. To them the older men in the universities often seem ' remote and ineffectual,' utopian, fugitives from life, irresponsible shirkers. So, since they cannot get guidance for action from their teachers, they will seek it from less reputable sources. It was thus that, fifteen years ago, the students of Germany fell victims to Hitler. To adapt slightly a sentence of Professor Collingwood's, they will infer that for guidance in the problems of life, since one cannot get it from thinkers or from thinking, from ideals or from principles, one must look to people who are not thinkers (but fools), to processes that are not thinking (but passion), to aims that are not ideals (but caprices), and to rules that are not principles (but expediency).

This reaction may be exaggerated. The ideal of detachment and ' irresponsibility ' (in Flexner's sense) may not be simply a vice. But it certainly needs to be rethought.[1] It needs this, if only because on many issues neutrality is impossible and the claim to impartiality cannot be sustained. The liberal ideal in its traditional form is based on a view of human nature, including academic human nature, that is naïve. This brings us to the second count in the indictment, which is urged with even greater vigour. Whether neutrality is desirable or not, it is alleged that, when probed, it is found to be a sham. It turns out to cover an uncritical acceptance of the common assumptions of the day or those of some particular social or professional stratum. In other words, so-called academic objectivity is a fraud; and the fraud is none the less disastrous and reprehensible because its perpetrators are commonly also its victims and deceive themselves as successfully as they deceive others.

This masked partisanship can be seen in the fields of politics, religion and ethics. In politics, to keep silence on controversial issues is, in effect, to acquiesce in the *status quo,* that is, in ' the institutions of the country,' the existing social order, whatever that may be. For practical purposes it is to side with conformists against nonconformists. So in Germany the universities have been tied up

[1] See below, pp. 61–68.

with the State, in the United States with the plutocracy, in England with the unwritten laws of a socially stratified society, as truly as in Russia to-day they are avowedly linked to the social revolution and in Spain to Catholicism. In England we are little conscious of this; and it is not quite so true as it used to be, for society as a whole is less stratified. But lookers-on often see what familiarity obscures for the participants; and that our universities reflect a hierarchical class-structure is certainly their impression. Thus Paulsen writes, at the turn of the century, 'In England . . . the scholars are enmeshed in the views and judgments of the governing class of society,'[1] and twenty years later Dibelius[2] expresses the same opinion.

In the field of religion the profession of neutrality is equally a pretence. It is related that the philosophical Faculty of a great American university, on acquiring a new building for their home, proposed to have inscribed over the main entrance the Protagorean saying, 'Man is the measure of all things.' The President of the university however thought otherwise; and when they returned to work after the long vacation, the words they actually found were, 'What is man that Thou art mindful of him?' Here is epitomized the fundamental religious issue; and on this issue the modern university intends to be, and supposes it is, neutral, but it is not. Certainly, it neither inculcates nor expressly repudiates belief in God. But it does what is far more deadly than open rejection; it ignores Him. Though Lucretius, Voltaire, and Marx agree in rejecting religion ('*Tantum religio potuit suadere malorum,*' '*Ecrasez l'infame,*' 'Religion is the opium of the people'), they regard it as pernicious but not as insignificant. Nietzsche proclaims defiantly that 'God is dead,' but to him this is an assertion having revolutionary consequences for life at a thousand points. But in modern universities, as in modern society 'some think God exists, some think not, some think it is impossible to tell, and the impression grows that it does not matter.'

Does it matter? If a negative answer to that question is silently assumed, the cause of atheism is won even before the battle is joined. The crucial question is not whether a man can assent *ex animo* to the Athanasian Creed or at the other extreme, whether he has 'lost his faith.' Theism is not just a speculative opinion, however assured, as e.g. that the internal angles of a triangle are together equal to two right angles, a conviction which one can

[1] *Op. cit.*, p. 262.
[2] *England*, p. 409.

entertain without doing anything about it. It is 'betting your life that there is a God.' Equally atheism is no speculative opinion. It is leaving God on one side, having 'no need of that hypothesis.' In that case one need not bother to deny the existence of God, one is simply not interested; and that is precisely the condition of a large part of the world to-day. It is in this sense that the university to-day is atheistic. If in your organization, your curriculum, and your communal customs and ways of life, you leave God out, you teach with tremendous force that, for most people and at most times, He does not count; that religion is at best something extra and optional, a comfort for the few who are minded that way, but among the luxuries rather than the necessities of life. 'Admit a God' says Newman 'and you introduce among the subjects of your know-ledge, a fact encompassing, closing in upon, absorbing every other fact conceivable.'[1] But in that case, since it is the habit of the modern university to study all other subjects without any reference to theology at all, the obvious inference is that it does not 'admit a God' in any sense that is of practical importance. It is a fallacy to suppose that by omitting a subject you teach nothing about it. On the contrary you teach that it is to be omitted, and that it is therefore a matter of secondary importance. And you teach this not openly and explicitly, which would invite criticism; you simply take it for granted and thereby insinuate it silently, insidiously, and all but irresistibly. If indoctrination is bad, this sort of condi-tioning and preconscious habituation is surely worse.

Two comments remain to be added. First this state of things is the result of no plot; no one has planned it. But if a planner of atheistic conviction and Machiavellian astuteness had been at work, he could hardly have wrought more cunningly. Secondly we are here arguing, not that atheism is untrue, but that, whether it is true or not, the modern university is not neutral. To persuade your-self that you are what you are not, is intellectually demoralizing; one need not be a theist to assent to this. A camouflaged partisan-ship is both more dishonest and more damaging than one which is open and avowed. Though Christianity has played so large a part in our national traditions, we do not claim that the modern university should base itself, like the older type, on acceptance of the Christian view of life. But this should not go by default as it does now. The challenge should be fairly and squarely presented to students. The decision they have to make is, in the highest degree, a

[1] *Op. cit.*, p. 26.

responsible decision, but to-day it is seldom presented or taken as such.

There is a yet more elemental issue in regard to which it must be asked whether universities are, or should be, neutral. That is the question whether the distinction of right and wrong is still to operate in affairs, both public and personal. For Europe to-day, and indeed for the whole world, this is a question of life and death. By a correct intuition, public opinion perceived that the recent war was not a mere struggle for existence and power. It perceived that Hitler had raised in a spectacular form the question whether any moral standards were to be recognized, of which the possessors of power must take account and by which they were to be judged, or whether justice is only ' the interest of the stronger ' and the so-called obligations of justice, good faith and humanity only rules of conduct for slaves, often convenient to their masters but never binding on them. But Hitler's challenge is only the most conspicuous instance of a general tendency. Long before the war amoralism had gone far on the continent of Europe. The violence of the war-years, the threat of the atomic bomb and even the experience of the resistance movements have deepened it. The best of our own young men are disillusioned, suspicious of idealistic appeals as ' baited by knaves to set a trap for fools,' disinclined to accept any moral code at second hand or from convention. They will not be held by any conventions which strike them as primarily designed for ' the maintenance of comfort and security as known to a suburban street in peacetime.' In nothing has Dr. Flexner's book more clearly ' dated ' than in his suggestion that morality, like cleanliness, can now be taken for granted. This is the fundamental question of our day. How are the universities oriented towards it ? Are they oriented towards it at all ?

But here too the universities have not only been irresponsibly neglectful. They have also escaped their own notice in covertly playing a destructive rôle. As is explained in the following section, we are coming to realize that much in their present structure militates against the development of responsible personality.

## 3   FRAGMENTATION

For many years the work of universities has tended to be done in an increasing number of separate water-tight compartments. Both for students and for staff the attainment of a synoptic view or map of the intellectual world and the relating together of the different disciplines of study, on which Newman laid so much stress, have largely dropped out. Here it is fair to recognize that the universities are in a great difficulty, since much of their human material is already warped in this respect when it first reaches them. In this warping both home and school play a part. Home tends to be set on the ultimate attainment of some job which will carry with it a measure of economic security and of social standing. Here the boy who arrived at school one day with a note, 'Don't teach my boy poetry, he's going to be a grocer' is representative; if he had been an intending teacher, his parents' outlook would have been no less narrowly vocational. School tends to be set on success in examinations, which is the shortest road to a good job; and such success is sought by concentration on the matter immediately in hand. During their last two years the cleverer pupils are working for Higher School Certificate or for College scholarships at Oxford and Cambridge. The quantity of information demanded of them is continually rising. Curricula are overloaded. For the great majority the only chance to cover the prescribed course is to keep severely to it and to explore neither to the right nor to the left.

Thus the student is apt to arrive at the university with his mind already set in an attitude of incuriousness outside his own restricted field. In any event it would be hard to counteract this, and all too little effort to do so has yet been made. At the university the same causes operate as at school and produce the same results. In the remoter distance the prospect of a job, in the nearer the examination class-list, dominate the student's mind. He concerns himself only with 'what pays for the schools.' Dr. Hutchins tells us of a friend who took an hour to explain to his law-class the economic and social background of the fellow-servant rule. At the end of the hour one student inquired 'What's this got to do with the law?' And Dr. Hutchins comments, 'There is a good deal to be said for the boy's position; he had come to the university under the impresson that it would prepare him for the bar examinations and teach him the rules of the game. He felt that he was being cheated.'[1] Almost any university teacher could relate a similar experience.

The effect of this tendency is narrowness in the individual and fragmentation in the university. In the words of Archbishop William Temple, a university becomes 'a place where a multitude

[1] *The Higher Learning in America*, p. 38.

of studies are conducted, with no relation between them except those of simultaneity and juxtaposition.'[1] The student is often confined to one of these; and even if he studies more than one, he is seldom led to reflect about their bearing on one another. It has been said that a lawyer's training is the worst possible for a Foreign Secretary. It is the barrister's business to work intensively on one case at a time and then to put it completely aside and go on to the next one, but the Foreign Secretary requires to have the whole field in mind all the time, since what is done in one plan may have repercussions everywhere else. In the graduate, as in the Foreign Secretary, grooviness is a grave defect, but it is also a common one. In a recent lecture Professor Woodward has pertinently contended that no one should receive an honours degree without showing evidence of that 'minimum of general understanding which differentiates education from technical skill.'[2] But few university teachers can feel any confidence that most honours graduates to-day fulfil this condition.

This defect has not passed unnoticed. It is, in fact, quite widely acknowledged and deplored, and suggestions for mitigating it are numerous.[3] But its full dimensions are rarely perceived and its true gravity is too little understood. It can indeed be viewed from a number of different levels. First the lack of general information and of wide reading and culture may be regarded simply as the lack of an attractive and desirable grace. Dons may often, and students sometimes, be heard to regret this; but the regret does not go very deep. Dons will not make big sacrifices, they will not for instance make radical reductions in the specialist demands of honours schools for which they are responsible, in order to leave more room for a culture of which, sometimes, they are themselves devoid. Students again are apt to regard such culture as a luxury which, whatever its charms, must be subordinated to more immediate necessities. Secondly, this 'atomism' may be felt to impair the character of the university as a community, since it prevents genuine communication between different sections. In particular it has resulted in an ugly rift between the scientific and the literary faculties. But even within the same faculty scholars have very often given up the attempt to understand one another outside the narrowest groups.

[1] In a sermon preached before the University of Oxford, *Freedom, Peace and Truth*, p. 5.
[2] *Towards a New Learning*, p. 4.
[3] See ch. VII below.

The President of a great American university once remarked that
the members of his teaching staff had practically nothing to say to
one another, for they had nothing in common. They had no common core of culture, no common frame of reference or stock of
fundamental ideas. This is becoming a feature of university life
everywhere. Trivialities form the only meeting-ground. Students,
it has been said, talk to one another only about athletics and the
Faculty only about the weather. Thirdly it may be seen to result
only too often in a narrow and arrogant departmentalism, which
takes for granted that 'there's nothing like leather.' This is the
'provincialism' described by Matthew Arnold as 'a serious, settled,
fierce, narrow misconception of the whole relative value of one's
own things and the things of others.' It produces a one-sided and
disproportioned outlook, and it disqualifies for judgment outside an
extremely limited field.

But beneath all these there is a further and a deeper level from
which the prevailing fragmentation must be regarded, and it is
with this that we are specially concerned. For it impairs not only
the outworks but the citadel of personality; and it does so not by
frontal attack, but by slow erosion of the foundations. So far as their
university studies are concerned, most students are nowhere confronted with the challenge or the opportunity to see life steadily and
whole. They are not stimulated to regard their own lives as a whole
rather than as a set of disconnected experiences, to make a plan of
life and to feel responsibility for it, to face a life-challenge and to
make a life-choice. Hence they may never come of age morally, as
persons able to decide and to act as responsible human beings. In
practice, of course, students must and do integrate their lives in
some degree, but generally the university does not help them. In
this respect it leaves them to the influence of agencies of a sub-
university grade, such as the cinema and the cheap newspaper.
Indeed by abstention it insinuates an impression that such integration is not a matter of the first importance.

It thus begs in advance the question of belief in God for it does
away with the only condition in which such a belief can have
meaning. You can have a strong sense of personal responsibility
without a belief in God, but you cannot have a living belief in God
without some sense of responsibility, some conception of your whole
life as coming under judgment. A conscious orientation of the whole
self to the whole universe need not involve theism; but, without it,
there can be no theism.

If this is true, the modern university is betraying its students. The more unthinking type of student simply drifts. Some sort of embryo of a working creed he must have; no one out of an asylum can live without it. But his version is uncritical and mainly unconscious, it is picked up at haphazard, and it is muddled and incoherent. He never faces as a whole the social problem or the problem of his personal life. Two books about British student life were written just before the war.[1] Their standpoints are sharply different, but each is based on wide contacts and on recent personal experience. They agree in emphasizing the pervasive triviality of corporate life for the majority. On the other hand, the thinking type of student is concerned, and often passionately, to find a working philosophy of life. He discusses major questions constantly. But since he has little help from the university, his discussion is often callow and has small reference to ' the best that has been thought and known.' Thus, of these two types, the former is not being helped to ask, nor the latter to answer, the really fundamental questions; and the university is doing its duty by neither. Here, as Christians, we have to admit that we ourselves have a bad record. We are as deeply implicated in this fissiparous and disintegrating tendency as anyone else and have as little understood its true import. We are in no position to say, ' This comes of your not listening to our warning.' On the contrary, if our present diagnosis is true, we, of all those concerned in universities, are specially called to an extremely thorough ' Metanoia.'

# 4  UNCRITICIZED PRESUPPOSITIONS

Mr. C. S. Lewis begins his Riddell Lectures, *The Abolition of Man*, with a scathing exposure of the misuse of suggestion as illustrated in a certain school textbook on English. The authors of the textbook had commented on a particular aesthetic judgment in such a way as in effect to ' debunk ' all judgments of value. ' We appear,' they say, ' to be saying something very important about something : and actually we are only saying something about our own feelings.' This implies, as Mr. Lewis points out, that judgments of value are only subjective and are unimportant. Further ' it is not a theory they put into his (the schoolboy's) mind but an assumption, which ten years hence, its origin forgotten and its presence unconscious, will condition him to take one side in a controversy which he has

[1] David Paton, *Blind Guides?* and Brian Simon, *A Student's View of the Universities.*

never recognised as a controversy at all.' For Mr. Lewis's immediate purpose—and for ours— it does not matter whether the belief so implanted is, in fact, true or false; in either case the procedure is wholly irresponsible. The teacher is doing something which is liable to have a profound effect on the pupil, but that is probably unintentional and unconsidered. The pupil is being subtly conditioned, by a form of suggestion which invites no critical thought, to think and feel in a particular way on an issue of the first importance. This is educationally disastrous and indefensible.

We have already emphasized the immense effect which is in fact exercised by unconscious assumptions. The major part of most people's conclusions rests on unformulated major premises. Thus there is acute need of a far greater attention than most of us pay to the latent assumptions underlying our own and other people's reasoning. To stimulate this, is one of the university's most urgent and most neglected tasks.

To recognize the part played by presuppositions is, on one side, to recognize fallibility. We all see the world through, more or less, coloured spectacles, and many factors have contributed to determining the colours. First we are finite beings, each of us living at a particular time and place and having a limited mental power. This involves inevitably that we see things from a particular angle and our preconceptions reflect that. Secondly the personal equation cannot be eliminated. What I think will depend in part on the kind of person I am. I am not only a finite being, but I have a particular psychological bias, derived from my particular temperament. According as I am a natural optimist or pessimist, sentimental or ' hard-boiled,' the same events will take a different colouring for me. Mark Tapley or Mrs. Gummidge, Mr. Pickwick or Mr. Gradgrind, will undergo different experiences in the same conditions. What they actually see is affected by what they expect to see. Thirdly, not only my psychical make-up but also my social background determines the character of my vision. The class to which I belong, my economic interest, my political party, my church, all contribute to tinting my spectacles. It does not require abnormal penetration to trace with some clarity the influence of such factors on those who differ from us; but it is only with extreme labour and pain that we can detect them in ourselves. Fourthly, along with the whole of our generation, our insight is subject to the limits of a particular historical period. Here too we can detect this quite easily in the writers of earlier periods, but at best only dimly in our own. It has been pointed out that even the Cambridge Modern History gives a totally inadequate consideration to economic influences. It does not require a historian of Lord Acton's penetration and range of knowledge to see that to-day; but his plans were laid fifty years ago. Again we speak of the ' Whig interpretation of history.' But we are only conscious of that because we have, to some extent, outgrown it; Macaulay did not think he was writing Whig history but objective history. Finally we are biassed, imperceptibly but constantly, by emotion. ' Perverse emotions combine with twisted reason to enchant and enthral us.' Naturally this is truest in fields such as history, literature and philosophy in which value-judgments are involved and emotions are stirred. But, even in more abstract subjects such as textual criticism or mathematics, a scholar tends to be biassed in favour of any opinion to which he has publicly committed himself. Professor Smith's quest of truth is insensibly coloured by an impulse to defend his original thesis against the wrong-headed and ill-natured criticism of Dr. Brown. In recent years it has become so notorious as to be a commonplace that what purports to be objective thinking is commonly a ' rationalization,' that is the finding of ingenious reasons for believing what we want to believe; while a system of such rationalizations constitutes an ' ideology.' But few people have the fortitude to apply this painful truth to themselves and, as yet, it has had a quite inadequate influence on educational practice.

The part then played in our thinking by preconceptions, often emotionally engendered, is certainly enormous and frequently sinister. One of the chief functions of education, and above all of a university education, should be to provide some kind of prophylaxis against this distorting influence. But the universities are still organized on the basis of the old liberal view and that view is impossibly naïve. According to it, one can, and one should, divest oneself of all presuppositions. But we cannot do this if we would, and we should not if we could. Some presuppositions are not only unavoidable but indispensable. It is not indiscriminate proscription but a searching critique that is required.

For instance no science can get on at all without some working assumptions or postulates, whose validity for the purpose of the investigation is presupposed and not proved. Some of these such as the postulate of the uniformity of nature are common to all the natural sciences. Others such as the universal applicability of quantitative methods are peculiar to a single science or group of sciences.

Their justification lies in their working; that is, in their enabling the scientist to get on with his job successfully. Sooner or later, any that do not do this are discarded. The splitting of the atom and the manufacture of the atomic bomb are presumptive evidence that the physicist's working assumptions are valid, at least for his own purpose. Again all scientific investigation, whether in the physical or the human field, starts with the selection of certain objects or events for study. For example the historian deals not with all events but only with certain events or classes of event singled out as being significant, as being specially important or interesting. He attends only to what interests him as a historian. He isolates it from much of the context in which it actually occurs and which he assumes for his purpose to be irrelevant. Such pre-selection is indispensable; and it can only be made on the basis of some implied standard of values. Again, any particular investigation usually begins with some tentative hypothesis which is to be tested. A large part of the genius of the great scientist consists in his trained intuition which suggests the right questions to ask. Thus what he finds is determined in part by what he expects to find. The competent scientist does not approach an investigation without any antecedent expectation, but with one which is clear and definite and which dictates the questions which he asks. The scientist differs from the layman principally in having an elaborate technique, whereby he can carry much further the process of isolation and interrogation. He puts his material through the third degree.

What is essential to honest thinking is not that all presuppositions should be discarded, but that they should be uncovered, clearly expressed and thoroughly scrutinized. 'Inferences may be as dispassionate as logic or evidence can make them. But it is a wise student who knows all his own premises.'[1] In particular, the emotional factors in our judgments should be revealed to ourselves and to other people. 'We have to uncover our sub-articulate egoisms.'[2] Once this is done, it becomes possible to discriminate. Some cannot bear the light of day: to expose the influence of greed, antipathy, jealousy etc. is to neutralize them. Others have a dual character; they are valid within a particular field but not beyond it. This is true of the methodological assumptions of parti-

---

[1] Ministry of Reconstruction, *Final Report of Adult Education Committee*, para. 130.
[2] Follett, *Dynamic Administration*, p. 29.

cular sciences, for example, the insistence upon the use of quantitative methods. The scientist is amply justified in the use of such assumptions in so far as they enable him to get on with his own work; and any that do not are soon discarded. But it is an unproved assumption that they can be transferred to other fields. The myth that Latin Prose provides an adequate basic mental training for the engineer or the administrator is now discredited. But those who would simply, for ' Latin Prose,' read ' the experimental method of physics ' or ' a training in statistics ' are guilty of a similar fallacy. Aristotle long ago pointed out that it is as inept to demand geometrical demonstration of a moral philosopher as to put up with plausible rhetoric from a mathematician.

An open mind need not, and should not, be an empty mind. The scientist or historian has more preconceptions than the layman. To the ignoramus one event is as likely as another, to the expert it is not. If a reported event or the result of an experiment seems to contradict natural laws as hitherto understood, the expert will rightly subject it to unusually stringent criticism. Not only does the expert have superior knowledge of what is probable; he is also more fully aware of the various ways in which fraud and credulity have combined to disseminate unfounded beliefs. A miracle is not to be accepted on evidence which would be sufficient for establishing a normal event. The naïve proposal to dispense with all preconceptions seems to be due to a confusion between two different moments in scientific investigation. When an experiment is actually being conducted, the experimenter must—provisionally and for the moment—put out of his mind all previous estimates of the probabilities. He must conduct the experiment and observe the result as though the initial chances were equal; otherwise it would be worthless as a test. But when the experiment is completed, all that he believed before comes back into the picture; the new evidence has to be correlated with the old. It never leaves the pre-existing doctrine precisely where it was before. Either it confirms it, or it modifies it or it casts doubt upon it. In the last event, the experimenter may suspend judgment till he has further data. For the time being he may, on balance, adhere to the received doctrine, thinking it more probable that he has made some mistake in the experiment or has misinterpreted its results than that the received doctrine is fallacious. He will do so of course with a certain question mark; and if further evidence is forthcoming, his own experimental findings will be brought into the reckoning. But in no event will

E

he, at this stage, treat his preconceptions simply as prejudices to be disregarded. Otherwise ' quacks ' would have a glorious time.

Mental health then involves the avoidance of two extremes, the closed mind and the empty mind. It is possible to hold preconceptions in such a way that one's mind is not really open to entertain any fresh evidence that seems to contradict it. This is the notorious fault of the dogmatist; and for one open and avowed dogmatist there are half a dozen who are dogmatists unconsciously but quite as effectually. The great advances in science have generally been made by men who were ready to take interest in, and to concentrate attention on, the unexpected, and, if need be, to revise their presuppositions. On the other hand simply to jettison all presuppositions is not only impossible but absurd. What is required is, to integrate the new and the old, and not to ignore either.

Similarly, while emotion is dangerous, it is often indispensable. A literary critic who was all sensibility would be a very poor guide. But a literary critic who had no sensibility would be disqualified from the start; he would be like a colour-blind art critic. In history, politics, ethics and all humane studies, a ' judicial ' attitude is the first qualification for the truth-seeker. But this should not be interpreted too negatively. A judge who was run away with by moral indignation or by human sympathy would be a very bad judge; but even worse would be one who, in his own person, was a stranger either to moral indignation or to human sympathy. He would be a judge to shudder at, and he would be unable to understand a large part of what it was his business to understand. It was Burke who warned us, instead of girding at general prejudices, to employ our sagacity in discovering the latent wisdom that commonly exists in them; and who added that such wisdom was all the more valuable when bound up with an emotional attitude, an ' affection,' which much enhanced the likelihood of its being put into action. The relativity of knowledge has been much emphasized in recent years through the work of philosophers dealing with the methods of the humane sciences, such as Dilthey and many others in Germany and Collingwood in England. Writing in 1932 on the problems of the German university Dr. Doerne goes so far as to say, ' The conception of learning as operating without presuppositions is shaken to its foundations, the ideal of an exact objective knowledge of " reality " is revealed as a mere illusion.'[1]

[1] *The University in a Changing World,* p. 63.

But at this point the critical reader will rightly take alarm. ' Are you not ' he may ask, ' preaching dangerous doctrine? Your quotation from Doerne is apposite in more ways than one, for he describes the temper in the German university world which almost immediately led to capitulation to the Nazis. You are opening the door to " thinking with the blood," and similar nonsense, and to accepting, with avidity but on inadequate evidence, whatever may be comfortable or profitable or exciting or edifying; and this is mental debauchery. Because it is harder to think straight than we used to suppose, are we wilfully to allow ourselves to think crookedly? Because no historian attains absolute impartiality, are we to abandon the attempt to be as impartial as we can? For example, Stubbs and Acton are generally reputed to be more impartial historians than Macaulay or Froude. Is not this due to their keener conscience about objectivity, and is this the time to administer a narcotic? Your attitude strikes us as a form of devil-worship; for the scholar or scientist it is equivalent to saying, " Evil be thou my good." You are in the tradition, we grant. Christian apologists have often indulged in this type of wishful thinking; but that only makes us the more suspicious.'

This warning is salutary. The field of presuppositions abounds in pitfalls which none of us entirely escape. The temptations are real and insidious. But if many presuppositions are disreputable and most are liable to misuse, it is all the more important that they should be recognized and discussed and not ignored. And here it is necessary to press home the question, Who is the real obscurantist? The most dangerous preconceptions are those which are unrecognized and uncriticized. The most pernicious kind of bias consists in falsely supposing yourself to have none. If we say that we have no bias, we deceive ourselves and the truth is not in us. According to the familiar story, Socrates said that he was only wiser than other men in that he knew his own ignorance, while they were ignorant without knowing it. He is more judicial than other men who knows his own bias, while they are biassed without suspecting the fact. The first step towards a greater measure of intellectual integrity is to stop ' kidding ourselves ' that we are or can be wholly unbiassed, and to set ourselves to think how the dangers arising from this can be minimized.

Once our presuppositions are brought into the open, they are relatively harmless. We can discount them ourselves and so can other people. Their influence can be checked too by comparison

with judgments on the same set of facts made by those who start
with a different initial bias than ours.

## 5    NEGLECT OF MORAL AND SPIRITUAL FACTORS

Since value-judgments are indispensable to any rational organization of the life of individuals or of communities, a university
training should enhance the student's capacity to make such judgments intelligently. But does it in fact achieve this? Does it often
even attempt it? It is not easy to give a confident answer. Perhaps
this is because character-training has come to be thought a nursery
activity, beneath the attention of the university and an affront to the
dignity of the student. But Plato and Aristotle knew better. They
were well aware that understanding in questions of value is not a
special function unaffected by the quality of the personality as a
whole, but can only be attained where there is already a foundation
of trained sensitiveness and disciplined behaviour. To supply these
prerequisites of understanding is the first task of education. It has
been truly said that it is futile to talk of ' free will ' in the case of a
child who has not yet attained a ' will ' and is simply a bundle of
undisciplined impulses. Similarly you cannot attain ' practical
wisdom,' that is the faculty of habitual good judgment in questions
of values, without two conditions. First you must have attained a
certain mastery of impulse and emotion; not that you are wholly
devoid of these (which would be a disqualification), but that in you
they are rightly directed.   Secondly you must have had some
experience of the good and some disposition to care for and aspire
to it. It is for lack of this sort of training that so much juvenile
discussion of major questions is mere talk, because it has little basis
in moral experience. It is too little related to the real springs of
action.

But at this point we may be met with a strong protest. You
are suggesting, it will be said, a return to a servitude from which the
university has slowly emancipated itself. You ignore the specific
task of the university which is education of the mind, in effect, and,
in effect, you subordinate it to edification. You want the university
to do the work of the Church. There is no need to decry moral
excellence or social reform, but they are not the university's distinctive job. What is wanted of the university teacher is not that he
should be a good husband and father, an active citizen or a pillar
of his church. It is the scholar's distinctive equipment and con-

science, a critical sense trained to the finest discrimination, a thorough mastery of his subject, together with the gift of lucid teaching and of stimulating his pupils. Indeed the quest for edification is not only irrelevant, it is actively harmful. It is likely to lead to bias and wishful thinking, and to result in scholarship less finished, enquiry less far-reaching and fearless, and graduates turned out with a slenderer intellectual equipment than they should be.

In such a protest there is an element of truth. The university's special task is to promote intellectual understanding rather than moral goodness. Some university authorities, such as Archbishop Laud or the Pilgrim Fathers who founded Harvard, have gone wrong through insufficient recognition of this distinction. Not all that makes for edification is suitable to a university, much less incumbent on it. But two principles must be insisted on. First, as we have seen, value-judgments are indispensable to the special work of the thinker as they are to any rational life. An education which omits all training in making them is an education maimed. Secondly some moral qualities are essential to intellectual understanding and some moral defects are fatal to it. To cultivate those qualities, and to eradicate those defects, is not irrelevant but deeply germane to the whole work of education. In the fields of the humane and social sciences at least, knowledge is not independent of our fundamental personal attitude. 'Certain dispositions of the will . . . enter into all deep and delicate apprehensions, be they of the life-history of a clematis-plant, or of the doings of a spider. A certain disoccupation with the petty self is here a *sine qua non* condition of any success.'[1] Something of a parental temper, von Hügel adds, is required for the full understanding of what is below us and something of a filial temper for the understanding of what is above us.

Why is not the output of creative work from the universities bigger and better than, in fact, it is? There is a penetrating discussion of this question in the chapter on 'The Conception of a Catholic University' which Professor Hildebrand contributed to Dr. Kotschnig's symposium. He attributes much of the sterility of modern academic thought to defective attitudes of mind, primarily moral, such as these. The first is *indolence*—' a strange dull insistence on remaining rooted to the spot one is accustomed to.' This induces blindness to whole ranges of reality and is con-

[1] Von Hügel, *Essays and Addresses in the Philosophy of Religion*, p. 12.

trasted with ' a certain winged alertness of the mind ' which is the condition of insight. The second is *pride*—a supercilious repletion and smugness as contrasted with wonder and ' the respectful desire to penetrate things.' The third is *resentment*—an egoistic revulsion from what is objective and resistant, which entails a reluctance ' to face unwelcome and exacting truth ' and so misses illumination because at heart it does not want to be illuminated. The fourth is *distrust*—a shrinking from the responsibility of decision and recognition and ' an unwillingness to venture and to let oneself be carried along by things.' In this analysis, Professor Hildebrand is saying something of the utmost pertinence to the work of universities and relevant far beyond the bounds of his own communion.

Once it is agreed that much of our troubles is due to defects of the kind here described, rather than to lack of natural ability or to gaps in technical equipment, the inference is clear. For the sake of its own distinctive work, the university is vitally concerned to promote ' winged alertness ' as opposed to indolence, wonder as opposed to pride, docility (that is, a hospitable attitude to fact, however unpalatable) as against resentment, and the power to make intellectual commitments as against an inhibiting distrust. Indeed if it simply leaves such things to chance, it is guilty of a great refusal—a refusal ' to be the university.'

Our predicament then is this. Most students go through our universities without ever having been forced to exercise their minds on the issues which are really momentous. Under the guise of academic neutrality they are subtly conditioned to unthinking acquiescence in the social and political *status quo* and in a secularism on which they have never seriously reflected. Owing to the prevailing fragmentation of studies, they are not challenged to decide responsibly on a life-purpose or equipped to make such a decision wisely. They are not incited to disentangle and examine critically the assumptions and emotional attitudes underlying the particular studies they pursue, the profession for which they are preparing, the ethical judgments they are accustomed to make, and the political or religious convictions they hold. Fundamentally they are uneducated.

# IV

# SPURIOUS REMEDIES

## I  SCIENTIFIC HUMANISM

To-day many of the younger teachers and of the abler students find their inspiration in a blend of Francis Bacon and Karl Marx. They seek to complete the scientific-democratic movement which has been going on for some time beneath the surface and to make it the basis for the official policy of the universities. The present anarchy would then terminate in a new 'conversion of Constantine;' the universities would capitulate to a young, vigorous and revolutionary creed, in tune with the *Zeitgeist;* the heresy of yesterday would become the orthodoxy of to-morrow. Among the articles of the new creed are the following. The universities must be planned. The plan must be based on the practical needs of a changing world. The criteria used in assessing those needs must be social welfare and social justice instead of the stability of a class-society. In place of the present chaos universities must again diffuse a definite culture; but that should be, not the classical culture of the ancient world, but the scientific culture of the living world of to-day. Thus only, it is held, can the university be re-integrated and re-vivified.

First, it is urged, the university must be better organized. This involves the abandonment of *laissez-faire* liberalism and the substitution of planning in this as in other fields. Capable administrators abhor waste and inefficiency and earnest reformers abhor avoidable delay. The university must become something more than a congeries of faculties, the faculty something more than a congeries of departments in which each professor can go very much his own way while the university as a whole has no master plan. This holds good not only of the individual university but of the universities of the country collectively. Otherwise they cannot be expected to meet the needs of the time.

Secondly, its bias must be more practical and its teaching more topical than they have been. Such sentiments as 'Learning for

71

learning's sake' or 'Truth for truth's sake,' once applauded, are now severely reprobated. If sincere, they are regarded as the indulgence of idle curiosity. But their sincerity is suspect, they are held to be anti-social and only a cloak for the vested interest of the scholar. Here wartime experience, it is suggested, points to a better way. During the war both research and training were directed to a single and universally accepted end, and there was an imperious sense of urgency. This over-mastering purpose gave élan and a sense of significance to all concerned and to everything done. A similar concentration, intensity, and pooling of effort are required if the university is to be harnessed to the no less exacting, but constructive, tasks of peacetime.

Thirdly, a thoroughgoing rationalism is demanded. The rigorous critical methods of the physical sciences should be applied, consistently and ruthlessly, over the whole field of knowledge. That some eminent scientists still see no incompatibility between religion and science and allow themselves to be influenced by ' mystical and metaphysical intuitions drawn consciously or unconsciously from pre-scientific beliefs' is a backsliding. It is due to the fact that, outside their own science and in regions where ' biassed motive and preconceived opinions' are influential, they have abandoned rational criteria in favour of uncritical belief.[1]

Fourthly, the pretence of neutrality must be abandoned. ' The proponents of knowledge and culture must ally themselves actively with all the forces making for social progress.'[2] We have learned lately that in some wars there can be no neutrality. Just as once the universities served the Church, so now they should openly serve the masses in their struggle with the classes; the only alternative is, consciously or unconsciously, to side with reaction. On this fundamental issue they must draw a line between orthodoxy and heresy, though the new orthodoxy will be very unlike the old. Reproaches on the score of totalitarianism are met by the reply that to-day equality is more important than liberty. Liberalism is a bourgeois creed and the freedom it guarantees is only nominal since, whatever the legal position, the great majority are bound by the iron laws of economics. ' In an integrated and conscious society this conception of freedom is bound to be replaced by another— freedom as the understanding of necessity.'[3]

[1] Bernal, *op. cit.*, pp. 233, 333, 389-90.
[2] Brian Simon, *op. cit.*, p. 110.
[3] Bernal, *op. cit.* p. 38.

It would be futile to criticize our academic colleagues who argue in this way until we have recognized the strength of their case. Christians, like other people, have much to learn from them. They have been the first to see and to demonstrate to others how wide is now the gap between the professed ideals of the university and the actualities of lecture room and laboratory, hall and common room. They have ruthlessly exposed its uncertainty of aim and the degree to which it has, in fact, been grounded in privilege. They have forced on our attention skeletons in our cupboard of whose presence we had already a lurking, but repressed, suspicion; and the penetration of their diagnosis is attested by its power to make us wince and to react with a mixture of resentment and a reluctant sense of guilt. Further, they exemplify, more than other people, two things that have a wide appeal. The first is the intellectual stimulus which comes from linking the universities with what is most vital in contemporary culture. Applied science goes from triumph to triumph; every day its frontiers are being extended. Here alone Field-Marshal Smuts's dictum is patently true: 'Humanity has struck its tents and is once more on the march.' The second is their passionate concern for human welfare and their sense of social responsibility, in which they excel both traditionalists and liberals. Through science preventible evils are daily being grappled with; scarcity, disease and distance are being overcome. Tractors and irrigation, insulin and penicillin, aeroplanes and wireless; such things are only symbols, for the list could be indefinitely multiplied. Thus their appeal is deservedly strong. Indeed they offer the only alternative to chaos which is 'getting across' to the younger men on a large scale. The haunting trouble of the student to-day is a very deep-seated doubt whether in the modern world, so impersonal and so insecure, his life can have any significance. Existing university courses do little to reassure or to stimulate him. 'Scientific humanism' alone seems to offer him a philosophy of life he feels to be relevant and a superpersonal cause to which he can devote himself wholeheartedly and with a sense that—

something from his hand has power
To live and act and serve the future hour.

Here there is much which it is vital to assimilate. But there is perhaps even more which it is vital to reject. In the first place reaction from academic complacency too easily results in an underestimate, and even a repudiation, of the intellectual values proper to a university. Certainly *Theoria* is not superior to *Praxis,* and academic people need to be reminded of this; but it does not follow that it is subordinate. The intellectual life is not to be esteemed as merely a means to social welfare; it is an integral part of that welfare. Academic people are not wrong in feeling that they have a distinctive treasure to guard, whose worth is not purely instrumental. Professor Bernal recognizes candidly that the scientist or scholar, having an aptitude for his work, enjoys what he is doing and finds an intrinsic interest in it quite apart from its practical consequences. But he belittles the objective value of this interest, ranking it with a game or hobby. Yet to equate our awed hush of wonder in presence of a great poem or picture or symphony with our enjoyment of a crossword puzzle, shows an odd insensitiveness to values. To take greater examples, the attitude of Darwin transported with intense interest in watching the habits of earthworms and humming birds, or of Kant contemplating the starry heavens and the moral law, is widely removed from that of a dealer, a collector or a preacher. It is neither patronising nor proprietorial, but humble and reverent; it is a glad recognition of what is independent of, or above, us. For the Christian of course contemplation and praise are, no less than self-devotion, essential parts of worship. The analogy of art is instructive; for, if we must repudiate the æsthete, we must also repudiate the philistine. Art is not simply ' for art's sake,' but neither is it simply for the sake of profit or relaxation or edification. Its character and worth cannot be fully understood in terms of something other than itself.

Similarly the university as an institution must not be simply the instrument of State, Church or Industry, it must not be the ' tied house ' of the social reformer any more than of the Vatican. The crime which the Nazis committed against the universities of Germany was not only that they made them tools in a wrong cause but that they made them tools at all. The rightful autonomy of science and scholarship, and of universities as their homes and guardians, has recently been re-emphasized by Sir Henry Dale, speaking as President of the British Association. ' He emphasized the vital importance of the universities maintaining in Britain and elsewhere their full independence, and reiterated that the proper function of the universities is to promote research with no immediate objectives but to widen the boundaries of knowledge, in contradistinction to prescribed research undertaken for the particular

purpose of solving an immediate practical problem.'[1]  In this utterance Sir Henry is not showing a scientist's ' provincial ' over-
estimate of his own importance; he is voicing an intellectual
conscience whose authority is widely recognized.

The nemesis of extreme utilitarianism is that it defeats itself.  The
great contributions of science to social welfare have commonly been
based on the creative work of men like Darwin and Rutherford,
whose primary concern and inspiration was theoretical.  In outstanding creative work of this stature, ' the wind bloweth where it
listeth.' If such men had been organized and set down to work of
which the practical end was apparent, it is unlikely that their major
discoveries would have been made.  There would have been no
golden eggs, for the geese would have been sterilized in advance.

But the ' scientific-humanist ' integration suffers from more
radical defects.  Their nature may be indicated by reference to
the series of ' Talks ' broadcast in the early spring of 1946, entitled
' The Challenge of Our Time.' Here the main issue lay between
two sets of speakers. The one consisted of ' scientific-humanists,'
who regard the world's chief need to-day as being further technical
advance.  Since the industrial revolution, they argued, human life
has been revolutionized and human welfare has been immensely
augmented by the triumphs of applied science.  Our most urgent
requirement is that these advances should go further and faster,
and that hunger, cold, disease and distance should progressively be
overcome.  Against them others, including some scientists, contended that our primary problem is one of human relations; it is
how we are to live together in reasonable peace and amity in a
world where destructive power has grown beyond all imagination.
Our worst trouble is not that there is too little to go round, but that
there is not a sufficiently general will that, whatever there is, should
go round.  It is epitomized by the phrase, *Homo homini lupus*.
That is a trouble which an increase in material resources may as
easily enhance as allay.  No doubt the human relation between two
starving men is likely to be strained, but there is little presumption
that the human relation between two millionaires will be more
happy.

Here is the most vital question of proportion for our time.  How
are universities to be oriented towards it?  On which set of questions is the contribution of university thinkers most urgently needed?
Which kinds of training for students are most indispensable?  There

[1] *Nature*, No. 4047, p. 699.

is grave danger that these questions may be begged and that the influence of the 'scientific humanists' will tend that way. In particular they shirk—or at most face quite inadequately—three major problems; the problem of values, the problem of power, and the problem of the transcendental.

### a.  The Problem of Values and the Problem of Power

These two problems are intertwined; or rather, they are the same problem seen from different angles.  They are the problem of the magician, the superman, seen either from his own angle or from the point of view of everyone else.  Professor Toynbee symbolizes our predicament in an illustration from road transport. There, he says, the technical problems of speed and haulage have been solved, and have been replaced by the problem of collisions. '. . . the problem is no longer technological but psychological. The old challenge of physical distance has been transmuted into a new challenge of human relations between drivers who, having learned how to annihilate space, have thereby put themselves in constant danger of annihilating one another.  Everything that is now done in our society is done for good or evil, with tremendous " drive," and this has made the material consequences of actions and the moral responsibility of agents far heavier than ever before. . . . It is a moral challenge rather than a physical challenge that confronts our own society to-day.'[1]  Scientists have lately been made acutely aware that the blessings of technical advance can easily become curses and that they have a responsibility in this matter extending beyond the frontiers of their own science.  The most spectacular example is, of course, the atomic bomb.  A little earlier the average scientist was apt to plead that he must stick to his last.  His business was to make discoveries.  If some other persons made an evil use of such discoveries, well that was too bad; but it was not his responsibility.  But for some time now, and with a more painful emphasis since Hiroshima, the stirring of the con- science of scientists, both in Great Britain and in the United States, has been notable; they have felt impelled to apply a new, and non- technical, criterion to their work.

But both the invention of the atomic bomb and the scientist's moral reaction to it are only the climax of an uneasy questioning which has been going on for a long time.  Sir Alfred Ewing's presi- dential address to the British Association in 1932 was a landmark.

[1] *Study of History*, III, p. 210.

'In the present-day thinker's attitude towards what is called mechanical progress we are conscious of a changed spirit. Admiration is tempered by criticism; complacency has given way to doubt; doubt is passing into alarm. There is a sense of perplexity and frustration, as in one who has gone a long way and finds he has taken the wrong turning. To go back is impossible; how shall he proceed? Where will he find himself if he follows this path or that? An old exponent of applied mechanics may be forgiven if he expresses something of the disillusion with which, now standing aside, he watches the sweeping pageant of discovery and invention in which he used to take unbounded delight. Whither does this tremendous procession tend? What after all is its goal? What is its probable influence on the future of the human race? . . . Man was ethically unprepared for so great a bounty. In the slow evolution of morals he is still unfit for the tremendous responsibility it entails. The command of nature has been put into his hands before he knows how to command himself.'[1]

For those scientists and for others who are impelled to ask such questions, the Baconian criterion is not enough; the 'fruits' are too liable to be bitter to the taste. But if so, by what further standard are they to judge? They are involved at once in questions of valuation. They have become moralists in spite of themselves; and they must review their equipment for such an enterprise. Some of the painstaking attention and delicate discrimination which they have been used to give to technical problems they must now give to questions of good and evil; or, at the very least, they must ensure that it shall be given by colleagues whom they trust. Here the gospel of 'scientific humanism' is defective.

But the problem of power is equally urgent and is indeed bound up with the problem of valuation. This is, in effect, the problem of Frankenstein. How are men to avoid being destroyed by powers which they have themselves brought into existence for their own purposes? How is the creator to avoid becoming the slave and the victim of his own creation? It arises from the dual fact that the quantity of power in the world has in recent times undergone a staggering increase, and that *this power is a power over persons as well as over things.* The expression in common use, 'Man's power over nature,' obscures the fact that, in practice, this is largely a

---

[1] Quoted Toynbee, *op. cit.* III, p. 211. It is due to Professor Bernal to point out that he recognizes the existence of this disillusion. In the opening chapter of *The Social Function of Science* he gives a lengthy excerpt from Sir Alfred Ewing's address.

power of some men over other men; and nowadays this is unprecedented in extent. Alexander or Cæsar, Charlemagne or Akbar, did not possess a tithe of the power over most of their subjects which rulers possess to-day. ' President Lincoln attained his objects by the use of a degree of force which would have crushed Charlemagne and his paladins and peers like so many eggshells'[1]; and as was Lincoln to Charlemagne, so is the force at the disposal of the President of the United States to-day to that which Lincoln commanded. But more far-reaching, and more formidable still to the contemporaries of Dr. Goebbels, is the equipment now available for swaying men's minds; compulsory education, the press, the cinema, and the wireless are weapons possibly even stronger than the atom bomb, and the art of using them for the ' conditioning' of men's minds and characters is much enhanced by modern developments in psychology and sociology. Most portentous of all is the prospect, now opening up, of a power to produce particular types of men by selective breeding, as scientists can already produce particular types of pigeon. ' At present,' says Professor Bernal, ' man attempts to control every part of the universe other than himself.'[2] But ' we shall find many new means of controlling life to an extent at present undreamed of . . . At last we are beginning to understand, and at some time may be able to mould, the development of living matter . . . Genetics furnishes us with another quite independent means of modifying life through selective breeding and even by the creation of mutations.'[3]

What is really significant in these passages is the writer's apparent unconsciousness that there can be two opinions about the attractiveness of the prospect he unfolds. Yet to many it will be repulsive. When the giant and the wizard are rolled into one, it is time for ordinary folk to tremble. To be clay for human potters is a degraded form of being. The conviction is deeply rooted that a man who has been fashioned to a specification by some other man or group of men lacks something of manhood. A patient under hypnotism may go through correct motions and feel appropriate sentiments, but he is not a responsible agent. It is an intolerable

[1] Fitzjames Stephen, *Liberty, Equality and Fraternity*, p. 29.

[2] *Op. cit.*, p. 354. Observe how the use of the singular 'man' obscures the fact that what is in question is the control, by some men or governments or scientific experts, of masses of other men and indeed of whole future generations.

[3] *Op. cit.*, pp. 338, 339, 340.

presumption and outrage for any men so to play the god to their
fellows.

This is true even if the planners are disinterested. But there is
no guarantee, and small likelihood, that they will be so. Notoriously history suggests that power in large quantities tends to go to
the head and corrupt. *Quis custodiet ipsos custodes?* No doubt
the bishop who suggested to the British Association a ten-year
moratorium in scientific progress did not intend his words to be
taken literally. They were a light-hearted way of indicating that
the gifts which science brings are double-edged and that there is
no automatic correspondence between the advancement of science
and the advancement of human welfare. Men like Aldous Huxley
and Gandhi are so conscious of this that they would have us abjure
power altogether, a policy, which, as a general rule of life, is hardly
consistent with responsibility. But a bland unconsciousness that
there is any problem to solve is still less helpful or worthy of respect.

The difficulty is apt to be concealed by two factors. First, the
participants in such discussions seem always to assume tacitly that
they themselves will be among the conditioners and not among
the conditioned. This is an exhilarating prospect, and they have
usually a serene confidence in their own good intentions. Secondly,
the present academic champions of scientific humanism happen also
to be men with an urgent concern for social welfare. But, it is far
from self-evident that a desire for the scientific organization of
society and a desire for social betterment are inherently bound up
together, or that education on the lines proposed will supply a
sufficient ground and incentive for disinterested conduct to anyone
not already predisposed to it. Professor Hogben contemptuously
dismisses moral philosophy as being ' merely a relic of the
ecclesiastical foundations' and unworthy of ' the attention of a
twentieth-century audience.'[1] But he does not make clear what
is his own ethic, or how he proposes to commend it, or how he
would answer the challenge, ' Why attempt to be moral or disinterested at all?' Yet that question has nothing scholastic about it.
It is *the* life-and-death question of the day, underlying all others,
in Europe, in India, in China, in every disturbed part of the world.
How is the ' scientific humanist' to meet it in terms of his own
categories?

One way is to belittle the importance of the question. The aim
of social organization, it may be said, is to satisfy fundamental

[1] *Dangerous Thoughts,* p. 214.

human needs; and everyone knows what these needs are, except those who first raise a dust and then complain that they cannot see. They are simple things like food, clothing and housing, gardens, ' beer and baccy '; there is no reason why, with the help of science, they should not be made available for everyone. So the scientist can take ultimate ends pretty well for granted and can devote his care and attention to the improvement of the methods by which they are pursued. But this is over-simplification. It is a gratuitous assumption that what people ought to have is identical with what they happen to want, that pushpin is as good as poetry, that the satisfaction of a fool in his own way is as important as the satisfaction of Socrates in his way; in short, that there is no such thing as an order of values in which people need to be, and can be, educated. It is a further assumption that, once supplies are ample, there will be no further conflict, and that men will be ready to treat their own family's or caste's or nation's claim, even to ' beer and baccy,' as being simply on a par with that of everyone else.

Another and better way is taken by Professor Bernal. He looks to science to produce finer and more harmonious ways of living. ' So far science . . . has accepted the crude desires of a pre-scientific age without attempting to analyse and refine them. It is the function of science to study man as much as nature, to discover the significance and direction of social movements and social needs. The tragedy of man has too often lain in his very success in achieving what he imagined to be his objects. Science, through its capacity of looking ahead and comprehending at the same time many aspects of a problem, should be able to determine more clearly which are the real and which the phantastic elements of personal and social desires. Science brings power and liberation, just as much by showing the falsity and impossibility of certain aims, as by satisfying others.'[1] In this passage there is much truth. Its author recognizes that, both for individuals and for communities, there is an art of living, proficiency in which is only acquired by taking pains. He recognizes also that, for the technologist who feels his social responsibility and aspires to guide social development, technology is not enough; he must become a moralist and a politician. But in two respects he fails to satisfy. He assumes that what is required is the application of the methods of natural science to the fields of psychology and sociology, and does not allow enough for the possibility that quite different categories of interpretation

[1] *Op. cit.*, p. 411.

may be required. He assumes, too, that the mere fact that something is desired, provided that it is attainable without the frustration
of other desires, is conclusive proof of its desirability, that things
are good because they are desired rather than desired because they
are good. But both these assumptions are highly disputable and
are, of course, widely disputed. They are certainly not axiomatic
and they require defence.

There is a further ground on which Professor Bernal claims that
science is an adequate basis for the life of a university or a nation.
This, too, deserves respect but will not sustain all the weight that
is placed upon it. Irrespective of its conclusions, he argues, science,
as a way of life, diffuses an ethos which is just what the world at
large requires. Scientists get their results through team-work and
through a spirit of comradeship, discipline, patience and humility
before fact. If they do not preach fraternity, they commend it
powerfully by example. It is the layman who attributes scientific
progress to the occasional work of individual genius. The scientist
knows that it depends more on the little-noticed co-operative work
of a great multitude who ' rest in unvisited tombs.' ' In science
men have learned to subordinate themselves to a common purpose
without losing the individuality of their achievements.'[1] ' Science
has been at all times a commune of workers, helping one another,
sharing their knowledge, not seeking corporately or individually
more money or power than is needed for the pursuit of their work.
They have been at all times rational and international in outlook,
and thus fundamentally in harmony with the movements that seek
to extend that community of effort and enjoyment to social and
economic as well as intellectual fields.'[2] A university permeated
by this spirit, selfless and equalitarian, will foster these qualities in
its alumni. Within the wider community it may thus act as the
leaven that leavens the lump.

This claim has substance. But genuine and admirable as is this
scientific ethos, it is not strong enough to sustain unaided the strains
and stresses of the world to-day. It is too frail to bind the giant
passions unloosed; or, to change the metaphor, it has not the head
of steam that can ride out a hurricane. Antagonisms such as those
of Jew and Arab, Hindu and Moslem, Orangeman and Sinn
Feiner, white man and black, where race feeling is acute, yield, if
at all, only to something on a still deeper emotional plane. The

[1] *Op. cit.*, p. 415.
[2] *Op. cit.*, p. 323.

scientific ethos did not save the general body of German scientists from succumbing to the Nazi flood.

The gospel of salvation by increase and application of scientific knowledge is less plausible to-day than it seemed ten years ago. War, says Professor Bernal writing in 1938, is one of those preventible evils which ' continue solely because we are tied to out-of-date political and economic systems . . . War in a period of potential plenty and ease for all is sheer folly and cruelty ';[1] and he seems to infer that therefore it will not happen. But the futility of war has been demonstrated over and over again. Since Bernal wrote we have had a second world-war, and we now live in apprehension of yet a third waged with atomic bombs. The most cogent demonstrations of war's irrationality have not been enough to prevent it. It is impossible to rule out of court those who urge that it is less ignorance that is at fault than ' the unruly wills and affections of sinful men.'

Salvation is not to be had by bread alone. Scientific humanists seem sometimes to argue that, if you can remove scarcity, you will have removed the main cause of contention; if you look after supplies, morale will take care of itself. Undoubtedly you will have made a contribution. Anyone who could provide starving Europe to-morrow with a sufficiency of food and of transport for its distribution would be a major benefactor. But when one devil is expelled, others even worse than the first are prone to take possession. Certainly greed is a prolific source of contention; but there are many others, such as lust for power, envy, vain-glory, etc. Perhaps Hobbes was a shrewder psychologist than Professor Bernal when he placed first among ' those qualities of mankind, that concern their living together in Peace and Unity . . . a perpetuall and restlesse desire of Power after power, that ceaseth onely in Death.'[2]

In this field, if Professor Bernal may be taken as a fair representative, it is difficult to acquit ' scientific humanists ' of utopianism and of a singular naïveté springing apparently from that sort of wishful thinking which they would generally be the first to condemn. Objections which threaten their whole scheme of things are impatiently brushed aside and are not genuinely faced and grappled with. Indeed one wishes that they would apply to themselves and to their own tenets a little of that acute psychological analysis

[1] *Op. cit.*, p. 410.

[2] *Leviathan*, pp. 62-3, Cambridge English Classics Edition.

which they employ so effectively against others. Thus Professor Bernal writes as follows: 'There are large tasks still for mankind to undertake—the ultimate conquest of space, of disease, and death, most of all of their own ways of living together . . . It will no longer be a question of adapting man to the world but the world to man . . . The terrible struggles and difficulties of our time are largely due to the difficulty of man's learning his new powers . . . The reason why people believe that a scientific world-order is impossible, or that even if it were possible it would not be worth while, lies in a deep-seated lack of faith in humanity . . . The new world . . . will be made by men, and the men who have made it and those who follow them will know what to do with it.'[1] Here indeed is a short, confident and dogmatic way of settling fundamental questions. That the convulsions of our day are merely growing pains, that if you attend to men's brains and their stomachs you need not worry seriously about their hearts, that human nature can be trusted with the terrific powers which natural science is making available without any re-making more radical than science can supply; these are tremendous assertions, to be justified, if at all, only after profound examination and enquiry. But neither Professor Bernal nor Professor Hogben makes any serious attempt to prove them; they only assert them defiantly. If challenged, Professor Bernal appeals, as here, to faith (in human nature) and Professor Hogben to hope.[2] In these matters 'scientific humanists' are entitled to their own beliefs. But if they proclaim them as established truths, henceforth to be taken for granted, and so as foundations on which a university system can safely be built; if they number them among those propositions which, as Professor J. B. S. Haldane puts it, science from time to time takes out of the hands of the metaphysicians and settles once and for all; we are bound to point out this is simply a piece of bluff of really titanic proportions.

There is yet another reason why a scientific outlook is not enough for salvation. That outlook is itself two-sided. For the great scientists themselves it may have mainly the ethical quality, selfless, humble and co-operative, which Bernal so well describes. But to the wider public which is being impregnated with it, and which acclaims and greedily avails itself of scientific achievements, science

[1] *Op. cit.*, pp. 379, 382.
[2] 'To sneer at hope is the cloak of snobbery with which outworn scholarship conceals its own mediocrity.' *Dangerous Thoughts*, p. 282.

is first and foremost the road to power. That is, it is only a new means of attaining a pre-scientific end. The craving for domination is indeed one of the most elemental of all human urges. It is shown in primitive society in the cult of the medicine man, in folklore, in the hero who can command the services of the genie of the bottle or the lamp. In a more sophisticated form it is exemplified in the ' Faust ' legend. It is, as Hobbes suggests, an insatiable appetite. By all ordinary moral standards it is at best amoral and it easily becomes immoral. In this aspect, science may be no antidote but even a stimulus to the poison. But it is this aspect of science which gives it its popular appeal; and it is this which is stressed when the ' scientific humanist ' insists that ' knowledge is power ' and that the utilitarian motive controls, and ought to control, its development. Yet this can clearly become a social danger. The fanatical will to live, passing into imperialism, is notoriously one of the chief threats to the world to-day. Concentration on the pursuit of knowledge as primarily a means to power seems more likely to aggravate than to counteract it. It opens the way for the adventurer or the gangster of genius; it opens the way also for the ' Kommissar ' or the Grand Inquisitor.

But here we may properly ask ourselves whether we are not spoiling our own case by exaggeration. Before the General Election of 1945 Mr. Churchill attempted to scare the British public by representing the Labour leaders as committed to the methods of Moscow. But the argument proved a boomerang; the British public simply could not see Messrs. Attlee, Bevin and Co. in the uniform of Kommissars. Similarly, we know Professors Bernal, Hogben and Haldane, familiarly in Common Room and Faculty. We know that, when we talk with them about truth or humanity, they and we mean substantially the same thing. We know they have a social conscience and ardour which puts most of us to shame. Can we then seriously regard them, for practical purposes, as being concealed agents of the Cheka? If not, does not our argument refute itself by a *reductio ad absurdum?*

We gladly acknowledge the absurdity. But it arises from the fact that the unformulated working philosophy of life of these thinkers is much richer than their own statements would convey and is not exclusively derived from natural science or by use of its methods. There is, in fact, a hiatus between the different parts of their creed. There is no inherent connection between the proposition ' Knowledge is power,' on which they ostensibly rely, and the propositions ' The exploitation of any human being is vile ' or ' The poorest he that is in England hath a life to live as the richest he ' to which they give whole-hearted allegiance. Their deepest convictions—those for which we most respect them—are really based on faith; but they do not explore the grounds of this faith or examine its congruity with their other beliefs. The reason may be that, for them, the paramountcy of social justice is simply taken for granted *ex hypothesi,* because they are within, as e.g. Mr. Molotov is not, a western Christian ethical tradition which, as a whole, they do not question, though they criticize severely its apparent inconsistencies and backslidings. Our well-founded assurance that Professor Haldane would never behave with the ruthlessness and lack of scruple symbolized by the figure of the ' Kommissar ' may be related more directly to his upbringing in a Christian tradition than he likes to suppose. Similarly Bertrand Russell, in a recent broadcast talk on ' The Faith of a Rationalist,' made ' kindly feeling ' and ' veracity ' the foundations of his ethic. Of course no one can doubt the genuineness and intensity of Bertrand Russell's humanitarianism; in all conditions, and regardless of an indifferent universe, he will go to the stake rather than surrender to cruelty or deceit. But any listener must have been struck by the contrast between the strength and impressiveness of the faith avowed, and the feebleness of the naturalistic reasons for it actually given. These were such as a tyro in moral philosophy could easily puncture.

The educational shortcoming of the ' scientific humanist ' then is this. There is little in his teaching, though there is a good deal in his practice and his implicit assumptions, to deter his pupils from becoming adventurers or Kommissars. But, in crises like the present, unformulated and uncriticized assumptions are not enough: to build on them is to build on sand. No doubt such assumptions play a large, and sometimes a beneficent, part in the life of any community, for most men are not thinkers. But in a revolutionary epoch like ours they cannot long hold their own, and in a university they are anyhow out of place and do not deserve to hold their own. We come back then, still unsatisfied, to the problem of power. What is the relation between Might and Right? What is the criterion of right and what authority does it carry? These questions are not ' academic,' they deal with matters of life and death to our society. We quarrel with ' scientific humanism,' not because it gives the wrong answers, but because it never seriously puts the questions. It finds them embarrassing, and in the main it shirks them.

What is required is a rational ethic for planners. By methods drawn from psychology, sociology or biology, the scientific legislator may be enabled to determine the moral judgments of later generations, but will he share those judgments himself? If he does, it must be on independent grounds; for *ex hypothesi,* he will not himself have been played upon by forces he sets in motion.[1] By what moral principles, if any, is Prospero to be guided? By his art he can raise or allay storms, mental as well as physical, in the other persons in the drama; he can produce in them a sense of obligation or an inhibition. But is he himself to recognize any obligation, and, if so, to what or to whom?

The great dividing line is between those for whom, in effect, all law is 'what the sovereign commands' or 'the interest of the stronger' (in which case the sovereign or 'the stronger' are themselves free of obligation) and those who recognize some kind of superior 'Law' that is binding because it is intrinsically right and reasonable and not because it is the fiat of any potentate or is backed by any sanction. In *The Abolition of Man,* Mr. C. S. Lewis has trenchantly pointed this contrast; and he has collected a large variety of quotations from many sources, Egyptian and Babylonian, Indian and Chinese, Greek, Roman and Palestinian, Norse and Anglo-Saxon, to illustrate how wide-spread in time and space is the recognition of some objective and binding, higher Law. Embodied in ancient custom and later in the 'Common Law,' the rule of law is rooted deeply in our national tradition. In the words of the Song of Lewes—

> *Legem quoque dicimus regis dignitatem*
> *Regere, nam credimus esse legem lucem*
> *Sine qua concludimus deviare ducem.*

No doubt the recent World War was no crusade, but was, in large part, a struggle for survival. But the plain man rightly divined that, for the Western Powers, it was something more than this and that the recognition of any law superior to naked power was at stake. Whatever their defects, the Nuremberg trials were at least an attempt to assert the existence and the binding character of a higher law, which is not merely an emanation of power, but to which, *de jure,* all power is subject; and this is the issue, dwarfing

---

[1] That is true, at any rate, of the original planner.

all others, for the 'Great Powers' to-day.[1] That 'scientific humanists' fail to push home this question is a grave flaw, for, with uncertainty here, they fail us at our point of greatest need.

Over and above the recognition of moral law, there is another indispensable principle deeply imbedded in our tradition. It is expressed in the title of a series of B.B.C. Talks—'People matter.' This is a value-judgment, not derived from natural science; but unless its authority is recognized, scientific planning might easily take a form which would shock most Englishmen. Here the term democracy' is ambiguous. For instance Professor Bernal[2] speaks of 'maximal welfare' as the end to which social planning should be directed; and, in view of his concern for social justice, he would probably himself interpret this in the light of Bentham's rule, 'Everyone to count for one and no one for more than one.' But there is no necessary connection between the two propositions. It is quite possible to argue that, to attain maximal welfare, the welfare of considerable minorities should be entirely disregarded. For the sake of posterity, even the majority of those now alive might have to be sacrificed. So Robespierre or Lenin or Himmler, with ruthless logic and unruffled equanimity, are prepared to liquidate or to sterilize or to 'condition' great multitudes of men. You cannot make omelettes without breaking eggs, they say, and that is that. But, to our tradition, such cold-bloodedness is abominable. We look askance at 'social engineering.' The engineer is concerned with shaping and manipulating things for the general convenience, but persons and even juvenile persons cannot rightly be so treated. 'What is of most importance to the educator is a respect for the soul as well as the body of the child, the sense of his inmost essence and internal resources, and a sort of sacred and loving attention to his mysterious identity, which is a hidden thing no techniques can reach.'[3] To many, even of those who have no religious beliefs it would seem natural to describe as 'sacrilegious' any attempt to play upon other people, to know their stops, and to pluck the heart out of their mystery; for any person has a claim to be regarded by others with some reverence.

[1] Looked at from another angle, the question for communities and for individuals, is whether, at any point, they will spontaneously 'draw the line.' It is in fact drawn at bewilderingly different points. Some draw it at Belsen, some at Hiroshima, some at taking part in war at all, some at vivisection, some at slavery, some at sexual promiscuity. But the major question is not *where* such a line is drawn but *whether* it is to be drawn at all.

[2] *Op. cit.*, p. 342.

[3] Maritain, *Education at the Crossroads*.

'Scientific humanists' do justice neither to the heights nor to the depths of human experience. Their utopianism is due to their ignoring the element of sheer perversity in human nature. Thus they underrate the degree, and in part misconceive the quality, of the remaking that is required. Both for good and for evil, their philosophy of life seems to omit the dimension of depth; it has about it a certain flatness. Their planning is thus liable to be at too superficial a level. Like the 'Women of Canterbury' in Mr. Eliot's play, many of us all the time, and most of us some of the time, are only 'partly living.' Our experience is insensitive, our thinking does not commit us as a whole, and we need to be stabbed into a higher order of personal life. Little provision for this is attempted by scientific humanism.

Here again our national temperament may mislead us. We have a temperamental aversion to unbridled emotionalism and to the sort of exhibitionism which parades and vulgarizes what should be intimate and delicate. But we go easily to the opposite extreme. We live on the surface and instinctively shrink from the deeper experiences. Recoiling from the pinchbeck imitation, we miss the reality.

## b.　The Problem of the Supernatural

The final challenge which 'scientific humanism' shirks is the challenge of the supernatural. For a large part of its history this country has professed to be, and has believed itself to be, a Christian country. To-day it is largely, but not entirely, secularized. Yet the claim of religion is so tremendous, that some decision about it is essential; and, on any showing, this will be a momentous decision.

It is claimed that, over and above the dimension of personal life of which we have been speaking, there is yet another, and that human life is not self-contained but is impinged on from outside and above. Our personal relations are not only horizontal but vertical; we are challenged to meet not only our fellow-men but God, and all lesser challenges and responses culminate in this. This is a declaration about human nature. It is asserted that man is so made as not to be self-sufficient, and that, for a healthy development, he needs to be in a right relation with God. *Fecisti nos ad te, Domine, et inquietum est cor nostrum donec requiescat in te.* If this need is unsatisfied, strains and stresses are set up, he becomes stunted and distorted; and the morbid forms which the religious impulse sometimes takes are a natural result of the thwarting of its normal and healthy development. Everything then depends on whether this extra ' dimension ' is fact or fancy. We all agree that it is fatal to mental health to live in a world of phantasy. But we need to remember that there are two kinds of phantasy, the phantasy of the mirage and the phantasy of the ostrich; if the one adds to reality, the other subtracts from it. If the atheist is right, the whole world of religion is phantasy. If the theist is right, the whole world of the atheist is phantasy, for nothing is simply what the atheist thinks it is.

Between these two world-views it is necessary to choose. It can be plausibly argued that the religious view is false, but it cannot be plausibly argued that, if true, it is less than all-important. The decision is as momentous as any decision could possibly be. It should be made as the Prayer Book says of the decision to marry, ' not unadvisedly, lightly or wantonly . . . but discreetly, advisedly and soberly.' But, as things are, for a large part of the world the issue is burked and the decision goes by default; and ' scientific humanism ' does little to hinder this.

Once God is brought into the picture, light is thrown on the recoil of many besides Christians from the ambitious—one might say, the grandiose—character of the programme proposed by scientific humanists. This recoil does not indeed presuppose a theistic outlook; it may proceed from ordinary human good sense. Whether in the individual or in the community, overweening self-assertion was condemned by the Greeks as ' Hubris ' and was regarded as justly provoking Nemesis. One remembers too the megalomania of a Napoleon or a Hitler. From a Christian standpoint this judgment is ratified and explained : it is impious for the creature to usurp the functions of the Creator in regard to his fellow-men. It is true that we need to walk warily here and to avoid exaggeration. The accusation of impiety was once brought against many attempts to find a cause and cure for the major diseases. We have also to remember that ' Son of man, stand upon thy feet ' is an adjuration given in a religious context, and that, in this sense, modern science may have been driving home a Christian truth which had been obscured. In the true biblical tradition, man made in God's image is entrusted with a measure of God's creative prerogative in being given dominion over nature. Submission to reality is not his whole duty. He should ' show himself bold, inventive and masterful,' and in his degree should carry on the work of his Maker. To Zeus, Prometheus was an impious upstart, but there could be a Christian Prometheus.'[1] But when we come to the more ambitious elements in the programme, selective breeding, psychological conditioning, etc., we cannot but repudiate the assurance and temerity with which they are proposed. Neither scientific humanists, nor we, nor any other persons are good enough for such a job; and the Christian conception of the ingrained perversity in human nature confirms and deepens our reluctance. There is thus between us and the scientific humanist a fundamental difference of emphasis. ' Modern man, or the typical man of our age, wishes to exploit the world for his own delight, whether individually or collectively, and this for him is the meaning of life. Christianity sees the meaning of life in personal relationships, and especially in relationships with God, which all other relationships reflect. Modern man therefore puts his energies into the struggle with nature and with other men who get in his way. The Christian puts his energies into the struggle with that in himself and others which unfits them for real community. The modern man takes his character and aims for granted and works to perfect his tools. The Christian is concerned to bring his character and aims constantly under judgment in the light of God.'[2]

Much of the force of the scientific humanist lies in his realism. He has shown pungently how liable the rest of us are to indulge in various forms of ' escapism '; and he constantly forces us to face unpalatable facts. But, by following him, we may very easily fall into the same pitfall. In the first place decay and death are awkward facts for any form of secular utopianism; and it is not easy to see that he has any way of dealing with them other than by trying to ignore them. In this he is like an eminent American literary critic, part of whose rule of life is—' Never allow oneself even a passing thought of death.' Even if we pin our hopes not on the individual but on the future of the race, it remains true that, in any long view, the works of man do not endure. On purely secularist assumptions, in planning for the future we are plaiting a rope of sand. *Tout casse. Tout passe.* In the now famous words of one of the leaders of modern thought, ' all the labours of all the ages, all the devotion, all the inspiration, all the noonday brightness of human genius are doomed to extinction in the vast death of the solar system and the whole temple of man's achievement must

[1] See de Lubac in *Dublin Review*, No. 442.

[2] Professor Hodges, *Christian News-Letter*, No. 120.

inevitably be buried beneath the débris of a universe in ruins.'[1]
This, he says, is practically certain. 'Only within the scaffolding
of these truths, only on the firm foundation of unyielding despair
can the soul's habitation henceforth safely be built.' This strain of
thought was familiar to the Preacher two or three millennia ago.
But neither to the ancient nor to the modern pessimist have
'scientific humanists' any convincing reply. The physical catas-
trophe is a very long way off; we, and our descendants for countless
generations can afford to ignore it. That is, they counsel us to avert
our attention from the awkward fact and in effect to forget it.
Happily that is not a procedure which they practise in their
laboratories.

Again they are impressive in so far as they impel us to get beyond
irresponsible theorizing to effective action. But action itself can be
a mode of escape from a deep personal challenge. It may distract
attention from a challenge which a man naturally shrinks to face,
because it threatens to pierce his innermost defences and to entail
disconcerting demands on the very citadel of his personality. He
has a strong natural disposition to hold off such an intrusion at all
costs. To plunge into social activity may be an attempt to find a
less exacting alternative, which, however arduous, does not involve
a drastic re-fashioning of himself. In the last analysis an energetic
doing may be a cheap substitute for being and becoming. 'To
keep myself to myself' is an obstinate and semi-instinctive impulse.
I may be ready even to give all my goods to feed the poor and my
body to be burned, but still shrink from giving away myself. Such
shirking the challenge of the transcendental, in its bearing on the
mission of the university, is admirably characterized by Ortega y
Gasset.[2] 'Man is habituated to living on subterfuges with which
he deceives himself, conjuring up around him a very simple and
arbitrary world, in spite of the admonitions of an active conscience
which forces him to observe that his real world, the world that
corresponds to the whole of actuality, is one of enormous complexity
and grim urgency. But he is afraid—our ordinary man is timorous
at heart, with all his brave gesticulations—he is afraid to admit
this real world which would make great demands on him. He
prefers to simplify his life, and keep it sealed up in the cocoon of

[1] Bertrand Russell, *The Free Man's Worship*, reprinted in *Philosophical
Essays*, pp. 60–61.

[2] *Mission of the University*, p. 67.

his fictitious, over-simplified conception of the world.'[1]

In conclusion we must make quite clear the nature of our com-
plaint against ' scientific humanists ' and the reason why we cannot
accept their philosophy of life as an adequate basis for the integration of the university. We do not claim that Christian assumptions
should be substituted for secular assumptions, but we have a right
to demand that the issue between them should not go by default.
We do not assert—and it is not true—that anyone who studies the
issue thoroughly and is adequately equipped with knowledge and
imaginative sympathy will necessarily reach a conclusion favourable to the religious claim. But we do assert that what mainly
confronts us, in the universities as outside, is not reasoned rejection
after honest and competent examination. It is a vague impression
that belief in God is no longer tenable and that the Christian
gospel is an exploded myth. We assert too that those who have
made no serious attempt to discover what leading Christian
theologians to-day do really hold and teach are not entitled to make
a dogmatic pronouncement, or even to hold a confident opinion,
about the Christian claim.

A great intellectual offence is being committed, and, by a
dramatic operation of nemesis, it seems to be an offence of precisely
the same order as that for which Bishop Wilberforce was deservedly
castigated by Huxley on a historic occasion more than eighty years
ago. The bishop's crime was that he dogmatized, confidently and
contemptuously, on questions which he had made no serious
attempt to understand. He relied on a hazy recollection of such
science, or of subjects bordering on science, as he had come in
contact with at school or college and on discussions carried on at
the level of the magazine or popular newspaper; he made no
serious attempt to think himself into the scientific attitude and
approach or to understand the scientist's methods and criteria or
to distinguish caricature from reality; and he employed the
resources of an agile brain and a ready tongue to excite popular

[1] I believe this argument to be profoundly true and important. But
' escapism '—and self-deception in escapism—is protean ; and we need to
be on our guard against falling into the very fault we denounce. The
' scientific humanist ' himself is likely to regard our argument as only a
familiar piece of counter-revolutionary technique. It has been said that
one of the most useful devices of the academic conservative is to urge that
' the measure proposed would block the way to a far more sweeping
reform ' ; and that, on enquiry, this reform always turns out to be something which nobody is proposing to do anything about just now. This
consideration does not lessen the intrinsic force of the argument, but it is
a warning to be honest in using it and not to make it a cloak for inertia.

prejudice against those whom he ignorantly criticized. In short, he showed an almost complete intellectual irresponsibility. But to-day it is the spiritual descendants of Huxley who are guilty of exactly the same offence against the representatives of religion. They dogmatize confidently, they appeal to popular prejudice, they suggest that all educated people have made up their minds that the foundations of Christianity, like the foundations of astrology, are demonstrably false and that the issue is now *chose jugée;* they adopt the attitude of Browning's ' Cleon ' to St. Paul :

> Oh the Jew findeth scholars ! Certain slaves
> Who touched on this same isle, preached him and Christ;
> And (as I gathered from a bystander)
> Their doctrine could be held by no sane man.

Yet, so far as can be judged from their writings, they have made no serious attempt to equip themselves to make any pronouncement on the subject of religion. For their conception of Christianity they rely on their recollection of such religious teaching as they encountered in childhood or at school, or in popular journalism. They have not attempted to think themselves into the mind of the major Christian thinkers or saints. But in their dogmatic pronouncements they grossly misuse the argument from authority. They ignore the fact that many of those whom they sweep aside—theologians, philosophers, or scientists who are also believing Christians—are, by any neutral academic test, their equals in intelligence and have given to religious questions a far greater quantity and quality of attention than they.

The university should be a place of resolute and untiring pursuit of truth in matters of the highest significance. The nature of man and of the world, and its practical implications for conduct, are on any showing foremost among such matters. Questions concerning them are difficult; they are also disturbing and unsettling. But to ignore or gloss over them, or to be content with slovenly treatment and answers at once superficial and dogmatic, is unworthy of a university.

## 2   CLASSICAL HUMANISM

If ' scientific humanism ' fails to satisfy, what alternative sources of integration are available? One is a return to our historic, ' classical,' tradition. This is, in the main, the policy of our older

humanists, as represented in this country, e.g., by such an outstanding and honoured figure as Dr. Gilbert Murray or a little
earlier, Lowes Dickinson; in the United States, Dr. Hutchins' *The
Higher Learning in America* exemplifies a similar trend. They base
themselves on our western cultural heritage, derived originally from
Athens, Rome and Jerusalem, but attested by its acceptance among
thinking men throughout European history.

The following are some of their tenets. First there is an art of
living, which can be taught and acquired; to impart it is the
supreme aim of education. A reasonable life, for individual or
community, is one in which the raw material of impulse and
emotion is shaped in accordance with a pattern, and conduct is
governed by principle. The danger of the world to-day is that it
should be without rudder or compass; for guidance we should
recur to a healthy tradition. According to that tradition there are
fixed laws of mental as of bodily health, which in broad outline
are the same for everyone and are independent of individual
idiosyncrasies, being based on a systematic understanding of the
structure and functions of the human mind. Its well-being is seen
to depend on its conformity to certain norms which it recognizes
but does not make. When we call anything true, good or beautiful,
we purport to measure it by an objective standard. Such goodness
is intrinsic and does not require to be buttressed by some external
prop. Honesty may or may not be the best policy; but its goodness
does not depend on its expediency but is self-evident. The university exists to pursue αὐτὸ τὸ καλόν, and that pursuit is its own
justification. It belies its own nature if it subordinates that pursuit,
either to money-making (as according to Dr. Hutchins do a number
of American universities), or to reasons of state and the rise to
power of the proletariate, (as on Professor Pinkevitch's showing do
the Russian universities under the present régime) or to edification
(as did the early Puritan universities in the U.S.A. and, at various
times, those under ecclesiastical influence in this country and in
Europe).

Secondly, the structure of the good life and the nature of the
cardinal virtues were described in outline once and for all by the
Greeks, and have ever since been part of the common stock of
European culture. Moral progress has consisted only in filling in
the outline and in widening the area of personal life to which, and
of persons towards or between whom, these norms apply. There
has thus come into being an understanding of what is a reasonable

way of living on which humanists and Christians can unite. In the
'ages of faith' Christians have, as it were, added an upper floor,
consisting of the theological virtues of faith, hope and charity; but
the ground floor stands and is habitable, irrespective of the fate of
this addition.

Thirdly there is a hierarchy of values, recognized by common
consent of good and sensible men. Games and circuses are not as
good as art, music and literature, and, if anyone thinks they are,
he is an ignoramus. In Plato's terminology this is a matter of
'knowledge' and not only of 'opinion.' Education then, whether
at school or university, must communicate this discrimination. It
must disseminate the cult of excellence and the power to distinguish
between the expert and the quack, between the first-rate and the
shoddy, in taste, in conduct and in reasoning. To do so, it must
ensure constant and intimate contact with persons and books of
the highest excellence. 'The habitual vision of greatness' is the
thing most needful. Burke has expressed this principle in his
'essential rule' of criticism—'If ever we should find ourselves
disposed not to admire those writers or artists, Livy and Virgil for
instance, Raphael or Michael Angelo, whom all the learned had
admired, not to follow our own fancies, but to study them until
we know how and what we ought to admire; and if we cannot
arrive at this combination of admiration with knowledge, rather
to believe that we are dull than that the rest of the world has been
imposed on.'[1]

Finally this point of view is called 'classical,' in distinction for
example from 'romantic' or 'modernist'; not because of its
reliance on Greek or Latin writers, but because of the claim that
its principles are objective rather than subjective, universal rather
than local, permanent rather than temporary. *Quod semper, quod
ubique, quod ab omnibus. Securus judicat orbis terrarum.*

> Greece and her foundations are
> Built below the tide of war,
> Based on the crystalline sea
> Of thought and its eternity.

It proposes to build on 'the man in men' rather than on individual
idiosyncrasies.

Thus our classical humanists would recall us to what is central

[1] *Works,* vol. III, p. 455.

in our tradition. They invite us to regain a sense of perspective, to distinguish between what is normative and what is exceptional or even pathological. Of course, they do not deny the immense scientific gains of the modern age or the propriety of developing applied science in the universities. But they do demand some change of emphasis and a restoration of balance between technical and humane studies. This is illustrated by Sir Richard Livingstone's dry remark, ' The Greeks could not broadcast the Aeschylean trilogy, but they could write it.'

This standpoint has very great attractions. Its sanity, balance and ' magnanimity ' are impressive and its protagonists are men who command high respect. But regarded as a complete philosophy of life on which our universities to-day can be built, it is gravely deficient. One sign of this is its undoubted failure to grip the great mass of students.

Most students feel in their bones that their older teachers, admirable as they often are, are living mentally in a vanished world, altogether simpler, less tangled and less unmanageable, than that with which they are themselves confronted. The classical outlook strikes them as disembodied and as sitting too loose to the material substratum of life. Its intellectual climate, they feel, is rarefied; it resembles our own no more than the pellucid air, the white buildings and the brilliant colours of the Mediterranean area resemble Manchester or Birmingham. For good or evil, we live in a ' Great Society ' which is thoroughly urbanized and industrialized, and whose life and outlook are profoundly affected by improvements in the instruments of production. Such a book as Trevelyan's *Social History* is one long commentary on this theme. The classical world is too remote to serve as our chief model.

Classicism is also too naïve a philosophy of life to be convincing to those who have grown up in the era of world-wars. They are acutely conscious of the grim reality of the struggle for survival and for power going on behind whatever decent façade civilization still maintains. The classical, like the scientific, humanist makes no sufficient attempt to recognize and to provide for this. Hence arises a curious inversion in the normal rôles of the generations. Usually it is persons of the older generation who smile at the hopeful illusions of the young; to-day it is the young who smile at the hopeful illusions of the old, for there is a sense in which they have ' been through the mill ' as their seniors have not. *Angst,* an uneasy anxiety, is too deeply ingrained in them to be allayed by any idealism. In a world of jagged edges, volcanic passions and daemonic centres of power such as ours, the cult of Sophrosyne, or sweet reasonableness, and the provision of a harmonious pattern of living are not in themselves sufficient for salvation. Platonism, whether pagan or Christian, does not plumb the depths; something at once more realistic and more dynamic is needed.

Classicism also overrates both the possibility and the value of stability. It is notorious that the Greeks inevitably confused the permanent conditions of civilized life with the local and temporary features of the Greek city-state. We have the advantage of an immensely greater comparative knowledge of different civilizations. But that only goes to establish how partial are all our perspectives. Classicism exaggerates both our power to disentangle and to formulate the permanent element underlying all changes in valuation and the degree of its embodiment at any one epoch. Archaism, in all its forms, is a policy which transgresses the laws of our temporal existence. The same conditions never recur. ' Back to Sophocles ' or ' Back to Aristotle ' are policies no more justifiable than any other form of reversion. Here Christians should be wiser. They should know that

> man is hurled
> From change to change unceasingly
> His soul's wings never furled.

But in this matter they have often been untrue to their own insight, and, in different forms, gnosticism has been a constantly recurring heresy.

In the last analysis classical culture is deficient in catholicity since it has too little room for natural science and underrates its significance. Of course our classical humanists are not obscurantists. They are neither ignorant of the modern physical conception of the world nor resistant to its diffusion in the university. But it does not make any deep dint in their minds; and to them the new forces remain secondary and peripheral. Their attitude may be symbolized by the status given to natural science at Oxford at the close of the nineteenth century. The battle for admission had been won a good deal earlier. The scientists were there and carried on their activities at a number of laboratories in ' the Parks.' But in effect they were still rather an appendage loosely attached to the University than an integral part of it. The general life of the place, its organization and its working philosophy, were unaffected.

G

They were not really admitted to the Brahmin caste. ' Stinks ' had not the same rank in the hierarchy as *Literae Humaniores*. Yet if industrialism and democracy are the outstanding and significant forces in the modern world, no philosophy of life or of education which gives to them only a secondary place and a subsidiary function can hope to convince.

Again the classical tradition is bound up with a society based on privilege. Within that tradition it is the university's function to train the ruling classes. It is concerned with a select and segregated minority, the brain-workers, and not with the vast majority who labour with their hands to get their bread and to do the world's work. The intellectual, whether student or teacher, leads a life of learned leisure, and that puts him in an exceptional and favoured position. He is relieved of drudgery; he toils not neither does he spin. He can afford to be disinterested simply because he can rely on other people to do the dirty work for him. Thus university students and teachers are, in effect, a chosen people with an appropriate retinue of hewers of wood and drawers of water to minister to their material needs. But the ordinary man must earn his bread by the sweat of his brow, ' not without dust and heat.' Such a class-division is typical of Greek rather than of Hebrew ideas, but it is exemplified very clearly in Ecclesiasticus.[1] ' The wisdom of a learned man cometh by opportunity of leisure . . . How can he get wisdom that holdeth the plough and glorieth in the goad, that driveth oxen and is occupied in their labours, and whose talk is of bullocks? . . . So every carpenter that laboureth night and day . . . the smith also sitting by the anvil and considering the iron work . . . So doth the potter sitting at his work and turning the wheel about with his feet . . . All these trust in their hands . . . Without these cannot a city be inhabited . . . They shall not be sought for in publick counsel, nor sit high in the congregation : they shall not sit in the judges' seat, nor understand the sentence of judgment . . . But they will maintain the state of the world, and all their desire is in the work of their craft.'

In the classical tradition people are not troubled by this class-division, they take it for granted. But it is just here that the modern conscience is most profoundly troubled and distracted. It cannot find a remedy for its distraction in going back to any primitive paradise in which men had not awoken to the unsatisfied demands of social justice. In that tradition the university is too

[1] Ch. xxxviii, vv. 22ff.

exclusively engaged in producing cultivated gentlemen, too little concerned with ' men unblest.' If universities were now to base their governing philosophy of life on the classical tradition, would they not be anachronisms like the ' country-house ' life which flourished in Victorian and Edwardian times? That was a singularly gracious as well as an opulent institution. But that particular form of graciousness was bound up with the opulence, and such opulence of a privileged caste is no longer possible nor tolerable. To speak of ' opulence ' in connection with university teachers may well seem ironical. But as compared with the great majority and with the homes from which an increasing number of students come, they have been accustomed to enjoy a modest degree of economic and social ' security,' in the strict sense of the word; they have had comparative freedom from care.

Assuredly we have, and shall continue to have, invaluable lessons to learn from the classical strain in our cultural tradition. But, as a complete philosophy of life on which to base university education it is too rarefied, too naïve, too static, too limited and, in a sense, too parasitic.

## 3 BACK TO THE CHRISTIAN TRADITION

If a humanistic philosophy of life, whether scientific or classical, is discredited, are we free to urge on our universities a return to an explicitly Christian basis, such as all the older European universities once acknowledged? In regard to schools, the Archbishops of Canterbury, York and Wales issued a statement in 1941, entitled ' Christian Education : A Call to Action.' In it they quoted and endorsed words addressed shortly before by a County Education Authority to the headmasters of its secondary schools.

' Religious instruction should not be looked on merely as one of a number of subjects to be taught, but as the foundation of the education given at the school. Its purpose should be to influence a child's whole attitude to life, not merely to impart religious knowledge but to teach religion. It thus becomes the real centre of school life determining its character and tone . . . Religion should be the basis and foundation of the whole curriculum of the school.'

Should we work to-day to make the Christian religion the basis and foundation of the whole curriculum of the university? The argument for such a programme might run as follows.

The crisis in human affairs needs little stressing. It is only too plain that we have reached a condition of near-anarchy in the interrelations of powerful groups and nations. But, as Christians, we hold—and this is our distinctive contribution—that men's relations with their fellows have gone all awry, just because all relation with their Maker has been neglected. In effect the modern world, including the Christians in it for a great part of their time, are living stunted lives and have their mental being in an artificially restricted world; but this is just what is characteristic of the insane. Secularism is practical atheism and it does violence to human nature. Hence come false and distorted religions like Nazism; they arise because a fundamental need of human nature is denied its normal and healthy development. Of course these assertions are, in the highest degree, controversial; but it is to these that Christians are committed. To wrap them up or to burke the issue is hardly consistent with integrity.

For many centuries now the civilized world has been gradually drifting away from any genuine awareness of God, and so from realism and sanity. This awareness was once so basic that the medieval historian could write a work under the title *Gesta Dei per Francos*. For him the interconnection of events was found in the will of God and secondary causes were neglected. To-day it is secondary causes that fill the scene. Modern writers of history would regard all kinds of things as important, but it is quite certain that the will of God would not play the slightest part in their treatment of the subject.[1] May not Christians rightly claim that the only way to recover meaning and purpose, other than that of a totalitarianism from which we rightly recoil, is to reverse this drift and to recover that ' deep, disturbing sense of the living God ' which has so largely been lost; and that Christ, as the ultimate source of all wisdom and all truth, is the only possible basis for a genuine unity of outlook and aim for the university? If the ship is to reach port, the neglected chart must be brought again into use. In that case our message to the university as to the nation must be, ' *Convertere Jerusalem ad Dominum tuum*. The motto of the University of Oxford, *Dominus Illuminatio Mea,* must be taken as the guiding principle, not only of one university but of all. The older universities have never ceased to be formally Christian. Let them become so again in spirit and truth; and let the modern universities learn the same lesson. ' Back to Newman,' if not to St.

[1] See a penetrating article by Hans Schonerus on ' Thinking Anew ' in *Theology*, Vol. L, p. 124, from which the preceding sentences are taken almost verbally.

Thomas, will be the slogan of the Christian university reformer. The organic structure of our universities, the selection of their teachers, the assumptions underlying their social life will be shaped by this supreme aim. Theology will once again become the master-science, which holds together and gives meaning and direction to all others.

Obviously such a conclusion has a powerful appeal to all genuine Christians. But, for the contemporary university as a whole, it is emphatically not the conclusion which we feel able to draw. It embodies a policy which in present circumstances we are bound to reject. First it is impracticable. Secondly, even if it were practicable, it would be inequitable. Thirdly, even if it were equitable, it would, from a truly Christian point of view, be disastrous.

First it is impracticable. When the older universities took their shape, the imagination of the European community as a whole was dominated by Christian ideas and the Bible was the primary source of culture. Even a hundred years ago the nation was still, in intention, a god-fearing nation. Newman and Whewell could appeal to the common assumptions of our history and literature and to normal social practice. For instance Whewell defended compulsory chapel by pointing out that at home the ordinary undergraduate would have been accustomed to attend family prayers. To-day all this is changed. In the Middle Ages an atheist was a peculiar person, probably persecuted and anyhow a misfit among his fellows. To-day it is the Christian believer who is the peculiar person, having special assumptions of his own which the man in the street does not share. To say that the end of man is to glorify God and enjoy him for ever, is to say something that for most people is, not so much false or pernicious, as balderdash. This is almost certainly true of the majority of those who enter our universities as students and of those who teach in them. But it is impossible that the body should be warm when the members are cold. Our real situation is not unlike that of the United States. In the Harvard volume, *General Education in a Free Society*, it is stated quite clearly that, a century ago, the unifying purpose and idea of education was to train Christian citizens; but, ' This solution is out of the question in publicly supported colleges and is practically, if not legally, impossible in most others . . . Whatever one's views, religion is not now for most colleges a practicable source of intellectual unity.'[1] It is true that, both in England and in Scotland, we differ from the

[1] p. 39.

United States in still having an established church, and that in our
school system some form of religious worship has long been practically universal and has recently been made statutory. But at the
university stage it is less possible to evade the difficulties. You may
conceivably get a majority of adults to think religion is good for
children; you will not get a majority to think it is good for themselves. It is unthinkable that in any near future our modern universities will profess Christianity as their basis. At the older universities
many of the forms of religion have survived; but in reality the
ethos both of dons and of undergraduates is little less completely
secularized than at 'Redbrick.' Until the 'climate of opinion' is
changed, outside as well as inside the university, it will not be
practical politics to look for a general adoption of an explicitly
Christian basis. 'Real Christianity,' it has been truly said, 'has
gone almost dead on the modern mind.' We Christians in the
universities are ourselves profoundly affected by this secularist
climate. To demand a consciously Christian university as part of
any short-term programme, is vastly to underestimate the magnitude
of the change required, not least in ourselves.

In the second place such a programme is inequitable. So long
as convinced Christians are a minority of our people, it is unfair
and unreasonable to ask that the universities shall be dominated by
Christian belief. Though the British universities are not state-
universities, they are, in a real sense, national institutions. They are
under at least a tacit obligation to be communal and not sectional.
They are no longer supported only by particular groups or intended
for the use only of particular groups or for the propagation of particular opinions. They ought therefore to reflect the national mind,
unless they reflect a mind even wider. But the national mind is not
now Christian in the sense that it once was; and, at best, it cannot
again become Christian by any speedy process. There is a real
danger that we should, unwittingly, lend ourselves to a policy whose
morality is dubious and which would leave the rationalist with a
quite legitimate grievance. There is such a thing as a 'Christian
racket.' It is one thing to demonstrate, with a good deal of acceptance, that the present state of universities is chaotic or that materialism is bankrupt; but, to 'cash in' on this and to assume that the
re-enthronement of the Athanasian Creed is the only alternative, is
quite another. In anything like the present state of opinion this
would be tantamount to the imposition of an 'ideology'; that is,
of an over-simplified outlook achieved by the domination of one

type of thinking over others. A Christian institutional framework would be so far divorced from the opinions of the majority, that it could only be set up by force or by dexterous diplomacy. But to use political manœuvres and stratagems in the cause of Christianity is perhaps the worst treason that Christians can commit; and it is no less a treason because, in history, Christians have so often committed it. Success, even if achieved, would be unhallowed and would bring a speedy nemesis.

Lastly, it is a delusion to suppose that the adoption of a Christian platform by the university to-day would really further the Christian cause. However well-intended, it would inevitably be a sham. The plausibility of such a programme depends on the ambiguity of the word ' Christian.' It is constantly used in a diluted sense, as when Sir Alan Herbert's ' Topsy ' says, ' I *always* believe in *always* doing the *Christian* thing.' Here the word signifies an ethos which as a matter of history was generated by Christianity, which has had a strong hold on the European mind and has lasted longer in this country than elsewhere, which now is threatened, and which it is most needful that we should recover and strengthen. It implies a belief in truth and goodness and a sustained effort to attain them. But though it is an offshoot of Christianity, it is not Christianity; it possesses no power unto salvation. Sharply distinct from this is authentic Christianity. The true Christian life consists not in keeping commandments, however stringent, nor in following principles, however lofty, nor even in the imitation of Christ. It is a life in grace—that is of prayer and sacrament, of daily and hourly dependence on power from on high, a life lived within the context of the worshipping community and based on faith in the great acts of God in Christ recounted in the Bible—Incarnation, Redemption, Resurrection. This is the religion of power, but it is unquestionably the religion only of a comparatively small minority of the people of this country or of the members of our universities. Of necessity it is only diluted (or debased), and not authentic, Christianity which either nation or university could adopt in any near future as the basic principle of its life; and the effect would be to obscure a difference which is vital. The plausibility of any such proposal depends on a substitution of the reflection for the reality. The Law is substituted for the Gospel and is itself much diluted to bring it within the range of practical politics.

Behind this lurks a still worse danger. Religious sentiment may be fostered as a means to an end for the purpose of ' moral rearmament,' as a bulwark of the institutions of the country and a counter-weight to communism or to other revolutionary forces. For such purposes emotional awareness of a purpose at once transcending and governing the life of the individual and the whole contempor-ary and terrestial scene may be cultivated, while all theological doctrine is left in a convenient haze. But such exploitations of the Christian religion for ends other than its own would be the ultimate profanity.

Yet again while we are ourselves assured that the whole truth is to be found in Christ, we have to recognize that it is not in the possession of Christians, either individually or collectively. It never has been, and at no historical time is it likely to be. As we look back at the battles of the last two centuries, we cannot but see that the champions of Christianity have often been in the wrong on particular issues. When fighting the Enlightenment, or ' Liberalism ' or Marxism, they have stood for fundamental truths. But, from our vantage-point of later knowledge, we can now see that they un-wittingly fought also for privilege and for obscurantism. The history of European thought since the Renaissance is not simply the history of a corporate going astray, for which the remedy would be to retrace one's steps. This is as true of academic as of wider issues. But, as Christians, we ought not to be surprised by this. Histori-cally, this is what we find; doctrinally it is what we ought to expect. An honest intention to fight the Lord's battles is no guarantee against mistaken objectives or illegitimate methods of warfare. Also Gnosticism, the claim to know more than the creature can know, has always been recognized as a heresy in principle, though in practice the champions of orthodoxy have often been guilty of it. It ignores the inevitable limitations of all partial perspectives, limitations of temperament, of place and of era. Idolization of the ephemeral—whether self, institution or technique—has been a major cause of the breakdown of civilizations; and the most Christian groups are not immune from it.[1] Domination by theologians is no less objec-tionable than domination by any other group. Any implied claim to infallibility is unchristian, since it clashes with Christian insight into human creatureliness and human corruption. Milton has pro-claimed unforgettably that it is not till our Lord's second coming that all the scattered fragments of truth will be re-assembled.

It follows that an all-Christian university, if we could have it,

[1] This is the theme of much of Professor Toynbee's great work, *The Study of History*.

would be defective. We have indispensable lessons to learn from the heretic, however wrong he is on fundamental issues. He is needed both as a test and as a contributor. Until the strongest adverse case has been faced, faith cannot be secure; and this can only happen through personal contact with the unbeliever. What is merely secondhand and unassimilated needs to be purged. To shrink from such exposure to the most trenchant criticism, such trial as by fire, may be a form of recreancy, for true faith is no ' fugitive and cloistered virtue.' At this moment some of our Christian brethren in other countries, having passed through fiercer trials than we, can speak with a higher degree of authority than ours. But it is still more essential to recognize that God may speak, and often does speak, through what we should have thought very improbable voices, through men who do not consciously know Him and who are disastrously wrong in their main contentions. As of old the heathen peoples might be instruments of His judgments on Israel, so Marx or Nietzsche or Freud may have a word for our generation, to refuse to hear which would be to be deaf to the voice of God. Professor Hodges has stated very clearly the principle which should guide us :—' No one, not even our most Christian selves, can have the whole truth and there is no one who may not become to us a vehicle of God's truth.' It is a mistake to try to root out all tares; not merely because they cannot be accurately identified but because the tares are not a hundred per cent weeds any more than the wheat is a hundred per cent good grain. In the present state of the world Christians themselves ought not to want an all-Christian university.

# V

# AIM AND BASIS

We come now to the most crucial, and the hardest part of our task. At this time of crisis, in the middle of the twentieth century and after two world-wars, what positive convictions, if any, should the British universities embody? In our earlier chapters we have painted a picture of disintegration, and we have disallowed various attempts at re-integration. What then is our own alternative? To what extent should a university concern itself with philosophies of life, and should it stand positively for any particular philosophy of life? If so, what should that be; and in what way should it be exemplified (e.g. by inculcation to students, tests for teachers etc.)? What responsibility has a university for the philosophies of life of its members? We ourselves are writing as Christian believers, desiring to bring Christian insight to the problem, ' How can the university be the university?' but we have already ruled out the view that definite Christian conviction can, now or in any near future, be the basis of integration. At what then can we legitimately aim, and what can we reasonably ask others to concede? These are the most fundamental questions that can possibly be asked about universities; and yet it is just on these issues that, both within and outside the universities, there is most obviously confusion or disharmony.

We confess frankly that in answering these questions we can only make a small beginning. At best what we have to offer is an interim report. As we see it, neither the general intellectual situation nor the mind of the general body of Christians in the university world, admits at present of anything more. Much further thinking and experimenting needs to be done, and the most we can hope is to contribute some stimulus towards it. But to shirk this central question altogether would make nugatory everything else we have to say. However crude or superficial our treatment, all that we have said so far leads up to it and all that is to follow springs from it.

# I   THE OPEN FORUM

As a minimum, even if the university is officially neutral on ultimate issues, its neutrality should be ' positive ' and not ' negative.' That is, it should not exclude or discourage discussion of these, frequently burning, questions but should actively promote and stimulate it. We borrow the term ' positive neutrality ' from International Student Service, whose experience in this respect is highly relevant. In addition to its relief work, I.S.S. has for many years brought together in conference groups of students and staff, for frank discussion of the most controversial and explosive questions. In this way it has successfully brought together such apparently unmixable groups as Jews and Arabs, Orangemen and Sinn Feiners, Dutch and Indonesians, etc., to discuss the very questions which divide and inflame them. The basis of unity which makes possible the plainest of speaking without rupture is, first, solidarity as university men and women, and, secondly, personal fellowship engendered in living together throughout the conference. Such conferences are, in a high degree, educational to all who take part in them. There you meet face to face those who hold opinions and sentiments antagonistic to your own. You become aware of such views not only at long range, as something misguided and perverse to be refuted, but as the sincere convictions of men with whom you are in immediate personal fellowship. They come alive to you and the members of each group take a notable step towards imaginative understanding of just those factors which they have been most liable to overlook. Disagreement may still be deep, but much misunderstanding will have been removed; and when, in later life, some of these students hold key positions, their decisions are likely to be more intelligent and responsible than they would otherwise have been. But, in order to perform this function, it is necessary that I.S.S., as an organization, should be uncommitted to any side in regard to the vexed questions debated at its conferences. Otherwise it would be unable to assemble the parties.

This analogy may be applied to the university. The university ' must be a community within which the chief contemporary intellectual positions . . . may enter into a living encounter with one another.' At the very least, fundamental questions must not be ignored but must be asked and examined radically. How shall a man live? What are the things which really matter and what is their relative importance? To what sort of world have we to adjust ourselves? ' Here arises the responsibility of the universities. They are inheritors of the Greek tradition of candid and intrepid thinking about the fundamental issues involved in the life of the individual and of the community and of the Greek principle that "the unexamined life is no life for man" . . . Certainly it is no part of the duty of a university to inculcate any particular philosophy of life. But it is its duty to assist its students to form their own philosophies of life, so that they may not go out into the world maimed and useless. It should stimulate and train them, not of course necessarily to think alike, but at least to think, and to think strenuously about the great issues of right and wrong, of liberty and government, on which both for the individual and for the community, a balanced judgment is essential to a rational life.'[1] The vital principle of democracy is that differences are hammered out in discussion. But the discussion which goes on in a university may be defective, either because it omits the really vital issues or because it treats them only at a superficial level. The radical discussion that is required is difficult and daunting, because it may not leave oneself unchanged. Yet of course to say this is easier than to mean it; and, to mean it in occasional 'hours of insight,' is easier than to do so steadily and effectively through 'days of gloom.'

How does one live? Every sane and civilized man must perforce have some rudimentary working philosophy of life, however unconscious or uncritical. From hour to hour he must make decisions and do what seems best to him. Not to take such choices seriously and simply to drift is infra-human; and it is unworthy of a university man or woman not to relate them to the live issues of the time or, in so doing, to be duller or more purblind than he can help. It ought to be impossible, though it is actually common, to go through a university without ever feeling this challenge at the deep level where real decisions are made. 'Upon leaving the university the foundations for an intelligent personal theory of the world and of life should have been laid.'[2] Here a university, however neutral officially, has a heavy responsibility. Somehow it should impress on its students the urgency of deliberation and decision. It may be unable to offer them an agreed *Weltanschauung*. But if it cannot speak with one voice, let it speak through its teachers with several voices. The one thing unforgivable is to be silent.

If this is our policy, we must recognize that it involves the frank

[1] U.G.C. Report, p. 32.
[2] Paulsen, *The German Universities*, E. T., p. 308.

abandonment of the old effort to protect the student from influences
that are dangerous and unsettling. In the latter part of the nineteenth
century Christian parents shuddered at the exposure of their sons in
the universities to infidelity and lamented the disappearance
of ' security from proselytism and infectious scornfulness ';[1] and
the Christian leaders fought long and strenuously against the admission of teachers without guarantee of Christian belief. Their attitude
is stated clearly by Liddon in a letter to William Bright written in
1868. ' Speaking absolutely, we know that religious truth can
take care of itself . . . But in the concrete and particular case of
young men living together, tempted to every sort of moral mischief,
and eager to get rid in their worst moments of the sanctions and
control of religion; it is no disparagement to religious truth to say
that it does need protection . . . To treat Oxford undergraduates
as in all respects men, appears to me the greatest possible mistake
. . . The question is . . . whether the sons of Christian parents are
for all time to come to be made over to infidel teachers of history
and philosophy, with an undisputed right to teach them infidelity.'[2]
Similarly, in Charlotte Yonge's novel, *The Daisy Chain,* when
Norman May while at Oxford reads some German criticism and
speculation by which his faith is temporarily shaken, his father
blames his rash folly; to meddle with the accursed books was to
run into temptation and to taste poison. Such an attitude is understandable, but it is misguided; and it is far less plausible now than
it was in Liddon's day. The dangers are incidental to growing up,
and the student is to be treated as an adult. Christian training at
the university level ought to include being confronted by, and not
being safeguarded from, other ways of thinking. This is a tension
which is inseparable from being an educated adult in a world so
deeply divided as is ours. No doubt it may be urged that such a
tension is all very well for the abler student, but that, to bear it, is
beyond the capacity of the weaker brother. But the answer must be
that such a ' weaker brother ' is probably out of place in a university, and certainly his needs cannot be allowed to determine university procedure. Faith, no more than virtue, should be ' fugitive and
cloistered.' Such a faith must be insecure for it is one to which
the holder has no real right. It is indeed Newman who, wiser than
his allies, denies that the best way of learning to swim in troubled
waters is never to have gone into them. In his famous tribute to

[1] Keble's words quoted in *Life of Pusey,* III, p. 400.

[2] *Life,* pp. 132, 133.

the Oxford of eighty years ago, Matthew Arnold enumerates among her charms that she was ' so unravaged by the fierce intellectual life of our century.' But that is a thing which no university has any business to be; for the university, intellectual innocence is not a virtue but a vice.

On the same fundamental educational principle—that the student is to be regarded as an adult—the tradition that the teacher should abstain from participation in radical discussion of ultimate questions, and should be reticent about his own views, must be rejected as a false idol equally with the tradition of protecting the student. The teacher of children may reasonably scruple to express to them opinions conflicting with the beliefs of their parents or the general sense of the community. But that is because children have not yet come to years of discretion and are not yet capable of weighing and judging for themselves. At the university stage there is no excuse for depriving students of the means and responsibility of judgment or of sheltering them from its difficulties. It is a boon to students to know ' what are the personal convictions of a sincere and serious man with respect to the great problems of life and the world to which such a man has devoted deep and serious thought.'[1] To communicate these frankly must not be regarded as a breach of professional etiquette, while to have none to communicate is a mark of professional incapacity. Thus, as Christian teachers ourselves, we claim freedom to express with a clear conscience our Christian convictions and our grounds for them. But we recognize that the same freedom must be conceded to those who differ from us. It is, for example, the right of Professor J. B. S. Haldane as of Mr. C. S. Lewis. This applies not only to ' out of school ' activities, to the evening meeting of the Conservative or the Labour Club, the Student Christian Movement or the Rationalist Society, but also to the lecture room.

It is true that there remains an essential distinction between university teaching and propaganda, a distinction which both Fascists and Communists have tended to obliterate. The teacher should not suppress his convictions for fear of being accused of proselytism; yet it is not his primary concern to make proselytes. His immediate task is to aid understanding rather than to impel his pupils towards, or away from, any prescribed type of action, to supply them with data for forming intelligent judgments of

[1] Paulsen, *op. cit.*, p. 241.

their own rather than to enlist them as disciples. But among those
data should be his own conclusions and the reasons which have
led him to them.

If university men must be deeply concerned with discovering a
working philosophy of life, the religious issue is unavoidable. For
every philosophy of life is either religious or secularist; it requires
God or it leaves Him out. The Christian asserts that the reason
why man is tearing himself to pieces is that he is out of harmony
with a Presence half hidden and half revealed by the façade of
physical things and processes, and that the only radical or lasting
cure for our disorders is to be found in the restoration of that harmony. This assertion is either, as we think, saving truth or, as
others think, fatal error. There is no third alternative. A choice
between these views is inescapable, and on any showing no more
momentous choice is possible; this is common ground to Kierkegaard and to Lenin. Religion, in the words of Donald Hankey, is
betting your life that there is a god; and he might have added
that irreligion is betting your life that there is not a god. You can
choose which way you will lay your bet, but you can neither
decline the wager nor reduce your stake. Whichever way the truth
lies, sitting on the fence must be futile; for it is in effect to choose
the negative side without intending to do so or realizing that you
have done so. We have refused to claim that universities to-day
should be Christian, even in the sense in which some colleges within
some of them still are Christian. But no student should go down
without having been confronted by the Christian challenge. There
can be no question of official pressure on him to accept it, but he
should be incited to take notice of it. What ought to be impossible
for him is decision by inadvertence, for that is really sub-human.

As Christians, we must realize that the supreme enemy of our
cause is not the ardent atheist, the serious-minded teacher or
student who, after due consideration, is impelled to reject Christianity. He is always to be regarded with respect, and in some important ways he is our ally. It is the man of trivial or merely conventional outlook who drifts through life without ever really facing
the question. And each of us has to admit that his own habit of
saying 'Lord, Lord,' is no guarantee that he is not himself one
of these drifters. As against such people are linked all those, however sharply opposed their creeds, who stand for intellectual integrity
and responsibility. There should be no place for such drifters in
the university, not because they are specially wicked (of which there

is no evidence) or specially profane (which may be irrelevant) but because they are uneducated, and apparently uneducatable in those issues which matter most.

Before we leave this conception of the university as an open forum for the thrashing out of ultimate questions, three reflections may be added. First the magnitude of the change would be great even if this were done and no more. Few who know the universities would venture to claim that fifty per cent of those who now go through them experience any such intellectual awakening as that which we are demanding, or ever make a responsible personal decision in adopting their working philosophy. Even with the minority which is alive to the larger issues discussion is often callow and superficial and does not touch the levels at which major decisions are made. This was exemplified by a University Union which once invited Dr. Joad and Father Knox to open a debate on the existence of God. Secondly, though some dons do take part with students in fundamental discussions, (e.g. in meetings of the S.C.M. or of various societies with Marxist sympathies) the amount of such assistance from seniors is still small, and the university takes no responsibility for promoting it. Thirdly, what is wanted is, that the university should press on the attention of students the urgency of attaining a convincing philosophy of life and should put at their disposal all possible resources for making an intelligent choice. The university authorities, Senates and Councils, Vice-Chancellors, Principals and Deans, should devote much attention to the question, ' Is this happening on a sufficient scale? If not, how can it be stimulated?' For this is an educational question more far-reaching and fundamental than most of those which now occupy their attention.

## 2    THE REOPENING OF COMMUNICATIONS

To be such a forum as we have described is a minimum requirement, but is it enough? Can a university rightly leave commitment to its individual members and confine itself corporately to holding the ring? This attitude has recently been sharply challenged by Mr. Arnold Nash, writing from a Christian standpoint. ' The liberal democratic university' he says ' by rejecting any real attempt to discern and then to teach a unified conception of life, refuses to be a university.'[1] Does not a university stultify itself if there is no

[1] *The University and the Modern World*, p. 35.

coherent scheme of life for which it stands, no coherent picture of the universe which it presents? Is not that intellectual anarchy? It does not behave so spinelessly in regard to the special sciences. When it is a question of the master-science to which all these are subordinate, is the university in effect to sit back and say, 'God bless you my boys, go to it'? On that showing it is all-important for the individual student or teacher to choose a way of life and, when so doing, to have heard the best that can be said for all sides; but, for the university officially, they are all on a level, whether fascist, communist, liberal-humanitarian or Christian. Students would then be like a jury which hears the witnesses and the speeches of the advocates but is without the help of any judicial summing up. But can anyone honestly believe this who to-day is a consenting party to the denazification of the German universities?

In the special sciences no one advocates so complete an embargo on corporate commitment. 'The accepted technique of teaching chemistry does not imply that the Phlogiston theory has as much to be said for it as the Atomic theory.'[1] Alchemy, Astrology and Phrenology are not given equal hospitality with the recognized sciences. Nor is it so in the homes and schools from which students come. Any philosophy of life may there be inculcated only half-heartedly and ineffectively, it may be implicit rather than explicit; but it can hardly be absent entirely. Are we then at the university stage of education tacitly to confess the insincerity of the earlier stages by our inability corporately to adhere to any consistent *Weltanschauung*? Would not such an inhibition be irresponsible and almost pathological? That is certainly the view of the ' scientific humanists.' The universities, says Brian Simon in the last words of *A Student's View of the Universities*[2] should ' ally themselves with the forces of progress all over the world to overthrow the enemies of culture and science.' This is also the clear implication of Professors Bernal and Hogben. The question here is not one of the use of tests or of proscription, that shall be considered later.[3] It is not whether the heretic shall be tolerated, or even in some sense welcomed, in the university. It is whether all distinction between orthodoxy and heresy shall, in principle, be annihilated.

In any case is not the supposed corporate neutrality quite unreal and impracticable? A university may indeed be neutral in theory.

[1] Hogben, *op. cit.*, p. 143.
[2] p. 142.
[3] See below, pp. 156ff.

H

It may abstain from identifying itself publicly with any particular philosophy of life. But in practice it is impossible to plan its studies or its corporate life except by reference to some standard of values, implied if not expressed. It is impossible to have a rational standard of values in the absence of any clear image of the ends of human existence, and that entails some conception of the nature of man and of the world. Without that, either the university will be merely chaotic——a conclusion in which no one can acquiesce —or its working philosophy will be surreptitious, unthought out and uncriticized. Such a university will be wanting in intellectual honesty; it will be too timid to make clear even to itself the body of convictions by which it is really animated. Now, in some forms of community, dominance by such a hotch-potch of sentiments, habits and archetypal ideas may pass muster. Thus Burke asserts the superior value of communal prejudices in comparison with reasoning; the presumption being that, through the operation of ' the survival of the fittest,' the prevailing prejudices are those which the course of ages has shown to be salutary. It is often maintained that the British temperament is such that our conclusions are more likely to be sound than our reasoning to be valid, and that it is therefore a mistake for us to try to rationalize too much. But can a university possibly be satisfied to base its attitude in regard to the deepest matters on sloppy thinking and conventional prejudice, and to substitute ' One does feel ' for ' I believe '? In adopting a *Weltanschauung* and commending a way of life, must not its thought be as thorough, intrepid and relentless as it is in the special sciences? If anything in this region is to be handed on to students, must it not be a coherent and articulate philosophy? Otherwise the university is involved in the absurdity which F. H. Bradley long ago pointed out, that it is permitted to think only so long as it does not think strictly.

In the Middle Ages, when the universities came into being and took their shape, it was of course Theology which supplied them with an intellectual framework. Both in Great Britain and in the United States it is widely admitted that the Christian faith cannot to-day be the common conviction on which the universities rest, and we have already subscribed to this view. But is it not then imperative that some substitute should be found? If faith and revelation must be omitted and the truth of Christian dogmas must be left an open question, may there not still be found a genuine basis of unity between Christian and liberal humanists in a philo-

sophy of life which embodies the traditional Christian values which
for so many centuries were ' drunk in by every Western child with
its mother's milk and inhaled by every Western man and woman
with the air they breathed?'[1] Thus Dr. Hutchins, after stigmatizing
most trenchantly the existing chaos in the American academic
world, urges that metaphysics should now take the place once
occupied by philosophy, as the master-science which gives coherence to all the others; and the context shows that he means by
metaphysics something very like ' the perennial philosophy,' that is
the 'natural,' with the omission of the ' supernatural,' part of the
system of St. Thomas. This is not Christian, but it has formerly
been in fruitful alliance with Christianity and might be so again.
Even if it is held that the perennial philosophy requires much more
revision in the light of modern thought than Dr. Hutchins would
allow, is not his principle sound? Is there not here a systematic
basis on which Christians can combine with others against the
major heresies such as atheistic Communism, as they once combined on the basis of Natural Law, and on which the universities,
at least of Western Europe and America, can build?

As between such a Christian-humanist philosophy of life and
others, is there not inevitably a war which must be fought out and
not shirked? Otherwise do we not cry peace where there is no
peace but only a crippling and stultifying incoherence? Our universities may in effect be national institutions, for which it would be
improper to go further in the way of commitment than does the
national mind. But must not the nation itself make up its mind
on this major issue, if it has not already done so? If it is too deeply
divided for this, is not the only honest and sensible course to have
more than one type of university; e.g. one which takes for its
foundation the Christian-humanist tradition and another which
stands for dialectical materialism? Each then can organize its life
and work with intellectual integrity and a measure of purposeful-
ness and need no longer be hamstrung by a vain and demoralizing
pursuit of appeasement.

It will be clear from Chapter III how keenly we sympathise
with this line of thought. But if by a unified philosophy of life is
meant a coherent system, even remotely reminiscent of St. Thomas's
*Summa,* it may be a legitimate long-term objective; but, however
desirable in principle, it is an impossible goal of practical policy
in the near future. The present chaos and division are such that

[1] Toynbee, *A Study of History,* V, p. 198.

no university or group of universities could adopt an agreed philosophy without doing violence to the intellectual situation as a whole. What is possible in the immediate future is largely determined by choices which have already been made.[1] In existing conditions any ' agreed philosophy ' could only be an ' ideology,' that is a pattern imposed on the situation and not growing out of it or organically connected with it. At the most it could be agreed between different faculties and different schools of thought only in the sense that it was not actively resisted; it could not command general, cordial and intelligent assent. ' The real problem is that our diverse worlds of thought do not make sense as a coherent unity, and probably cannot and will not do so for some time to come.'[2]

Vital as is the need for a common and coherent philosophy of life there is a prior and more modest but still more urgent task. Professor Emmet most pertinently continues—' We no longer live in a common civilization which speaks a common intellectual language. Hence we are beset by the problem of communication.'[3] There can only be a genuine integration where minds are really in touch with, and really meet, one another; and this is just what is not happening at present. The university, like the contemporary intellectual scene generally, is a Babel. There is no common means of intercourse because the different sections dwell in different intellectual worlds. The first need is to restore communication.

The situation is like that which at present exists between the Great Powers. They have no common philosophy and no hope of arriving at one in any near future. They must somehow work together; and yet it is all but impossible to do so when their objectives and presuppositions are diverse. Any agreements they make are in the highest degree precarious, since they are prompted by different motives and are differently interpreted; and, in case of divergences there are no common standards to which appeal can be made. In these circumstances the immediate object of statesmen from month to month must be to reach some *modus vivendi,* however temporary and unsatisfactory, so as to gain time in which some more thorough job may be attempted. And if all full and frank communication is prevented by the existence of an ' iron curtain,' that must be removed before there can be any real progress towards understanding. Similarly, in the university world, the

[1] See Maritain, *True Humanism,* p. 136.
[2] Emmet, *The Nature of Metaphysical Thinking,* p. 219.
[3] *Op. cit.,* p. 221.

equivalent of an iron curtain shuts off different groups from all but superficial mental contact with one another. They inhabit different imaginative worlds and have different sets of instinctive convictions.[1] Behind the differences in their conscious opinions lie those deeper differences in the habitual, and no longer noticed, mental categories in terms of which they think, and the unconscious assumptions and basic acceptances which largely determine their respective attitudes. In the ordinary way such differences are never resolved. Thus a Christian theologian or philosopher may enter into public controversy with a scientist of Marxist outlook, and each may in some degree impress other people. But hardly ever does either make the least impression on the other. This is not because they are impervious to reason, but because their minds never really meet. The ' man convinced against his will ' who refuses to change his mind need not be simply pig-headed or perverse. The reasons for his belief which he has been able to adduce may have been roughly handled; but he feels obscurely that his real reasons are more multifarious and elusive and that they have not been touched. It is what is at the back, rather than at the front, of the mind that is decisive, and this is rarely brought into the picture.

Here the question is no longer of teachers talking freely to students but of their talking freely to one another. One day at an educational conference a hard-bitten pagan administrator heard a divine speak in the traditional language of Christian devotion and was so bored and alienated that he barely restrained himself from walking out. But then there followed another representative of the Churches who spoke in the language of the plain man. The administrator listened with keen interest. At the end he whispered to his neighbour, ' You know, *I could talk to that man.* We might not agree, but I could talk to him.' A real contact had been established, where before there was none. That is what needs doing at a thousand points throughout the universities. The theologian and the engineer, the doctor, the chemist and the lawyer, Sir Richard Livingstone and Professor Bernal, Mr. C. S. Lewis and Professor J. B. S. Haldane, the Provost of King's and Professor Hogben, must learn how to talk to one another on the radical level at which their ' instinctive convictions ' are brought into the open and their minds really make contact. When they do, things will really begin to happen. Till they do, no talk of an integrated philosophy of life for the university will be more than talk. A deeper critical aware-

[1] *cf.* Whitehead, *Science and the Modern World*, p. 5.

ness of our own ' instinctive convictions ' and of those of our own group may be the first requisite for understanding those of others. It is a two-way traffic that is required. ' Real life is meeting,' and the university needs much more of it. It is the penetrative imagination which can go behind what another man says to his real mind that we most need to cultivate, and our chief object in so doing must be, not to refute him, but to understand him and to learn from him. The deep reverence for personality which is inherent in Christianity makes this specially incumbent on Christians. This will involve two things. The first is a deeper and more resolute self-analysis than most of us have hitherto attempted or are likely to find at all palatable; so that we may become aware of the real grounds of our thinking and feeling and behaving as we normally do. The second is a patient and sustained effort to enter into the minds of colleagues whose interests or philosophies of life are remote from our own, in order to understand and appreciate, not only what they believe, but why they believe it. Neither of these tasks can be accomplished quickly or easily. Merely to find a psychological formula by which to interpret our own or other people's minds, is not to perform but to evade them.

To make real contacts and to deepen understanding will not necessarily or speedily produce agreement. In the next stage different Faculties and different schools of thought, working out their special presuppositions, may have to go further down their several divergent ways than they have yet gone. But both agreement and disagreement will become far more fruitful when they are clarified and found to be real. Unity may well come in the first instance by the performance of a practical common task rather than by the formulation of a theoretical common minimum. With that may go the development of a sense of fellowship which already exists in germ and which will be the academic equivalent of what the British workman expresses when he addresses a stranger as ' Mate.'

## 3    SPECIAL ACADEMIC POSTULATES

Though the intellectual situation does not yet admit of any agreed systematic philosophy, certain basic values, elementary and elemental, are already implied in our common living and action. If it were not so, there would be no real bond between us. However highly we rate the importance of freedom of thought, we must rest it on some basis of conviction. The university is engaged in a co-operative quest for truth. But such a quest itself presupposes agreement

in some underlying value-judgment, held, not as a tentative hypothesis, but with absolute assurance. We cannot without absurdity
have an open mind about the value of having an open mind.

At ordinary times such basic principles may well be below the
threshold of consciousness. Habit and custom may supply enough
of a common pattern for practical purposes. Indeed it is arguable
that an institution such as the British Empire gets on better because
we do not try to work out its principles too precisely. But when
basic values are threatened, as they have been in the last ten years,
it becomes necessary to defend them, and to defend them we must
know clearly what we have to defend. It is necessary to disentangle
the essential values on which no compromise is possible from fortui-
tous and possibly undesirable accretions which may well be dis-
pensed with. As Karl Mannheim puts it, ' Our democracy has
got to become militant if it is to survive . . . The new militant
democracy will develop a new attitude to values . . . It will have
the courage to agree on some basic values, which are acceptable to
everybody who shares the traditions of Western civilization.' And
he enumerates ' those basic virtues and values—such as brotherly
love, mutual help, decency, social justice, freedom, respect for the
person, etc.—which are the basis of the peaceful functioning of a
social order.'[1]

What then are ' the basic values and virtues ' which our universities to-day should commend, for which they should stand, and
on which they should endeavour to build their corporate life?
What are the credentials by which they are to be recognized? They
have two sources. First, there are certain specific assumptions and
convictions without which the work of the university cannot go on.
They are inherent in the job; but they may be imperilled, either
from within by some ' treason of the intellectuals,' or from without
by political dictation as they obviously were in Hitlerite Germany.
It is only those with personal experience of the working of a university from within who can determine what these are. In this respect
there falls on them a special duty of vigilance; and here they have
to lead, and not merely to follow public opinion. Secondly, there
are other basic values, more general in character, which the
universities share with the whole community. It is true that the
British universities, though not State universities, are in effect communal institutions, inasmuch as they represent the whole community
rather than any particular section. Hence, in general, the basic

[1] *Diagnosis of Our Time*, p. 7.

values they presuppose can only be those acknowledged by the community in which they are set. For such a university to assume any special colour, whether Christian, Communist, or Bourgeois-Individualist, which is not that of the nation as a whole would be illegitimate. But Mannheim's contention still remains;—are there not some fundamental values, recognized and respected to-day by the British people? If so, should they not be acknowledged and exemplified by the British universities? In this Section we shall be concerned with the former set of assumptions; the latter will be discussed in the following Section.

Here we are concerned with assumptions on which, as academic people engaged in doing our job, we cannot be neutral, since that would be to saw off the branch on which we are sitting. The university is a Guild; it is perhaps the greatest of the Guilds which have come down to us from the Middle Ages. But every Guild evolves its own professional standards and principles of craftsmanship and its own professional ethic; e.g., the Goldsmiths, the Merchant Taylors, the Royal Colleges of Medicine and Surgery, the Inns of Court, etc. Of all such codes there are three characteristics to be noted. First, it is the members of the Guild rather than the public who are competent to be their judge and to decide what their code should be and what is, or is not, an offence against it. *Cuique in sua arte credendum.* The innovator has to make good his case before a body of educated opinion, a jury of his peers. It is true that professional opinion tends to be unduly conservative. But reforms, and even revolutions, can only come from within. If the practice of surgery is revolutionized, it is by no quack with his panacea, but by a Lister who has himself been subjected to the fundamental disciplines. Secondly, the Guild-members are not merely the judges, but the rightful guardians of their professional principles. Against the client who wants his lawyer or doctor to do something unprofessional, sometimes against popular clamour or governmental pressure, the Guild-members have a moral responsibility for maintaining their standards. For instance—to confine ourselves to illustrations which have ceased to be controversial—it is now clear that both Fascists in Italy and Nazis in Germany imposed on their universities procedures which were not only morally wrong but professionally disastrous. Thirdly, a Guild normally accepts responsibility for the professional training of its members. It initiates novices into the theory as well as the practice of the craft; and it teaches these with authority as a set, not only of tentative hypotheses, but of articles of faith.

The special quality of such presuppositions is that they are inherent and not extrinsic. With others we may be suspicious that some sectional or outside interest is trying to capture and exploit the university, to make it an instrument for the service of some purpose other than its own, to superimpose on it some particular pattern, political, religious, social, or even æsthetic, to force it into some framework which does not properly belong to it. But such natural resentment and resistance should not blind us to the fact that there are some presuppositions inherent in the undoubted task of the university, some postulates without which it cannot proceed. Some such postulates indeed each Faculty has peculiar to itself; related, that is, to its special field and method of study. But, over and above these, there are some which are common to the university as a whole. For instance, the engineer and the theologian may be largely ignorant, uninterested and even unsympathetic concerning each other's work. But they recognize each other as genuinely engaged in the pursuit of discovery and learning and as paying allegiance to some common intellectual standards; and, on that ground, they recognize each other as colleagues. If it were not so, they would have no business to be in the same university, and each must be striving to oust the other.

Apart from discussing *what* these presuppositions are, it is important to recognize *that* they are and that they may need to be defended. But if we are to defend them, we must seek to analyse them and to distinguish the authentic from the spurious. In what then do they consist? Much further thought needs to be given to this question. What follows is a tentative attempt to discern and describe some of them. But it is only a beginning; it is offered as the launching rather than the conclusion of a discussion.

First there is the conviction that the things of the mind are worth pursuing, developed to an intensity at which it becomes an intellectual passion. Without this intellectual passion the members of a university staff become only a kind of academic civil service, doing a routine job with reasonable efficiency, but uninspired and uninspiring. They communicate no glow because they feel none. Everyone who is acquainted with universities from the inside knows that here is the difference between mechanism and life. Of course this is a platitude, but it needs insisting on; for, in some ways, the utilitarianism fashionable to-day is against its recognition. In this matter we need to preserve a delicate balance. Only yesterday it was important to repudiate academic isolationism—the precious intellectual dwelling complacently in his ivory tower, content to keep himself unspotted from the world.   To-day it is equally important to repudiate the thoroughgoing utilitarian, who assigns to the pursuit of truth a function merely ancillary to the attainment of comfort or power by the community.   An institution whose interest in truth was confined to the knowledge how to do or to make or to mend things would not be a university.

As Christians we are specially concerned to maintain this balance. On the one hand we welcome an insistence that thinking should be responsible and should lead to action and engage the whole man rather than reflect a detached and merely speculative curiosity.   On the other hand, the supreme Christian experience is not in action but in worship (which includes contemplation, and even, in a sense, enjoyment, as well as action).   For the Christian, truth is one aspect of the being of God, and to treat with contumely the cult of truth for its own sake comes near to repudiating the cult of God for his own sake.   This has been put very clearly by the philosopher, F. H. Bradley, in a famous passage, ' Some in one way and some in others, we seem to touch and have communion with what is beyond the visible world.   In various manners we find something higher, which both supports and humbles, both chastens and transports us.   And with certain persons the intellectual effort to understand the universe is a principal way of thus experiencing the Deity. No one probably who has not felt this, however differently he might express it, has ever cared much for metaphysics.   And wherever it has been felt strongly, it has been its own justification.'[1]   Bradley is speaking primarily of philosophy.   But what he says, holds good of ' the intellectual effort to understand the universe ' in detail as well as in the gross.   That is, it applies to academic study as a whole.

A second postulate is the duty of intellectual thoroughness.   In the university, arguments must be followed wherever they lead, however unexpected, and they must be followed through relentlessly to the end, however unwelcome.   In the conventional detective story, the great detective, called in by friends of the suspected man to refute the police theory, warns them that, once engaged, he will

[1] Bradley is careful to preserve balance. For he continues on the next page, ' There is no calling or pursuit which is a private road to the Deity. And assuredly the way through speculation on ultimate truth, though distinct and legitimate, is not superior to others.   There is no sin, however prone to it the philosopher may be, which philosophy can justify so little as spiritual pride.'

regard it as his duty to discover and to reveal the whole truth whether that is favourable to his client or not; the university acknowledges the same obligation. In other departments of life there is room for conventions into whose objective basis no exact scrutiny is made, in which indeed there is often an undefined, but tacitly agreed, element of ' Let's pretend.' Examples are the rites of Freemasons and other Friendly Societies, the institution of Christmas as it exists for that large majority of our people who have no firm religious conviction, or the rights and powers of the Crown. For practical purposes it is needless, and sometimes undesirable, to probe or analyse these too precisely. Such a twilight between belief and disbelief has its legitimate place in some spheres of life, but it has no legitimate place in a university. For the university it is a canon that thinking must be of the utmost strictness that the subject-matter permits and slovenly thinking is taboo. Nor can there be any forbidden territory. Loyalty to this obligation is one aspect of intellectual integrity, as are the two or three which follow.

The next postulate, closely related, is the obligation to be meticulously accurate in dealing with empirical evidence. It is true that we have already disclaimed the simple-minded view that truth is attainable by nothing but faithful reception and reporting of empirical data, and we have laid stress on the vital part played by schemes of interpretation. But the empirical data are also vital, and even those whose schemes of interpretation differ widely may be held together by a common intellectual conscience in the observation, recording and taking account of such data. The classical scholar must reject the most ingenious or seductive emendation as soon as the manuscript evidence contradicts it. The historian must note and report evidence that seems to contradict the interpretation to which he has previously committed himself equally with evidence that confirms it. As to the scientist, Darwin's declaration is classical, ' I have endeavoured to keep my mind free so as to give up any hypothesis however much beloved . . . as soon as facts are shown to be opposed to it.'[1] Apart from such a conscience there could be no common ground, or even room for argument, between different schools of thought. As it has been put, ' there is a kind of inner dæmon which says " Come off it," when we are indulging in ingenious feats of explaining things away in the interests of our own point of view, political, religious or philosophical.' The evil consequences of the lack of such a conscience

[1] *Life,* I, p. 105.

were seen in an extreme form in Nazi Germany. According to Dr. Jaspers the Nazi biological theories were due to ' a closed mind, which translated all reasons to the contrary into confirmations.'[1]

Fourthly, there is the obligation to approach controversial questions with the temper of the judge rather than of the advocate or the notorious ' expert witness.' This is totally distinct from tepidity or from a disposition to compromise. It is the fruit of a passion for the whole truth as against half-truths, for proportion as against one-sidedness. It springs from a high sense of intellectual responsibility, whose possessor is on his guard against adopting an opinion more easily because, for instance, it pleases or shocks, amuses or impresses, and is doubly watchful and critical of the unconscious operation on his mind of his own pet prejudices and sympathies. This is an obligation more easily acknowledged than observed, for the influence of non-rational and mainly unconscious motives, even on minds of very fine intellectual quality, is much more pervasive than has been realized till lately. A rare example of self-knowledge and self-mastery is shown, again, by Darwin. In his autobiographical fragment he speaks of his ' golden rule that whenever a published fact, a new observation or thought came across me which was opposed to my general results, to make a memorandum of it without failing at once; for I had found by experience that such facts and thoughts were far more apt to escape from the memory than favourable ones.'[2]

An aspect of this judicial temper is fair-mindedness in dealing with the opinions of others, particularly those which are uncongenial and opposed to one's own. This is required, not only or mainly for the sake of courtesy and good feeling, but in the interest of truth. In controversial questions, all opinions held at all widely among persons technically qualified to form an opinion at all are part of the data for judgment. There is a prima facie presumption, not of course that each of these is free from error or amounts even to a half-truth, but that it is not mere nonsense, that there is at least ' something in it.' So long as views which we reject seem to us nothing but ' fool opinions,' we ought to feel uncomfortable and insecure; for the probability is that we have failed to understand them or to take account of the grounds on which they are held. We are only fully entitled to reject them finally when we have first

[1] See his inaugural address at the re-opening of Heidelberg University, October, 1945.
[2] *Op. cit.* I, p. 87.

understood why they seem plausible to those who hold them and then have seen further. A merely combative attitude is untrue to the university spirit. That spirit is expressed by Henry Sidgwick when, writing amusedly in his diary of a visit to Keble College and of his friendship with the Anglo-Catholic, Edward Talbot, he says, ' We agree in two characteristics which are quite independent of formal creeds—a belief that we *can* learn, and a determination that we *will* learn, from people of the most opposite opinions.'[1]

The fifth postulate insists on freedom of thought and publication. It is closely linked with the sense of responsibility on which we have just insisted; for responsible thinking must be allowed to find its own way, even at the risk of error, and be met by open argument. In Dr. Jaspers' words, the university ' claims freedom of teaching and learning as the condition of the responsible independence of professors and students.' If the intellectual conscience is to operate, it must not be constricted and hampered by extraneous interference. As the scholar or scientist will resist internal motives other than the pursuit of truth, so he will resist external pressure which must deflect it. This does not imply a reversion to the ' Liberal ' conception of the university in its old form, for the university need not be neutral or indifferent or take Gallio for its model. But it springs from a conviction that expulsion or silencing of heretics involves a worse evil than any which it can avert. The university is no place for the mass-production or mass-repression of opinion. The methods of the Commissar and the drill-sergeant are wholly out of place. The attempt to find a short cut involves a short-circuit.

This needs emphasis because it may be endangered. The besetting sin of academic liberalism, it is now widely recognized, was to shirk practical decisions because of the difficulty of reaching theoretical certainty; though in fact people are constantly called on to take such decisions on a basis of probability only. But that is not sufficient ground for pretending that greater theoretical certainty has been attained than the evidence warrants, for trying to manufacture it by non-rational means or for closuring the theoretical debate in the academic arena.

The university, as a community in pursuit of truth, needs the potential contributions of all its members who are capable of original thought. To rule out in advance those who quit certain prescribed lines, contradicts its central purpose. The Miltonic argument is still valid. ' They are the troublers and dividers of unity,

[1] *Memoir*, p. 403.

who neglect and permit not others to unite with those dissevered pieces which are yet wanting to the body of Truth. To be still searching what we know not, by what we know, still closing up truth to truth as we find it (for all her body is homogeneal and proportional), this is the golden rule in theology as well as in arithmetic and makes up the best harmony in a Church; not the forced and outward union of cold and neutral, and inwardly divided minds.' For *Church* read *University*, and this passage retains all its force. Any ' forced and outward union ' does not assist, but inhibits, the genuine union of tested conviction.

In his monumental study of the rise and fall of civilizations, Professor Toynbee traces a common cycle. Everywhere advances are due to the influence of some ' creative minority.' And everywhere the ' creative minority ' presently degenerates into a ' dominant minority.' Either because inspiration flags, or in the effort to get quick results and to secure the adhesion of the multitude more rapidly than the slow process of real conversion allows, the influential minority falls back on the method of ' drill.' Sooner or later this has two results. One is the ossification of the élite. The same policies and watchwords, even the same persons or at least the same organizations which once were the spearhead of reform, become the stronghold of reaction. The other is the eventual revolt and secession of the proletariate. The obvious moral applies with redoubled force to the university whose raison d'être is to think things out. To exercise the influence of a creative minority is a legitimate aspiration for every group in the university. But to seek to become a dominant minority and to ' collar ' the university, is to betray the university.

For Christians this postulate of university life is confirmed, illuminated and deepened by their faith. On the one hand this includes a profound respect for the individual, carried to a point which to most others appears merely quixotic, but is itself grounded in the astonishing patience of God and abundantly illustrated in the story of the life of Christ. On the other is the vivid sense of human fallibility and perversion. No group is so wise and good that it can safely be given a monopoly; no group is so besotted that it has certainly nothing to contribute. We may not proscribe the heretic lest haply on some point we be found to fight even against God.

Our last postulate is the conviction that the university has indeed a social responsibility, but that this is first and foremost a responsibility for focussing the community's intellectual conscience. No doubt it has also some measure of responsibility for the community's moral conscience. An eminent German scientist is quoted by Professor Bernal as saying, ' I do not know anything about politics and I do not want to know anything about politics, because if I keep out of it I do not see how they can do anything to me ';[1] and while such irresponsibility may be extenuated by the peculiar strain, most of us would agree that it cannot be justified. But that sort of responsibility falls on the individual teacher rather than on the university corporately, it falls on him as citizen rather than as professor, and it is one which he shares with multitudes of his fellow-citizens. But the university's distinctive responsibility—the task which no one else can perform—is to be the university; that is, to be a place where the criticism and evaluation of ideas is continually being carried forward, where nonsense can be exposed for what it is, and where the intellectual virtues rooted in sincerity of mind are being fostered and transmitted. Of course this intellectual conscience is not a monopoly of the university, but no other institution has an equal opportunity of engendering and of nourishing it. There are many other services which the university can render to the community,[2] but they will be ' Greek gifts ' if they are given at the expense of this quintessential service. The university will betray the community, as well as lose its own soul, if it allows itself to be so anxious and troubled about many things as to miss the one thing needful.

On these academic postulates there are two general comments to be made. First, of course it is not suggested that universities are places where these convictions are regularly lived up to and the appropriate virtues practised. On the contrary, if we say that, in these respects, we are blameless, we deceive ourselves; the evil that we would not, we constantly do. But they are the standards which, by common consent, we acknowledge and hold in honour, and to which we appeal in judging our own and our colleagues' performance. Insofar as we have offended against them, we repudiate and condemn our own action. Secondly, they are put forward as ' rules of the guild,' tacitly agreed working assumptions, found to be necessary to good workmanship in our craft. Probably most university teachers, at least in Great Britain, would assent to them. If they are criticized, it is more likely to be as platitudes than as paradoxes. But some, if not all, of them have far-reaching implications in the

---

[1] *Op. cit.*, p. 395.

[2] See Chapter IX below.

sphere of ethics, of anthropology and even of ontology. If their acknowledgment does not absolutely necessitate a particular philosophy of life, it is at least true that to some philosophies of life they are thoroughly congenial and to others highly antipathetic.

# 4 BASIC COMMUNAL VALUES

Those basic assumptions which the British universities share with the nation may themselves be subdivided.

### a. Universal

Some are common to all universities anywhere, to El Azhar, Peiping and Calcutta equally with Oxford, Paris or Harvard. The convulsions of the last fifteen years have made clear that there are some values or principles which are indispensable to civilized existence. This was typified at an annual conference of International Student Service shortly before the War. The German representatives were troubled by the relief work done in Great Britain and other countries, which at that time was mostly for refugees from Nazi persecution; but they were ready to be pacified by an assurance that the basis of this work was purely humanitarian and in no way 'ideological.' But at the critical moment the British relief secretary jumped up and, speaking with much feeling, said, 'Of course, I.S.S. is neutral, on ordinary political questions. But there are *certain elementary conditions of civilization* for which we do stand.' In the words of Dr. Kotschnig, the war was widely felt to be not only a conflict between different political and economic systems, but a 'clash of mutually exclusive worlds of thought and aspiration.'[1] It was a war not between one civilized Power and another, but between civilization and barbarism; and in such a war the real mind of all civilized persons and learned bodies, whether expressed or not, must perforce be on one side.

Deeper than all differences of moral judgment is the difference between those who make moral judgments at all and those who do not. It is the old issue between Socrates and Thrasymachus; and it is the issue on which, humanly speaking, the fate of the world in the next few years seems to hang. What is in question is, whether those who hold power will recognize any moral standards as objective and binding on them, and as having a *de jure* authority superior to their own inclinations or interests. The problem of power is the problem of our age. But all civilization has depended

[1] *Slaves Need No Leaders,* p. 11.

on the recognition of some restraint to naked power. The universality of the recognition of the ' Tao,' that is of the existence of ' moral law ' having authority, has already been pointed out in Chapter IV above. This recognition is part of the common cultural heritage of civilization. Here then is something for which the universities of the world must stand. For our own universities, this principle was applied eighty years ago by the chief philosopher of Liberalism. In his Rectorial Address to the St. Andrew's students, J. S. Mill laid down that the proper end of their studies was that they should become ' more effective fighters in the battle between good and evil,' and that universities should have a pervading tone of reverence and duty. In this he was at one with Carlyle, Shaftesbury and Pusey, and indeed with Confucius, Marcus Aurelius and Kabir.

Mr. Lewis's examples go to show that the traditional wisdom of different civilizations includes, not only a recognition of Duty as something peremptory and absolute, but a good deal of agreement about the kinds of conduct which Duty enjoins. Here only one or two examples can be given. One is the duty of reasonableness. When Hitler first came into power, a distinguished German who was then in this country remarked that this event was the triumph of irrationalism and betokened an uprush of forces from the psychic underworld. That is something towards which universities cannot be neutral, for it is a condition of civilization that the beast in man should be subjected to the man in man. Another duty is good faith. ' Keeping of faith,' says Locke, ' belongs to man as man and not as a member of society.' No reasons of State or business excuse a breach of covenant; without mutual trust, social intercourse becomes impossible. Another duty, important though hard to define, is that of a good will of man towards man, a certain freemasonry between fellow-members of the species which is the exact opposite of the natural enmity affirmed by Hobbes, a disposition to treat others as friends so long as they do not show themselves to be enemies.

On this basis the peoples of all civilized communities can meet. Here the universities of the world cannot be neutral, since civilization cannot be neutral. If any student or teacher advocates irrationalism or Machiavellianism or inhumanity, he may indeed be tolerated for reasons we have already given; but he is definitely a ' dissenter ' and unrepresentative, for in this respect his mind is in contradiction with the mind of any university.

I

### b. Western

Secondly, there are some further principles which are common to the contemporary civilization of the West. Europe and America have a common cultural heritage, derived mainly from Greece, Rome and Palestine. There are some truths concerning the good life and the conditions of attaining it on which these are agreed, and one function of Western education will be to pass them on. ' Our society, like any society, rests on common beliefs and a major task of education is to perpetuate them.' This is the contention of the Harvard Report, *General Education in a Free Society*. The writers are clear that an educational system must have some common purpose which holds it together; that, in the United States, this purpose once was to make Christians citizens, that in existing conditions it can be so no longer, and that some alternative must be found on which the Christian and Humanist, Professor Niebuhr and Mr. Lippmann, can unite and that the source of such an alternative is to be found in ' the intellectual forces which have shaped the Western mind.'[1] Of these forces Christianity is one, but it is one among others.

The Nazis proclaimed a ' war against the West.' In so doing they recognized, though by repulsion, that there was a moral tradition, common, e.g., to the Latin and to the Anglo-Saxon peoples, which constituted a standing obstacle and rebuke to their aims and methods. This again is more easily perceived than analysed. But it is not hard to identify some judgments characteristic of the Western mind. First there is a certain activism, a sense that it is normally right to be up and busy. An obstacle is something to be removed; an evil is something to be redressed. Fatalism is not a Western creed, and it is no accident that Applied Science is a Western product. Secondly, from Greece has come the conception of the good life as embodying the cardinal virtues of wisdom, temperance, courage and justice; and from Rome an ingrained respect for law and order. Fatalistic and irresponsible inertia, unbridled indulgence of appetite or self-will, cowardice in all its forms, injustice and anarchy, are decisively condemned by our Western tradition. Thirdly, there is a Palestinian element in our Western heritage. Though the extent of its survival to-day is disputed its place in the historic tradition is not. ' The Christian

[1] *Op. cit.*, p. 44.

virus or elixir is in our Western blood.'[1]  This deepens the Roman demand for even-handed justice by adding a respect for the individual as possessing rights and responsibilities.  The Harvard writers define their moral basis as being the dignity of man and his duty towards his fellow-men.  But, however defined, its practical importance lies in what it excludes.  Men are never to be treated simply as slaves or cannon-fodder, as beasts of burden or as material for scientific experiment.  Whoever holds otherwise is a heretic.  On such issues Western civilization has not an open mind but a firm conviction.  It is against this moral heritage that so much that has happened in Europe in the last fifteen years is a gross offence.

## c.  British

Thirdly, over and above those principles which they share with the universities of other countries, there are certain basic values for which the British universities may legitimately stand, since they are inherent in the British way of life.  They are a part of the heritage which, in 1940, our people rallied to defend.  Our political history notoriously suggests that there is some such common, national, basis of belief.  Our party-differences have not been carried to an extreme.  After a General Election, the party newly returned to power does not undo the bulk of the work of its predecessors.  The outlook which Mr. Churchill and Mr. Attlee have in common is more important than the things in which they differ.  The national unity in time of war only expresses and reveals an underlying unity of standard and of purpose which is there all the time.

From this unity there arises directly the first of these basic values. That is tolerance, or, as it has been recently described, ' our habit of not killing one another.'  The parties to our contentions are not implacable.  The sombre drama of Thucydides, Book III, has not been enacted ' in England's green and pleasant land.'  Class-war has not hitherto disrupted our society as it has disrupted others.  No doubt this trait has its reverse side, a lack of intellectual thoroughness and moral intensity.  But, primarily, it is based on tacit recognition of a fellowship more fundamental than all the Isms that divide us.  ' Fraternity ' is that one of the revolutionary triad which we rate most highly.

A second of our national basic values is illustrated by the paradox that this country is the home both of the ' Rule of Law ' and of the ' Sovereignty of Parliament.'  We can dispense with legal

---

[1] Toynbee, *op. cit.*, V, p. 190.

checks on the sovereign body because, in practice, the moral authority of tradition and the informal pressure of public opinion give sufficient security that it will not abuse its powers.  Similarly, we can dispense with the police-state, because we can rely on a general habit of spontaneous cohesion and conformity; people take their places in the queue without being hectored by someone in uniform.  Irrespective of party, we believe in ordered liberty and in self-discipline.  With this goes an ingrained belief that a balance between continuity and change is both needful and possible.  In making alterations the style of the building should be preserved; but ' a state without the means of some change is without the means of its conservation.'  So we cherish the *critic* on the hearth, and ' His Majesty's Opposition ' is one of our most characteristic institutions.

A third of our basic values is represented by the conviction that, ' Democracy is meaningful and right.'[1]  Of course ' democracy ' is a highly ambiguous term.  But, in this context, it clearly does not imply any particular political arrangement; it signifies a broad ethical test by which political arrangements are to be judged.  As such a test, it seems to be twofold.  On the one hand, it emphasizes the claim of every man to consideration.  Government should be ' for the people.'  ' The poorest he that is in England hath a life to live as the richest he.'  That strikes a chord to which something deep in our nature responds.  On the other hand, it expresses the community's need of the active co-operation of all its members in ordering the common life; and, seen from the opposite angle, this is the right—and obligation—of every man to a share in responsibility.  In some real sense government must be by the people.

All this is fairly obvious.  These are values which few persons of influence in our universities would question.  Humanists, whether theocentric or anthropocentric, can easily agree upon them.  But, so far, they are vague and superficial.  In quiet times they may supply a common ground on which we can get along without digging deeper.  But are they deeply rooted enough to enable us to stand against the impassioned communist or fascist at a time when events are forcing on us, in the most practical and insistent form, the question : Do we really believe what we have supposed ourselves to believe, and, if so, with what depth of conviction do we believe it ?  At this level a further question is unavoidable.  In

---

[1] We take this phrase from the Harvard Report, where it is used to express the basic presupposition of American universities.

the body of common conviction, unformulated but actually operative, which the British universities share with the British people,
how far, and in what sense, is there a definitely Christian ingredient? There is no suggestion here of reviving the idea of a ' Christian
university ' which we have definitely rejected in the previous Chapter. But, if there is any significant sense in which it was ' Christian
civilization ' that the nation defended in 1940, it may follow that
the culture which British universities diffuse should in some degree
be a Christian culture.

## 5  DO THESE VALUES INCLUDE A CHRISTIAN INGREDIENT?

Among the British universities to-day, broadly speaking, the
ancient do, and the modern do not, make formal acknowledgment
of a Christian basis. Which are right, and with which is the
future? Is the Christian profession of Oxford, Cambridge and the
Scottish universities only a historical survival, having no longer real
point or meaning, a venerable façade behind which there is only
emptiness? Ought Cambridge, equally with Chicago or even with
Calcutta, to preserve an official neutrality between Christianity
and other religions or between religion and rationalism? Or is the
absence of Christian orientation and Christian profession in ' Redbrick ' an unnecessary and crippling impoverishment? Behind
this lies the question: In what sense, if in any, is the British
people still a Christian people? On this the only comment which
can be made with confidence is, that the answer is not simple or
easy, and anyone who thinks it is rules himself out of court. In
the nature of the case, any answer must be impressionistic and cannot admit of demonstration, and, in attempting an answer, academic
people speak with no special authority; yet, in practice, some
answer must be presupposed.

### a.  Prima Facie Evidence of Christian Influence

Great Britain, unlike the United States, is officially a Christian
country. Both south and north of the Tweed there are ' Established
Churches,' whose dignitaries have an assured status in the realm.
The Coronation of the King is a religious ceremony. Assizes and
the daily sessions of Parliament are opened with prayer, and prayers
are said when foundation-stones are laid or ships are launched. On
great occasions national days of prayer or thanksgiving are

appointed, and, by at least a substantial section of public opinion, this is felt to be natural and right.  In his broadcast addresses to the nation, the present King constantly stresses a religious appeal; and, speaking as a responsible Minister in a time of crisis, Sir Stafford Cripps calls on his fellow-countrymen to refresh their hearts and minds with a deep draught of the Christian faith as the most potent source of their inspiration.  As regards their personal lives, a very large proportion of our people are still christened, married and buried under the auspices of the Christian Church. Nor are these Christian professions only survivals from the past. The Butler Act embodies a new national affirmation of Christian allegiance.  While it leaves full freedom to parents or teachers to contract out, it makes Christian worship and instruction a normal and statutory part of the life of the school.

Behind all formal observances Christian ' archetypes ' have, very noticeably, coloured the ethos of our people in a number of ways. For instance, the soldiers in the ranks during the last two wars showed often a personal warmth and a tenderness towards any of their fellows in trouble, which went far beyond recognising other men's rights and giving them their due.  In quality and motivation, this still falls very short of the true Pauline ' charity,' but it is doubtful whether it would be found in the same degree in men whose tradition did not include the story of the Good Samaritan. Similarly the marked readiness of the British soldier to succour and befriend his enemies as soon as they lay down their arms is not due simply, as critics would have it, to infirmity of purpose, but owes something to the peculiarly Christian ideal of forgiveness and to the New Testament record.  Both these traits are rooted in an understanding of human nature that is richer and deeper than their possessors can usually express.  They have a dim sense that 'man is more than can be known about him,' that there is something inexhaustible in their neighbour and in their duty towards him, and that the whole end of life and the whole hope of man do not consist in ' the being used for a purpose recognized by yourself as a mighty one, the being thoroughly worn out before you are thrown on the scrap heap'.[1]  The humour and humility, so commonly found in our fellow-countrymen and so antiseptic to megalomania, may be a rudimentary form of what, at a higher and more reflective stage, would pass into religious reverence.

This is not merely fanciful and sentimental idealization of our

---

[1] G. B. Shaw, *Man and Superman*, Epistle Dedicatory.

own people.   What is in question here is not a level of achievement
but a standard of judgment.   Always and everywhere the general
mass of people fall far below their own standards, and for our
immediate purpose it is enough if these are the qualities which men
sincerely approve and admire when they meet them in others and
which, in their hearts, they would like to be able to include in their
picture of themselves.

### b.   The Negative Case

The argument against the inclusion of any distinctively Christian
ingredient, among the basic values for which the British nation or
the British universities stand to-day is powerful.   As with the more
ambitious claim for an all-out Christian university, the attack comes
both from the secularist and from the Christian standpoint.   The
secularist will say to us something like this.   ' You exaggerate
absurdly the amount of genuine, as opposed to nominal, Christianity, that is of Christian modes of behaviour, feeling and thought,
which survives in this country to-day.   You are, almost wilfully,
blind to the ever accelerating rate at which the tide of Christian
belief is running out.   It is reasonably certain that only a minority
of the people to be met in the Strand or the Whitechapel
Road have any effective religious belief or practice.   But, if so,
what warrant is there for assuming that they still take for granted
any of the ethical implications of the Christian faith?   Till lately,
it may be, the Ten Commandments, or at any rate the last six,
entered deeply into the popular imagination.   But, decade by
decade, that is becoming notably less true.   From a Christian point
of view must you not confess;

> *Aetas parentum pejor avis tulit*
> *Nos nequiores, mox daturos*
> *Progeniem vitiosiorem?*

We agree that, as a people, we have a faith, though it is inarticulate
and unformulated; we fought for that faith in 1940.   But what is
agreed in it is not specially Christian; and what is specially
Christian is not agreed.   A Christian outlook and a Christian ethic
are now sectional and not national.'

When it is the university which is in question, the objector can
argue *a fortiori*.   It follows from the university's function as a
place of thorough intellectual enquiry that it must be more sensitive
to changes of belief and to contradictions, and less able to entertain

simultaneously incompatible doctrines, than is the general community. Beliefs, which may be treated as working assumptions outside the university must within it be freely canvassed and submitted to constant re-examination. Even if some degree of Christian belief may be taken for granted in the schools of the nation, it does not follow that it can be so taken in the universities. This is borne out by experience. Representatives of the National Union of Teachers and of the Association of Education Committees can join with representatives of the Churches in framing an agreed syllabus of Christian teaching for the schools. But all who know them must admit it is unthinkable that the Association of University Teachers, or the National Union of Students, or the Senior Common Room or University Union or Guild of Undergraduates of any particular university, should voluntarily include in its ' platform ' an avowedly Christian element. But, if so, is it not unfair to take advantage of any Christian vestiges or vantage points in the university's constitution, to inveigle it into going where the majority plainly do not want to go?

The ascription of any sort of Christian character or purpose to the university in its corporate capacity is denounced no less vigorously from the Christian side in the name of Christian integrity. It is held to involve a disastrous element of pretence. The organization of the Churches, and especially of the Established Churches with their parochial system, has been based on the assumption that this is a Christian country and that their main task is pastoral; and this assumption has now become a lie. There are a good number of decent people, at least in the upper and middle classes, having high principles with a Christian smattering, up to which they try, with fair success, to live. They form a healthy and honourable part of our community. But they are not Christians, though they are constantly mistaken for Christians both by others and by themselves. It is only the few to whom their Christianity is indeed a power of God unto salvation. These are now a small minority in a pagan country and theirs is a missionary task. The present, privileged status of the Churches in the national life is an organized hypocrisy, involving them in an atmosphere of continuous and soul-destroying make-believe. They need the bleak and bracing air of reality; in the universities, of all places, the pretence should be abandoned and not extended.

Further, dishonesty is, here as usual, the worst policy. The temper of the younger generation to-day is marked by ' a distrust of every kind of *Schwärmerei* and an almost brutal honesty in the analysis of experience.'[1] Many of the older generation, it is true, cling to long-standing moral and religious conventions. They

> keep hold of Nurse
> For fear of meeting something worse,

though with less than utter and unclouded personal conviction. But, to their juniors, such conventions, so sponsored, are contemptible and exasperating, and 'the decent drapery of life' is relentlessly to be stripped off. Much of the missionary work of the Church will have to be done all over again in new, and more difficult, conditions. It cannot be done by bluff or by adroit use of the force of inertia. For the gospel has to be presented not as 'news' to those who hear of it for the first time, but as an old story to those who suppose that they have long ago seen through it. In the modern vernacular, they believe they have once already 'been had for mugs,' and they do not propose to repeat the experience.

As regards the university, Christians will be on firm ground so long as they claim freedom of action for Christian, as for other, groups within the university, which is itself neutral and uncommitted on the Christian-secularist issue. But if they claim the university itself for 'Christianity,' in however attenuated a sense of the word, will not their ground be weak and their morality dubious? They will only be playing a political game such as is imputed to the Communists. The same argument which caused us to reject the idea of a fully Christian university will hold good against any attempt to fasten on it a demi-semi-Christianity. The very conception of such a partial 'Christianity' is itself heretical, since it implies that Christianity is a matter of more or less, when it is really a matter of all or nothing. It is not a water in which, if you please, you can dabble your toes; unless you plunge in out of your depth, you are not there at all. A 'Christianity' attuned to the receptive capacity of the greatest number is a fraud masquerading under a false name. 'What Jones will swallow' may have genuine moral value; and, so long as the Joneses are in a majority, it may afford the only possible basis for the university and for the co-operation of different groups within it. But things should be called by their right names, and the name of 'Christian' should not be applied to what is really sub-Christian. The right

[1] Emmet, *op. cit.*, p. 221.

model here is Grotius. When Christianity had ceased to be the working faith of 'Christendom,' he evolved a set of generally recognized principles, on the basis of which Christian and other states could combine. It is on something analogous to 'Natural Law,' rather than on the Christian gospel or on any derivative from it, that the university should to-day be based.

### c. An Alternative Diagnosis

Our present communal condition of mind is not simple but extremely complex. To depict it accurately and in due proportion is hard. It would certainly be false to represent the mind of the nation as still predominantly Christian, but neither is it clearly pagan or completely secularized. A penetrating diagnosis is contained in Mr. T. S. Eliot's *The Idea of a Christian Society*.[1] He starts with two propositions which are common ground to writers of different schools. On the one hand, much of our heritage is Christian. Our forefathers had a Christian map of the world. That is, their mental world-picture, or the frame-work within and with reference to which they saw particular events, was Christian. Their ' culture,' in Ortega's sense of the word, the body of convictions, conscious or unconscious, which underlay their moral judgments and by which they purported to direct their lives, was largely derived from the Bible. On the other hand the British nation is vastly less Christian than it used to be. It has undergone a drastic, and ever accelerating, process of secularizing. The traditional order of life, as it existed for instance for the villagers of Gray's *Elegy* and for countless earlier and several later generations, has been disrupted. Church and churchyard have lost their pivotal position. ' The bosom of his Father and his God ' is no longer a simple and natural climax for the poet. For the common mind indeed ' Nature ' has silently displaced God as the ultimate basis to which all other things are referred.

But Mr. Eliot adds three further propositions which, if accepted, must radically modify the reasonable aim of the body of Christians, both in the nation and in the university. First, though the destructive process has already gone far and may go further, it is still incomplete. Our present state is transitional and not pagan or wholly secular; it differs widely from that prevailing in India or China or again in the Soviet Union. It is true that it cannot be

[1] See also Professor John Baillie's Riddell Lectures—*What is Christian Civilization?*

long maintained; either the secularization will be completed or there will be a revivification of Christianity. But the issue is still open.

Secondly, ' we have to-day a culture which is mainly negative, but which, so far as it is positive, is still Christian.'[1] So far as there is a national conscience, it is still mainly Christian in colouring. With the majority of people for whom the Christian picture has faded out, no alternative body of convictions, serving as an effective guide to existence, has yet taken its place. There is only a vacuum; in practice they belong nowhere and give no whole-hearted allegiance to anything. ' The religion of the Englishman,' that is, the cause or causes for which, when roused, he is impelled to sacrifice everything, and even life itself if need be, is Christian in origin. In wartime it was often remarked that we were much surer of what we were fighting *against* than of what we were fighting *for*. But, when analysed, those values which we felt in our bones to be menaced by Hitler, and which Churchill incited us to defend, are what our nation first received as Christian values. It acquired them, not as self-subsistent truths but, as the consequence of certain beliefs about the nature of man and of the universe. The large number of our countrymen who sprang to their defence, but who have, individually, abandoned Christian worship and Christian belief, are putting their trust in a plant which has been severed from its roots, or as has often been said, they are living on their capital.

Thirdly, the issue cannot long remain open. Some of the factors producing the present precarious equilibrium are evanescent. The present residual Christianity will die out, so far as the public scene is concerned, unless it undergoes a revivification. ' The choice before us is between the formation of a new Christian culture and the acceptance of a pagan one. Both involve radical changes.'

Mr. Eliot's book was published in 1939, and, since then, events have moved swiftly towards a climax. In Europe, the war with its attendant atrocities, the overrunning of so many countries by the Nazi régime, and the resistance movements with their heroic and anarchic features, have combined to disturb rudely thick layers of convention and comfort which ordinarily conceal from men the reality of themselves and of the world. In this country we have experienced the imminent menace of annihilation, the awakening of 1940 bringing a renewed sense of mission, wide recognition abroad and a call to moral leadership, and the partial but still

[1] *Op. cit.*, p. 13.

retrievable lapse since the end of hostilities. In the next twenty or thirty years, the future of the world may depend, and the future of the British Commonwealth almost certainly does depend, on whether we are able to stand for a way of life, as coherent and as whole-heartedly embraced as any other, but saner and more convincing. That remains to be seen. Our own belief is that it will depend on a recovery of our Christian heritage and its bold re-adaptation to contemporary facts. The burden of proof seems to rest on those who think it can be done otherwise.

What is the upshot? The British people to-day is not ' Christian,' except in a debased sense of the word which is therefore better avoided. But its imagination, its ethos and its sentiment are, to a very substantial extent, *Christianized*. This is also true of the universities. The full Christian faith cannot now, or in any near future, be the working basis of the British universities any more than of the nation. But it is not impossible or necessarily illegitimate, that the pattern of their organization and studies, and the character of their corporate life, should be given deliberately a certain degree of consciously Christian orientation. It is not for the university, in its official capacity, to attempt the work of evangelization. The university cannot itself be the sower of the seed, though it can give him his opportunity. But it can, and should, provide a soil which will be favourable to growth and not so arid that the seed withers nor so full of thorns that it is choked.

But what is the moral? If the situation is as open as we have described it, have universities within the nation or Christians within the university nothing to do but to wait and see which way things will go? Are the determining factors wholly outside their control? Or is there any initiative which they can rightly and effectively take?

# 6   THE UPSHOT FOR THE UNIVERSITY

The British universities, we have agreed, are not sectional but communal institutions, and, in general, their basic assumptions must be those of the nation. In addition, as we have also seen, they pay allegiance to a number of fundamental, though unwritten, ' rules of the guild,' which are essential to the proper performance of their special function. Under each head we have enumerated some of these assumptions. At first sight they are not distinctively Christian; theocentric and other humanists, who attach a high value to personality, can unite on them. But, for us as Christians, both sets of values have deeper implications. They are not self-subsistent, but rest on a distinctive understanding of man and of the world, and in its absence they are precarious and 'in the air.' How far may we work to stress these implications in the ordering of our corporate life and studies? How far can we ask others to acquiesce in our doing so? In the current vernacular, 'where do we go from here?' We must soon go somewhere, for our present position is unstable and can only be transitional. 'The impersonal configuration of our common life' will inevitably become a good deal less, or a good deal more, 'Christianized' than it is at the moment.

There can be no moral leadership, of Western Europe or of the world, which is based on negations. It can only come from some group which knows its own mind and which has the courage of its convictions because they are firmly grounded in some coherent philosophy of life. At present every such group is a minority group. The question is, Which of them will prove itself to be the leaven which leavens the lump? Even if it should be the Christians, such 'leavening' would not be a matter of evangelization or of the restoration of a 'Christian university,' in the sense in which for example the University of Paris in the Middle Ages was a Christian university; a supra-national, scientific centre of Christendom, whose basis of unity was at the highest point of personal life, doctrinal, theological and philosophical. It would be a matter of deepening the Christian colouring and bringing into consciousness the Christian background of the basic values on which the university is built.

Within a democratic community, what sort of leadership is practicable or wholesome? We shall agree in rejecting the régime of the drill-sergeant or the spell-binder. But we need not fall back on the leader with his 'ear to the ground,' whose sole aim is to find out what his followers want and to give it to them, who indeed inverts the rôles of leader and followers. Our clue must be Professor Toynbee's distinction between a *creative* and a *dominant* minority. With regard to the shaping of policy, the organization of studies, and the quality of corporate life, can the Christians within the university legitimately aspire to become such a 'creative minority,' whose lead others will follow?

What is the mark of a 'creative' as distinct from a 'dominant' minority? It puts forward opinions which are novel, in the sense that the majority of us did not previously know that we held them, or policies which we did not previously know we intended. Yet we did hold, or intend them, in that, when they are propounded, we recognize, accept and acclaim them. They come to us, not as strange and alien but as a revelation of the deepest truth of our own minds, though we could never have articulated them for ourselves. 'Yes, that is what we think,' we cry with a mixture of surprise and delighted recognition. They both light up what is familiar and show us that there is much 'more to it' than we had realized. They are partly elicited from us and partly instilled into us. They explain us to ourselves. They represent our own real, but hitherto unconscious and ineffective, wills. May not the Christianizing of our common values bring, to university people generally, a similar sense of enlargement and enlightenment?

But here alarm may be taken. Is not this process, it may be asked, simply the hackneyed device of the salesman and the demagogue, of which Hitler was the supreme exponent? Is it not a technique for persuading people that they themselves have chosen what has been dexterously palmed off on them? And that is to add insult to injury; you not only manipulate people but also bamboozle them. You are only proposing to 'sell' Christian values to the university or the nation. But to criticize on these lines, is to confound two widely different processes. The one puts to sleep our critical faculties and operates as a drug; it appeals to our baser urges, to inertia, greed and fear, to 'envy, hatred and malice and all uncharitableness.' The other appeals from Philip drunk to Philip sober. It eschews all methods that are clandestine and crooked. It evokes and energizes our highest capacities.

This can be made clear by two illustrations. The policy of Broadcasting House has differed sharply from that of Hollywood. Hollywood played down to its public. It gave the masses what they wanted—or what it supposed they wanted. It did little to raise, and a good deal to debase, the public taste. The B.B.C. also had to cater for an enormous clientèle and could not be merely highbrow. It had, in the main, to give its listeners what they liked rather than what the Governors thought good for them; in its early days the Third Programme would have been quite impossible. But it was always a little ahead of its public; it gave listeners the best that they would put up with rather than something a little below the average. So it gradually raised the whole level of public taste, and opened to millions new ranges of aesthetic appreciation. This was genuinely emancipation rather than enslavement.

Another example is the contrast between Winston Churchill's (or Abraham Lincoln's) wartime leadership and the whole Hitlerian technique. His 1940 speeches gave his countrymen a moral lead which they could not have evolved for themselves. But he drew out their real mind and character and they responded from the depths of their being. In this there was no deception; he was not ' putting anything over ' on them or warping their nature. But he was able to evoke ' the common enthusiasm which brings into action the deep energies of the crowd.'[1] Even more relevant is Franklin Roosevelt's leadership of the American people in the years 1938-41. He saw earlier and more clearly than most of his fellow-countrymen the true nature of the issues in the struggle then developing. He led them by gradual stages into participation, which in advance they would have repudiated but which they came to see was necessary to the maintenance of all they held dear. In a sense he knew their minds better than, at first, they did themselves, but he brought them to this knowledge. History will justify him as a democratic leader, in so far as he is held to have opened and not to have closed their eyes.

The application of this conception of leadership to the present task of Christians in the British nation (and by implication, in the British university) is made by Mr. Eliot in the work referred to above. To the three propositions we have already noticed, he adds a fourth which is the most momentous of all. Our choice, he says, is between the formation of a new Christian culture and the acceptance of a pagan one. ' Both involve radical changes; but I believe the majority of us, if we could be faced immediately with all the changes which will only be accomplished in several genera-tions, would prefer Christianity.'[2] Obviously such a proposition admits neither of proof nor of disproof. But we see no warrant for ruling it out as improbable, and if it is admitted even as a possible hypothesis, the existence of established Churches in the national community or the conscious acknowledgment of Christian values by universities can be viewed in a new perspective.

How can this conception of the ' creative minority ' be applied to the practical problems of the university with which we are concerned? Can the British universities act in this capacity within the nation? Can they affirm, and ground themselves on, values not yet fully endorsed by the whole community, in the faith that the

[1] Maritain, *op. cit.*, p. 198.
[2] *Op. cit.*, p. 13.

community will come to endorse them, when really confronted with them and when fully awake to the issues involved? So far as the special academic values are concerned, those embodied in the unwritten ' rules of the guild,' they can and they must do so. In this region they must lead, and not merely reflect, public opinion if they are not to betray their trust. But what of the more general ' Christianized ' values, of which we have spoken? Here, the universities could in principle give a lead; but, in practice, they cannot at present do so, since their internal divisions are too great. But this carries us back to the prior question, Can Christians act as a creative minority within the university?

Those who would answer, ' Yes,' are under fire from two sides. Secularists urge that, for Christians to-day to claim any special majority-rights or representative capacity, is at best an anachronism and at worst a dishonest ' ramp.' On the other hand, many ardent Christians contend that a claim by, or on behalf of, the mass of our countrymen to any sort of Christian status, is hypocritical and must debase the intellectual currency. But to both these attacks weighty replies can be made. The former is misconceived; for the real question is not whether Christians *may* but whether they *can* act as a creative minority. It is not their abstract right to do so but their spiritual and intellectual capacity that is in question. Christians, in the early centuries or in the modern mission-field, have won their triumphs by the degree of reality, the validity, which other people perceived in them and in their way of life, and the same principle holds good to-day. Whether they can do so again, is an open question, which cannot be answered in advance for the answer must be wrought out in life. In no university do they yet look like doing so; and any claim, in advance, to be looked on as a ' creative minority ' would be drowned in derisive laughter. Such a status has to be earned before it can be claimed. But that does not close the question. We may be called to tasks which far exceed our human resources. To our reading of history God has, not once nor twice but many times, used the weak, foolish and base things of the world to confound the mighty and wise and noble, and the things that are not, to bring to naught the things that are.

But there is still the objection urged by some of the best of our fellow-Christians. They hold that the Christian minority could only become an operative influence on the university as a whole—or on the nation as a whole—by being ' subdued to that it works in,' that the same considerations, which are fatal to the project of a fully Christian university, apply equally to any attempt to write into its title-deeds some demi-semi-Christianity; and that, in the university as elsewhere, the policy of Constantine involves a concordat with the prince of this world. For strictly secular purposes, no doubt, Christians must often be prepared to work with half-believers and unbelievers, with whom they happen to agree on some immediate, practical, end. But, in such an enterprise, why drag in Christianity?

If the basic assumptions of the university are to have a Christian colouring at all, it is clear that, to-day, this cannot be the full gospel or anything closely approximating to it. In Maritain's phraseology, it will be 'secularly and not consecrationally Christian.' It will not, like the medieval ideal, aim at unity at the highest point of personal life. For example to make sacramental observance a condition of full membership, in university as in commonwealth, could only result in the profanation of the sacrament. The 'Christian' unity, so far as it exists at all, can only be a minimal unity; it is a unity not of faith and religion but rather of orientation. Yet it would be a mistake to drop the Christian reference altogether, and Christians should not advocate it. That would be to eradicate an element which is still present in the general consciousness, in however confused and embryonic a form, and which has the possibility of growth. The maxim, 'All or nothing,' represents one aspect, but only one, of the Christian attitude which has really a dual character going back to the New Testament. 'He that is not with me is against me'; but 'He that is not against us is for us,' and the disciples are not to forbid others who cast out devils in Christ's name though the status of their discipleship may be dubious. Over and over again in the Parables, instances of natural goodness and piety are treated as signs and tokens of genuine discipleship. Christians belonging to Churches which practise infant baptism cannot repudiate all communal propaedeutics to Christianity simply because they operate at a sub-personal level. Nurture in a Christian family is a great boon; the 'Freshman' of whom it was said, 'An atmosphere of holiness, not yet completely his own, hung about him,' was highly privileged. No doubt, the contemporary university cannot, like a Christian family, provide an atmosphere of 'holiness.' But it could provide a soil which is favourable to Christian thinking and living instead of, as at present, one which is resistant.[1]

[1] See Chapter III above.

K

## 7  CONCLUSION

If our universities are to rise to the height of the times, the first, and quite inescapable, requirement is that they shall concentrate far more attention on the deep and difficult issues of the day. There must be no more tacit conspiracy of silence. Convictions must be explored and tested to their roots. Next, communications must be re-opened. Contact must be made and the issue must be joined, not at the ordinary level of debate, but at the level at which convictions are really formed. If, at this level, agreement on a basic philosophy of life were possible, that would invigorate the whole work of the universities and their contribution to the world; but nothing like a modern 'Summa' is conceivable for a long time to come. Yet, though unformulated and unsystematic, the acceptance of some basic values is implied in the normal life-attitudes of British university teachers and students as of the British people generally, and there are others more special to the university; and for practical purposes these can be regarded as axiomatic.

So much very many critics would be willing to concede. 'But,' they will ask, 'why cannot you stop at that?' We agree in commending certain virtues and in condemning certain vices; and, on that basis, we can work in harmony on practical issues which come up for decision in Faculty, Senate or Council. We do not agree, and are not likely to agree, on ultimate questions. Why then force to the front questions which must divide us? This is a time of transition. The ground is still heaving, the day for permanent building is not yet. In intellectual, as in physical, construction we must still 'make do' with temporary expedients.

Such an attitude might be reasonable in less desperate times. But 'safety first,' to let well alone, *quieta non movere,* to wait for the saecular movement of thought to come to a natural climax, is no missionary policy for Great Britain in the world to-day, or for the universities in Great Britain. It may sound plausible in our own pleasant, and seldom war-scarred, Common Rooms; it would be much less so in the universities of Central Europe. If we are to 'withstand in the evil day, and, having done all, to stand,' there must be no gaps and no weakness in our armour. The 'truth' with which we 'gird our loins' must be comprehensive and thoroughly grounded. Otherwise we shall succumb to strange gospels which are more coherent, and more firmly held than our own. Whatever our basic values are, national and academic, we need to make them much clearer and to develop and deepen them, if we are to play the rôle in the world, to which we were called in 1940, and to which leaders as far apart as Winston Churchill and Sir Stafford Cripps would agree that we are called to-day.

In these basic values there is certainly a Christian ingredient. No doubt it is extremely hard to estimate its present extent and significance. Equally honest observers may well differ widely in their estimates; and, even among our own group there is at least some nuance of difference. Christian teachers should not ask their colleagues to accept in advance any wider commitment of the university to a Christianized orientation than those colleagues are disposed to concede. But they should claim elbow-room to show themselves a ' creative minority,' if they can. All will then depend on whether they have enough spiritual energy and political wisdom to demonstrate to others that a growing Christianization of ' the impersonal configuration of our common life ' is what sound reason and the common good require.[1] Yet in their own minds, they will be well aware that they can only hope to have such energy and wisdom, if they open themselves in extraordinary measure to be vehicles of the grace of God.

Some of the lines on which such a policy may be worked out in practice will be considered in the later chapters. What is possible and legitimate varies from university to university. But for Christian teachers and students everywhere, if we have ears to hear, there is sounding, through the course of events, a trumpet-call for action. Almost audibly, the voice of the Lord is heard, saying, ' Whom shall I send and who will go for us?'

[1] cf. Maritain, op. cit., p. 168.

# VI

## FREEDOM AND INTEGRATION

If the university has some positive basis of principle, some 'platform,' however general, what bearing has that fact on its type of organization and its personnel? For instance must it satisfy itself that at least its officers, if not all its members, adopt that platform?

## I   WHAT MAY INTEGRATION ENTAIL?

We have already noted the painful contrast between the purposive planning of particular researches or of training for particular callings and the absence of a master-plan for the university as a whole. It is as though, in an empire, each provincial government had a policy, but there was no policy at the centre. How are all these separate policies to be fitted together in one whole, what is their proportionate importance, by what common standard of value are they to be judged, what is the university as a whole, or the university system of the country, 'out for'? On such questions there are no agreed principles. Some universities are, in effect, little more than a congeries of Faculties, going their several ways; they resemble England in the days of the Heptarchy. Their chief men have discordant philosophies of life or none.

This, it is urged, does not make sense at any time and in an era of crisis it is insane. Have we not to learn from the experience of wartime? Then the universities had a clear, overriding, common purpose, given them from outside—to win the war. As a result there was effective co-ordination and team-work, an immense quickening of tempo, and a new 'drive' and concentration of effort; and these proved extraordinarily fruitful.[1] In a peacetime which is no less critical do we not need a Five-Year or Ten-Year Plan on similar lines? But such a plan presupposes that the major objective is settled in advance. In detail the plan may be very flexible and constructive criticism may be encouraged. But the main objective is *chose jugée*. It is not to be further debated, but only to be got on with. 'When the fire alarm calls out the municipal fire engines [people] recognize that unbiased statement of the

---

[1] See Sir Henry Dale's presidential address to the British Association 1947.

case for a voluntary salvage corps is not what the situation demands.'[1] To call in question the accepted main purpose of the institution is not helpful but sterilizing.

The analogy of wartime experience suggests that, to get the most out of a university, it must be enrolled in the service of some cause beyond itself. In other countries the rightfulness of such enrolment is common ground. In Russia the end is the building up of a socialist society and the furtherance of the interests of the working classes.[2] The Fascist university aimed at ' the formation of a definite type of Italian.'[3] The American universities have sought to nurture protagonists of a liberal democracy, of which the distinctive spiritual impulse was found in the crucial experience of the pioneers. Even the more traditional types of university acknowledged an overriding communal obligation. With Whewell this is the maintenance of the social structure, ' the institutions of the country.'[4] With Paulsen, writing it is true in Germany, it is the political structure; a teacher who is radically hostile to the whole existing structure of the State has no business in a communal university.

This principle, it may be suggested, has negative implications; in practice it involves some exclusions. But must not that nettle be grasped? Really basic doctrine is for application and not for criticism. Christians may dispute among themselves, with the utmost freedom and tenacity, about the interpretation of the Bible, Communists about the interpretation of *Das Kapital;* but neither will question the validity of their foundation documents. In comparison with the Christian Church or the Cominform the intellectual basis of the university may be much less elaborate. But, such as it is, is it not authoritative, and how can the university absorb any one who challenges it? In foreign universities such exclusiveness is common. The Fascist says, ' Liberty, by all means; but not liberty to destroy the creations of liberty. The universities must not betray the nation by " the poisonous injections of corrosive theories." '[5] The Communist, as of course, purges his universities of counter-revolutionaries. The traditional Roman Catholic attitude regards the heretic as one who attacks the life-spring of the whole

---

[1] Hogben, *op. cit.*, p. 144.

[2] Pinkevitch in *The University in a Changing World*, p. 195.

[3] Fantini, *ibid.*, p. 176.

[4] *Op. cit.*, p. 133.

[5] Fantini, *op. cit.*, p. 174.

socio-temporal community[1] and so the Irish bishops claimed
the ultimate control of all appointments in the Catholic University. The basis of the modern university may be a good deal
wider and less exclusive than any of these. It may be wide enough
to include ' Jews, Turks, infidels and heretics.' But so long as we
recognize any basis at all, have we not an irreducible minimum to
which we must demand loyalty? Even the most famous historical
protagonists of liberty and toleration have recognized this fact and
have made inevitable exceptions to their generalizations. Milton
says, ' I mean not tolerated popery and open superstition, which
as it extirpates all religious and civil supremacies, so itself shall be
extirpated.' Locke excepts atheists on the ground that promises
and oaths, which are the bond of civil societies, have no hold on
them, and Roman Catholics because their primary obedience is to
a foreign jurisdiction. These are indeed ' exceptions which prove
the rule,' since, were they not excepted, they would stultify the rule.
For instance to tolerate the intolerant would be a *reductio ad
absurdum* of the principle of toleration.

No doubt even to mention ' tests for teachers ' is to touch a raw
nerve. But is it not sheer muddle-headedness to assume that,
because such things as the maintenance of the Christian faith or of
the tenets of the Conservative Party are outside the purpose of
the university, it has no coherent purpose at all, or that, because it
is irrelevant and monstrous that a university teacher should be
asked to subscribe to the Thirty Nine Articles or the Westminster
Confession, he therefore must not be asked to adhere to anything?
Is not that mere liberal sentimentalism? If it were valid, why are
Nazi teachers now being thrown out of German universities? Such
questions are asked with the subdued impatience with which a
teacher confronts a dunce.

If our main argument has been valid, does it not follow
that candidates for appointments in universities should undergo
a scrutiny of their *Weltanschauung* more stringent than has been
customary in recent years? Technical qualifications however
high will no longer be enough. If the university stands for any
definite values, the furtherance of those values will be among the
objects for which it appoints its staff. No doubt stronger grounds
are required for terminating an appointment than for refusing to
make it in the first instance. But even here does not the same prin-

---

[1] Maritain, *op. cit.*, p. 144. Maritain himself regards this attitude as unsuited
to the present age.

ciple hold good? If a man devotes his professional career to the service of a certain cause and, later, comes to disbelieve in it, his life is in ruins; he must start again. In mid-Victorian times Leslie Stephen and Henry Sidgwick, of their own motion, felt it incumbent on them as honest men to resign, the one his College Tutorship and the other his Fellowship, when they had ceased to hold the Christian faith. To-day there would be no such obligation, for universities are not Christian in the sense in which Trinity Hall and Trinity College were Christian eighty years ago. But if—*per impossibile*—a university teacher did become a convinced disciple of Sir Oswald Mosley, denying those obligations and attacking those liberties which are among the fundamental university assumptions, would not his university belie itself if it allowed him still to officiate?

## 2 COUNTER ARGUMENT FOR FREEDOM

The cult of integration can be carried to a degree which is deadening. There are other values equally to be maintained by Christians. Not unison but a harmony is required. It is important to stress this, because it has frequently been ignored by Christians in the past when they were more in a position to call the tune than they are to-day. In the eyes of Cardinal Cullen or of Pusey, the university's function is not to cultivate true religion *and* sound learning. Sound learning is only ancillary; all studies should lead directly to the promotion of religion. 'All the sciences,' says Pusey, 'move like planets round the sun of God's truth,' and again, 'All things must speak of God, refer to God, or they are atheistic.'[1] In this spirit Charlotte Yonge refused to be associated with the founding of Lady Margaret Hall, because of the absence of 'a decided religious object.' 'This scheme,' she wrote to the Warden of Keble, 'seems to be Lectures plus Church, not like the original conception of a College, education primarily for the direct service of religion to which other students were admitted.'[2] To Cullen zeal and piety were the essential qualifications of teachers; their intellectual equipment was of secondary importance. This attitude, says von Hügel, might be parodied by saying, 'Since religion is true and supreme, religion is all we require: all things else must be bent or broken to her sway.'[3]

[1] Quoted in Mallet *A History of the University of Oxford* III, pp. 331, 319.
[2] Quoted in Georgina Battiscombe's *Charlotte M. Yonge*, p. 146.
[3] *The Mystical Element of Religion* I, p. 46.

A quite different and much wiser strain of Christian teaching is found in Newman, and, to confine ourselves to Roman Catholics, it is echoed in von Hügel and Maritain. Literature and science, Newman insists, must be allowed to develop on their own, according to their own laws, without being perpetually worried on the score of possible collisions with theology. No premature synthesis should be attempted; that should be left to time. There must be a generous confidence that truths in each sphere will, in the long run, be found to be consistent. ' He who believes Revelation with that absolute faith which is the prerogative of a Catholic, is not the nervous creature who startles at every sudden sound and is fluttered by every strange or novel appearance which meets his eyes.'[1] Literature represents all the beauty and all the fierceness of the natural man, and to bowdlerize would be to impoverish. We are not to be for ever pulling ourselves up to ask whether St. Bernard or Savonarola or John Knox would approve. The study of science is bracing and deprovincializing just because of the severity and impersonality of its methods. Each of these provinces has its own domestic laws which must be pushed as far as they will go. Newman quotes the analogy of the Roman Empire, which blended different peoples in one great social establishment and yet left to each its own privileges and its own national sentiments. For the Christian the ultimate end of the university, as of every human institution, is to serve the Kingdom of God, but its immediate end and the ordinary object of its attention is different. It is ' to secure the due disposition according to one sovereign order, and the cultivation in that order, of all the provinces and methods of government which the human intellect has created.'[2] The scientific investigator needs elbow-room. He is not to be, every moment, adjusting his course by the maxims of any science other than his own.

Baron von Hügel makes three points with great force. (1) Religion is the most important and universal of things, but it is not everything. Science and art, morals, and politics, have each its own ' inside,' its own law of growth and existence, and are not simple departments or dependencies of religion. He would agree with Dorothy Sayers that the first duty of a Christian carpenter is to make good tables. (2) Human free will furnishes an analogy. God has somehow alienated a portion of His own power and has given it a relative independence of its own. (3) For self-centred and

---

[1] *Op. cit.*, p. 466.
[2] *Op. cit.*, pp. 459-60.

sensually sentimental natural man there is a positive value in the experience of what is impersonal and resistant, and in the consequent sense of friction and ' non-fit.' This tension cannot be entirely outgrown at any point in this life. In the last resort of course, but only in the last resort, collisions may have to be faced. In that case we must put first things first; if our eye offends us, we are bidden to pluck it out. But blindness, though not the greatest possible, is yet a major calamity, and surgery is not required by a man in normal health.

We have dwelt on instances where the basis of integration has been religious, because that is where our own bias is liable to be strongest. But in these days some secular basis is more usual. In most countries this tends to be political, but in Britain perhaps a more likely form of pressure is that of public opinion, well-meaning but unenlightened, and operating at the level of its lowest common denominator, to produce an undue standardization, pushing the universities against their better judgment into the use of mass-production methods. But every form of strait-waistcoat is to be avoided.

In order to be useful to the community, the university must retain a large measure of autonomy as against the community. This is a paradoxical, but quite vital, fact. It is only so far as Balaam serves God first, and Balak only incidentally, that his word is worth anything to Balak himself. This has been expressed clearly by Paulsen, ' " Science " would manifestly lose its value even as a means of power if it appeared as the dogma of the party in power. It influences the opinion of men only so long as it seems to be an independent product of the intellect.'[1] The same point has been made by the University Grants Committee : ' A university which allowed itself to become the " tied house " of any special interest or calling, would lose the world as well as its own soul, for it would soon be found that every limitation of its academic freedom was accompanied by a weakening of the very qualities which originally made its services seem so desirable to secure.'[2] An essential part of the service of the university to the community is to aid it to resist the almost overwhelming pressure of the immediate and ' to break the stranglehold of the present on the mind.'[3] All sorts of

[1] *Op. cit.*, p. 244. He continues very significantly, ' The dominant party will therefore always desire to have a form of science that is really dependent, but publicly boasts of its independence.'

[2] *Quinquennial Report*, 1930, p. 53.

[3] *General Education in a Free Society*, p. 70.

social service are possible and valuable only so long as ' the university is the university ' and has a mind, a conscience and an individuality of its own.

No less essential is the freedom of the individual teacher *(Lehrfreiheit)*. There are weighty reasons for laying stress on this, of a general as well as a specifically Christian kind. First, there is a sense of the limitations of deductive logic. For instance, as we have seen, inferences from the existence of a double allegiance were long regarded as being a fatal obstacle to Catholic Emancipation. But, in the main, the event has belied this reasoning, which, in retrospect, seems doctrinaire. What has actually happened, is not what the critics contended it logically must be. The living sense of human fellowship within the nation has proved too strong for the logicians. It is likely that similar inferences about heretics within the university will be similarly falsified.

Secondly, there are the limitations of planning. Here the success of wartime planning for short-term, very obvious and clearly defined, objectives may easily be misleading.[1] The most fundamental discoveries and contributions to knowledge have generally been made by men who were not looking for rapid solutions to urgent, practical problems. It is at least highly doubtful whether Kelvin or Rutherford, Gilbert Murray or G. M. Trevelyan would have produced equally outstanding results, if throughout their careers they had been working within the limits of corporate plans. The wind bloweth where it listeth. The masters in science and scholarship need elbow-room. The planner can help them best by freeing them from hampering conditions and ' giving them their heads.' Again they will only do their best work if, in controversial questions, they feel they are free to say whatever the Lord puts into their mouths and not only what is required of them by their university or by the powers behind the university. Karl Mannheim has popularized the conception of ' planning for freedom.' That is based on a distinction of spheres. To plan a railway timetable demands absolute precision; but in the world of art such precise regulation is absurd, because it is inhibiting. The wise planner will recognize this and in the appropriate regions will, of set purpose, leave freedom to the individual. The higher work of universities is certainly one of these regions.

Thirdly there is a good deal of empirical evidence that regimentation defeats its own purpose. Professor Toynbee's estimate of the

[1] See Sir Henry Dale's presidential address to the British Association, 1947.

ultimate futility of the work of 'dominant' minorities is much in point. Looking back, Christians as well as others can see that when the Church has called in 'the secular arm' for spiritual purposes, the result has been a de-spiritualizing. What you believe —or rather profess to believe—because you will suffer for it if you do not, is unlikely to have the quality of 'saving faith.' Indeed for you, the area in which such faith is possible is being reduced. Nor is it only the use of the big stick which has this effect; indoctrination and habituation also have it in some degree. What you believe mainly because it is constantly dinned into you and you never hear anything else, ways of thinking and feeling and acting which you have acquired mainly through suggestion, do not constitute a creed or a philosophy of life which is worthy of a university graduate. The restriction of criticism and of the free play of mind to details as opposed to first principles, such as used to exist in Christian universities and is rumoured to exist to-day in the Russian universities, has two evil effects. The faith it is designed to safeguard remains insecure, because it has never been submitted to a rigorous test. It is also intellectually debasing. It makes disciples, not as do the great teachers, of those whose faculties, including the critical faculty, are at full-stretch, but of those whose higher faculties are lulled to sleep. The impatient reformer is always under the temptation to turn his colleagues into 'auxiliaries for battle' rather than 'counsellors for deliberation,' but he should not yield to it.

There are also specific Christian grounds for the freedom of the individual teacher. This must be insisted on, because, in reaction from the present disintegration, Christians can easily go astray. Any kind of authoritarianism should be approached by them with suspicion. The fact that authoritarianism is now coming to be 'in the air' is an additional reason for vigilance. It is significant that, in the last few years, the Christian Church has often appeared to be the most effective remaining barrier against totalitarianism, and that it has found itself morally obliged to take this attitude, not through thinking in the study, but under the strong compulsion of events.[1] The chief reason for this is a strong Christian sense of the responsibility of the individual, of which we have spoken earlier. As Maritain puts it, what needs emphasis to-day is, less the holy empire of God than, the holy freedom of the creature. With this goes the

[1] The cynic says that the Church only takes a stand when its own interests are threatened, e.g., to defend freedom of worship, but not to denounce anti-semitism. But this is far from being the whole truth even in Germany.

Christian sense of human fallibility. We are, or ought to be, specially conscious of the gulf between the creature and the Creator and of the limits to what human scheming can effect. Once perhaps Christian thinkers could be fairly charged with taking the problematic out of life; now it is rather the materialist scientist who is guilty of this presumptuous folly. But no section is wise enough to be entrusted with a monopoly.[1] As Christians we have also to recognize not only human fallibility, but also the destructive part played by human perversity. We are, none of us—majorities or creative minorities, Christians, dialectical materialists or liberal humanists—a hundred per cent honest or disinterested. It is a pity that even would-be realists mostly talk as though this were true of all other groups, but, for some unexplained reason, not of their own.

Christians should work for an 'open university.' This does not mean a university which is shapeless or neutral. But it means one in which even academic 'infidels' are not, as such, aliens or outlaws; one which is hospitable to dissident minorities, even if they do not accept their university's integrating principle. No thinking will be suppressed as 'dangerous.' Above all there will be no 'tests for teachers,' no articles of faith, however widely drawn, which will be prescribed as a condition of service. This will not be because a teacher's philosophy of life is irrelevant to his fitness for his job; sometimes it is relevant in a high degree. But 'tests' are to be repudiated for two reasons. First they notoriously put a premium on hypocrisy; that is one reason why they are so offensive to school-teachers. Even more important, apart from conscious hypocrisy, they do not test the right things. At most they can assure the university authorities that a candidate for a job is prepared to say, 'Lord, Lord,' and we have the highest authority for believing that this does not carry us far.

## 3    APPLICATION TO APPOINTMENTS

'Freedom' and 'Integration' are rather vague and general terms. Perhaps we can get a little further in trying out our principles by applying them to the crucial case of appointments to the staff. We have just rejected formal 'tests' or terms of subscription. But behind this there is a further, and vital, question in regard to which

[1] This wholesome sense of fallibility is shared by many democratic thinkers who are not necessarily Christians. See *General Education in a Free Society*, p. 105.

there is no agreed ethic. When we serve as members of appointing committees, Boards, Faculties, Senates, etc., how far should we confine our attention to the technical and professional accomplishments of a candidate for appointment? How far should we also take into account what seems to be his general attitude to life and its relation to the basic principles of the university, however those may be defined?

The present position is unsatisfactory. Large numbers of individual electors do, in fact, take these wider questions into account. They consider a candidate's interest in the social background and consequences of his science or art, his conception of its relation to other subjects, his probable relation to pupils and colleagues and influence on the university's corporate life. In short they try to ascertain, and they give weight to, his philosophy of his subject and his working philosophy of life; but sometimes they do so with an uneasy conscience and a little surreptitiously. Their own vote is influenced by these things, but that is unacknowledged, except perhaps to one or two like-minded colleagues. They regard them as considerations for the ' lobby ' rather than for general discussion in Committee, Faculty or Senate. But obviously such questions should be brought into the open and thrashed out, whatever the conclusion.

The issue may be narrowed by ruling out two extremes which most thinking people would agree in rejecting. The first is the position of Pusey. For him, soundness in the university's faith (however that may be defined) is the first essential; intellectual ability and technical qualifications are of minor importance. In 1842 when Keble's term of office as Professor of Poetry came to an end, the succession lay between two clergymen of whom one was a Tractarian and one was not. In fact the Tractarian, Isaac Williams, seems to have had the better literary qualifications. Unfortunately Pusey issued a circular asking for support for him on the ground that ' his known religious views would ensure his making his office minister to religious truth.'[1] Nemesis quickly followed. The election was fought almost entirely on ecclesiastical rather than on literary issues, and it soon appeared that the majority of the electors preferred the ecclesiastical affiliations of the other candidate.

The other extreme is represented by the old liberal assumption that it is illegitimate to take anything into account other than a candidate's technical excellence and that such excellence is entirely

[1] Church, *The Oxford Movement*, p. 274, cf. Mallet, *op. cit.* III, p. 270.

detachable from his moral constitution and his general philosophical attitude. In a speech in the House of Commons on theological tests in Scottish Universities, Macaulay directed some rather heavy raillery against those who 'talk in horror of the danger of suffering young men to listen to the lectures of an Arian professor of Botany or of a Popish professor of Chemistry.'[1] He easily carries the modern reader with him in this instance, because, whatever their ecclesiastical status, Arianism and Popery are not generally regarded as academic heresies. But if for 'Arian' and 'Popish' we read 'Nazi' and 'Russian Communist,' the case is by no means so clear. The exclusion of Nazis from the staffs of German universities is now being carried out with wide approval; and many will feel that the Communist of the straitest sect at least raises a problem.

From these illustrations it seems clear that, in principle, the question is one of relevance. In the case of the Chair of Poetry, Pusey was, from his own point of view, perfectly logical. He held that the purpose of the University of Oxford was to serve God according to the principles of the Church of England, and that the Catholic party in the Church was the true exponent of those principles. We reject his conclusion, because we reject his premise and think that sound churchmanship is not directly relevant to the work of a Professor of Poetry. We agree with Macaulay in thinking that Arianism or Popery need not be a barrier to successful tenure of Chairs of Botany or Chemistry. But we reject a possible further implication that to give competent instruction in these subjects is the only business for which their Professors are appointed, and that moral attitudes and general philosophies of life are necessarily irrelevant.

But, granting that these things are germane and that enquiry concerning them is legitimate, it must still be asked whether it is expedient. Should heresy, even on fundamentals, exclude absolutely from teaching office in a university? If not, should it exclude relatively? That is, should it be regarded as a reason for preferring another candidate, if one of adequate technical quality is available? Here we must remember that even for the Christian—and *a fortiori* for the modern university—the ultimate enemy, the enemy with whom there should be war to the knife, is not the ardent and conscientious atheist or totalitarian. It is the trivial-minded, irrespon-

---

[1] *Miscellaneous Writings* III, p. 136. In 1818 a Dissenter was rejected as an applicant for the Deputy Keepership of the Botanical Gardens at Cambridge (Winstanley, *Early Victorian Cambridge,* p. 85).

sible thinker who does not take seriously his obligation to seek truth and to ensue it. Accordingly the only irreducible minimum is good faith, the intention to play the game according to the rules. The only outlaw is the cheat; that is, the infiltrator who conceals his full view in order to gain admission, and comes in, not to argue his case and to convert others, if he can, by rational argument, but to ' collar ' the machine, who in short is a wrecker. Such intentions are not susceptible of precise proof. But if, on the best view we can form, we strongly suspect any candidate of entertaining them, we shall vote against him. In the academic field, his is the sin against the Holy Ghost. With that sinner, so long as he continues in his sin, the university can make no terms and have no fellowship. It is true that, as we have already argued, intellectual integrity is a less simple matter than is often supposed and that it is, at best, imperfectly achieved. Nevertheless, we must be like President Coolidge's preacher in the story. Asked what the sermon was about, the President replied ' Sin !' Asked what the preacher had to say about sin, the President replied, ' He was *against* it.' Any preacher who was not against sin would be out of place in the pulpit; any teacher who is not against intellectual dishonesty is out of place in the university. The reason for excluding Nazi teachers from the German universities at this moment, so far as it is valid, is not to silence honest advocacy of any doctrine however offensive, but to prevent a dishonest manipulation of university machinery for the subversion of everything for which universities stand.

With regard to honest heretics no doctrinaire rule can be laid down, but there are two guiding principles. First the university's fundamental orientation must be maintained. The admission to teaching posts of those who repudiate it in such quantities as to threaten it should be opposed. Secondly, as we have seen, heretics may have a genuine contribution to make, and subject to the above qualification should not only be tolerated but be made welcome.

The practical application of these principles will vary with different offices and different subjects. When the appointment in question is that of Vice-Chancellor or Principal, ' Head of a House,' Warden of a Hall, or—more doubtfully—Dean of a Faculty, it is to be remembered that, in his own institution, he is the only one of his kind. As its official head, he should be the most influential person in it. He may belong to any one of a large variety of schools of thought; but his basic values and outlook should be congruous with those of the university. The same holds good in a lesser degree of the Head of a Department. It is much less true of a Lecturer, particularly in a large Department, where there is room, and even need, for much variety. Similarly there is a great difference between subjects of study, in the degree to which high specialist excellence in the departmental field is detachable from a general outlook on life. Mathematics presumably marks the extreme in one direction (though even here mathematicians have responsibilities as members of the university community just as have others), and Philosophy in another.[1] But even in Philosophy, it is not mainly doctrine, however outré, which may form a barrier to appointment. What matters more is the teacher's whole mental approach to his subject. To accept the wrong answers is less serious than to fail to ask the right questions. For instance, if—*per impossibile*—any historian were really to share Henry Ford's opinion that ' History is bunk,' however great his erudition, he would be unfitted to hold a chair in history. So in philosophy. There is room for immense variety. Even if Hume, Marx or Nietzsche are regarded as dissenters from the basic principles of the university, there may well be room on the staff for any or all of them. But there is no room for anyone, however acute dialectically and however well he ' knows his stuff,' who regards philosophy irresponsibly as merely the playing of a dialectical game.

## 4   FINAL REFLECTIONS

(i) As Christians, we hold that nothing short of the Christian faith supplies a basis which does full justice at once to integration and to freedom. In our view Christ, as the ultimate source of wisdom and of truth, is the only possible ground for a genuine unity of outlook and aim. ' Only a Faith superior to reason, which vivifies at once intellectual and affective activities, can assure the existence among men of a unity which is not founded on compulsion but on interior assent.'[2] *Dominus illuminatio mea* is the only master-principle which can fully or permanently satisfy. We may too easily beguile ourselves with a utopianism which forgets this.

(ii) But in present circumstances and in any near future the university's common basis cannot be specific Christianity, and its

---

[1] This distinction is illustrated by the experience of the ex-service students. In most subjects their greater maturity of experience more than compensates for any rustiness in their academic equipment, but in Mathematics the break in their studies seems to be pure loss.

[2] Maritain, *op. cit.*, p. 154.

Christian members ought not to try to make it so. Yet the university should have a recognizable and conscious orientation. This should take the form of a common moral outlook or *Weltanschauung,* which sees the challenge of our time in personalist rather than technical terms, which, though not specifically Christian, is ' christ-ianized ' in that it has been deeply influenced by Christianity, and which is a basis on which Christians and large numbers of non-Christians can work cordially together. Admittedly, in our belief, such a basis will prove in the long run to be a precarious and un-satisfactory compromise, having in itself the seeds of decay. Yet it is an imperative Christian duty to work strenuously for that system, however faulty, which we judge to be the best practicable at a given time and place.

(iii) We reject the policy of conserving this orientation by any kind of formal ' tests ' or terms of subscription. But some legitimate regard for it may be had in making appointments, and particularly key appointments. There is a place and a use within the university for a dissenter even in fundamentals, but it is marginal rather than central.

(iv) We reject both the shapeless and the closed university and we require a large degree both of integration and of freedom. Where a ' higher unity ' is unattainable, this involves an application of the principle of the mean. But, for practical purposes, as Aristotle makes clear, this is not an absolute mean but a ' mean relative to ourselves,' and this will vary from time to time with variations in ' the climate of opinion.'

(v) To-day it is freedom which most needs emphasis. Only yesterday, in view of the prevailing chaos, it was integration, and if we confined our attention to the institutional facts, that would still be true. But the pendulum is swinging. Among those sections of staff and students who seriously concern themselves with univer-sity problems, and have any policy to offer—as in the world out-side—this is already the age of planning. In a sense far truer and more pervasive than Sir William Harcourt's, ' we are all socialists now.' The wheel has come full circle. Once again, as for Newman a century ago, ' liberalism ' has become a word of ill-meaning and is often used for purposes of abuse. But our emphasis is different. We feel the need of reacting not only against liberalism, but against the current reaction from liberalism. Our aim should be, not to bury liberalism, but to save it from itself and to give it a spiritual stamina which it has hitherto not possessed.

L

(vi) But one qualification must at once be added. It is not the old liberalism that is required but some kind of creative re-interpretation of the values for which it stood. The corollary of freedom is responsibility. For the university, some kind of effective self-criticism is the only alternative to forcible interference from outside. If there is some spiritual autonomy for which we must fight, that must be carefully disentangled from any mere defence of the *status quo*. Whatever is the intrinsic weight of the arguments for autonomy, they can all be used as a vehicle of falsehood, and indeed of self-deception. They were so used by last-ditchers in the unreformed universities of Oxford and Cambridge a hundred years ago. Our motto must not be, ' Hands off the Senior Common Room,' with its vested interests, prejudices and trivialities, its chronic rheumatism of the mental joints, and its ' strange dull insistence on remaining rooted to the spot one is accustomed to.'

At this point the reader may react with some impatience. He may say, ' Thank you for nothing; or rather, for a set of sententious platitudes, the like of which I have often heard before. You tell me that the university must be integrated but not closed, free but not shapeless. Is not this the very echo of Polonius (" familiar but not vulgar " . . . " thy apparel rich but not gaudy.") ?' Or, if you prefer a later parallel, you resemble the Bellman in the *Hunting of the Snark:*

> ' He was thoughtful and grave—but the orders he gave
>    Were enough to bewilder a crew.
> When he cried, " Steer to starboard, but keep her head lar-
>       board,"
>    What on earth was the helmsman to do?'

Such impatience is very natural and understandable, but the objector may be asking for the impossible. Students to-day are often disposed to demand ' solutions ' for the major problems of life; but ready-made and fool-proof solutions are not to be had. The military analogy is instructive. Manuals of tactics or strategy, such as Field Service Regulations, have a useful function. But they are couched in very wide and general terms and they provide no infallible recipe for victory. The practical decisions which a great commander, like Napoleon, makes on the field of battle or in planning a campaign, he makes not by deduction from first principles, but by a kind of intuition. But Napoleon wins his battles and campaigns—and differs from Hitler—just because his is a trained intuition. His mind is steeped in military history and in the lessons which writers of authority have drawn from military history and the principles which they have evolved. So with our university problems. In practical decisions, ἐν τῇ αἰσθήσει ἡ κρίσις. But it is the φρόνιμος, the man of educated sagacity, whose intuition is most trustworthy; and a large part of practical wisdom is to have learned to ask the right questions.

# VII

## STUDIES

All the reasoning of the preceding chapters might be valid, so far as it goes, and yet lead up to nothing more than an ' ideology.' This is because the discussion has been mainly on the level of conscious and avowed principles; but, as everyone familiar with schools and colleges knows, there is often a yawning chasm between the principles they profess, without conscious insincerity, and the real impact which they make on their pupils. This may easily be a hundred miles away from what the Head of the institution wants it to be, and, very likely, supposes that it is. Intimate talk with boys or students, past or present, will give a picture in startling contrast to that portrayed in the prospectus or the addresses of Principal or Dean. So, if we want to know what universities are in fact, what are their most serious shortcomings and how these might be eliminated, we must go below the surface and enquire into their actual institutional working. For example we have to ask whether even the soundest policies are being nullified in practice by such things as class-segregation (till recently a characteristic of Oxford and Cambridge), lack of time for genuine thought, (overcrowded curricula are met with almost everywhere), geographical dispersion (shortage of residential accommodation makes this an acute problem for urban universities), want of opportunity for frequent contact between staff and students (all too few lecturers have ' a room of one's own ' in or near the university), a philistine and crudely utilitarian attitude to study imbibed by students before they reach the university, etc., etc. If these defects exist, how can they be cured? In this chapter we are to pursue such questions with special reference to the formal studies of a university. What types of course ought a university to offer and why, and what sort of teaching should it provide? On what principles should a student select his course and on what lines should he set about it?

## I  AIM

### a. Broad Culture?

Here we must recur to Professor Dobrée's challenge already quoted. The university, he holds, has been neglecting its primary task, which is to train an élite for life, and not merely for livelihood; 'the creation, generation by generation, in a continuous flow, of a body of men and women who share a sense of civilized values, who feel responsible for maintaining and developing them, who are unified by this culture and who by the simple pressure of their existence and outlook will form and be enlightened public opinion.' On his view there has been an inversion of values. Primary things have been crowded out and forgotten in the 'drive' for the economic and social advancement of the individual student. Similarly the Harvard Report condemns much higher education in the United States as producing only the narrow specialist with trained skill but without responsible judgment or a philosophy of life. However strongly we reaffirm the essentials of liberalism, mere *laissez-faire* is an impotent reply to Fascist or Marxist indoctrination.

But 'culture' is an ambiguous term. Here it is not used in the sense of some polish, decoration or grace which is superadded to a working life, as a bad architect, having designed his building for use, adds some ornamentation in order to beautify it. Admittedly a kitchen is a necessity to a house, a parlour a dispensable—possibly even a dubious—luxury. We mean 'the repertory of convictions which become the effective guide to a man's existence' (Ortega); that is, a picture of the world and of man which serves as a map by which to find a way through life. It gives rise to a hierarchy of values, so assimilated as to become a part of the self.

The difficulty is that, throughout history, education for such culture has been the monopoly of a privileged minority. The majority have been trained as specialists or 'hands' to perform certain specific services. Some of these services may demand a very high degree of skill; but the skills are menial skills, 'banausic' since they pertain to the function of servants. The masters require and receive a more all-round training. The long-term result of such excessive division of labour is that the creative minority becomes a clique and the uncreative majority becomes lop-sided. Sooner or later there is likely to be a revolt or 'secession of the proletariate.' Thus it is arguable to-day that the educated classes in this country have so misused their power and privileges as to have been weighed in the balances and found wanting and that they are now due for liquidation by God or man. But, in that case, the proletariate which succeeds them will need to devise for its own members an education for leadership which, as yet, they have not had. Education for functions associated with a servile status, however highly skilled, is not enough for those who are called on to bear the responsibilities of government. Hitherto the technical expert in industry or in government service, however accomplished, has commonly found himself in an inferior position. He has been asked to give technical advice, but final decisions have not rested with him. It is beginning to be realized that this is wrong and that the 'gentleman-amateur,' who is still in control, is unequipped for much of the work of statesmanship in so complex a world as ours has become. But if the technical expert's responsibility is to be enlarged, so must his training be. He who is to exercise imperial functions must be educated to think imperially.

The experience of the Adult Education movement furnishes a corroboration. As a term of art, 'Adult Education' is distinguished from 'Technical Education.' While not minimizing the value of technical training, the workers have resolutely refused to be fobbed off with it. They have felt that any offer of a merely technical training was to deprive them both of some of their birthright as men and of the opportunity to fit themselves to exercise power. Whatever its intrinsic interest or financial inducement, a merely vocational education for the working classes would, they felt, be an attempt 'to keep them in their place.'

Finally the argument for a 'cultural' education must be judged in the light of the world-crisis. In such a time first things must come first, necessities before luxuries. How this truism is applied to the university problem, will depend on how we picture the challenge of our time. If the world's troubles are due first and foremost to failure to apply systematically appropriate means to agreed ends, then what we need most is more and better experts, and the first task of education will be to produce them. On the other hand if our most intractable divisions are concerned with ends, if they arise from the difficulty which two men find in living together peaceably in a house, or two nations in a world, even when food and warmth and clothing and the other material necessities of life are amply provided, if the most serious menace is not scarcity but 'envy, hatred and malice and all uncharitableness'; then the mental commodity most in demand will be practical wisdom rather than specialized expertise. In that case the most urgent and practical service demanded of the universities will be that they should turn out an élite who will be men of judgment and 'skilled considerers of human things.'

## b. Occupational Training?

Whatever the strength of the case for a broad cultural education, simply to drop the occupational, and revert to the cultural aim, will not do. Here the Harvard Report is significant. *Ex hypothesi* it is concerned with the provision of liberal education for those who are perforce giving much of their time to a specialized training. It demands and plans liberal education as well as, but not instead of, the specialism which has come to stay. Indeed the authors expressly avoid the term ' Liberal,' and speak by preference of ' General ' education. They think the term ' Liberal ' has been spoiled by its traditional association with the education of a gentleman; that is, of a privileged and leisured class, the product of a thoroughly inequalitarian order of society, which, in the United States at least, is no longer practicable or tolerable.

' Liberal ' education indeed, as an exclusive ideal, suffers from four major faults. First it is parasitical. It requires in students leisure and disinterestedness. But a student can have leisure only if he does not have to worry about his daily bread; and he can afford not to worry about his daily bread only because someone else does the worrying for him. He must be waited on and he must be freed from anxiety. Thus the traditional liberal education presupposes a substratum of servile or menial labour. Cardinal Cullen indeed let the cat out of the bag : ' Too high an education will make the poor oftentimes discontented and will unsuit them from following the plough, or from using the spade, or from hammering iron or building walls.'[1] As soon as the universities are peopled largely by the unprivileged it is no longer possible to neglect occupational training. It may be, no doubt, that for certain callings, e.g. the civil servant or the banker, a general education is the best preparation at the university stage. But to urge that, is to accept a vocational test.

Secondly, it is remote from reality. It disdains or ignores the processes of production and distribution. But it is in those processes that the great bulk of the population are engaged. It is in that field that the real business of the world is done, the vital moral tensions occur, and the decisions are made to which others are subsidiary and which determine major social changes. By comparison the liberal and learned professions are not in mid-stream but in backwaters.

[1] Quoted *Memoirs and Correspondence of Lord Playfair*, p. 213.

Thirdly, it is hypocritical. In the medieval universities the work of the Arts Faculty was only preliminary to the higher work of the professional schools of Theology, Law and Medicine. 'Many universities,' says Rashdall, 'were almost entirely occupied with professional education.'[1] They prepared students, not for lifelong research, but for careers outside the university. In fact what they really provided then—and have generally striven to provide ever since—was a technical training for the use of a literary ruling class. It is humbug to speak as if they have ever really disregarded the professional interests and ambitions of their students. They have simply tended to concentrate on training for those professions which have, or used to have, the most social prestige.

Fourthly, it is snobbish. It is a relic of the aristocratic contempt of the landowner for the tradesman or mechanic or of the brain-worker for one who works with his hands and, in so doing, becomes hot, dirty and dishevelled, of the artist for the artisan. The origin of this attitude is Hellenic and it is a grave mistake for the Christian to adopt it. The Hebrew tradition has none of this fastidiousness. Hebrew society was not constituted of masters and slaves, but of peasant agriculturalists, fishermen and craftsmen. In it there is no insistence on the part of any class that work must be interesting or a means of self-expression. Work is frankly recognised as drudgery. Man can only earn his bread by the sweat of his brow.

### c. ' Redbrick' and ' Oxbridge'

In their aims there has notoriously been some difference of emphasis between the ancient English universities and the modern ones. It is true that ' Redbrick' has steadfastly refused to be what it might have been expected to become—merely a glorified Technical College. But both in Arts and in Science the bias has been occupational. The great majority of Arts students are going to be teachers and have come to the university to qualify themselves for that job. In Science the proportion of intending teachers is much smaller, but most of the others hope to go into industry in a technical capacity. Anyone who sees the graduands year by year can be confident that most of them have received a sound training in their special crafts. But it is much more doubtful whether most of them can satisfy Professor Dobrée's requirements and whether, *as a result of their years at the university,* they have notably improved in the power ' to think effectively, to communicate thought, to make rele-

[1] *Op. cit.* III, p. 461.

vant judgments and to discriminate among values.'[1] So far as the bulk of their students are concerned it is to be feared that few teachers at 'Redbrick' would dismiss this doubt with any confidence.

The answer has to be unfavourable, largely because it is not on producing these abilities that the modern universities have concentrated. The attitude both of the student and, in the main, of the university, has been that necessities must come before luxuries, and bread and butter have been the criterion. The modern English universities have done what a Harvard committee of 1850 criticized Harvard for not then doing, that is, ' to give people the practical instruction they want, and not a classical-literary course suitable only to an aristocracy.'[2] The Harvard committee wanted the university to help young men to become better farmers, mechanics and merchants. Our more urban universities have turned out high-grade clerks, teachers, engineers, and technical chemists; but the principle is the same. Ortega's generalization about the universities of the modern world has much truth when applied to ' Redbrick.' If, broadly speaking, the university in modern times has abandoned the transmission of culture, ' Redbrick ' has only faintly attempted it.

' Oxbridge ' on the other hand has notoriously set itself to give a more general training of the mind through courses in arts and in pure science. It has aimed at turning out graduates widely read, flexible and judicious, but not, in the main, at giving specific technical training. The tacit assumption behind this is twofold. Either the technical jobs are lower-grade work, on which the best minds with the best training would be thrown away, or the necessary technical equipment can speedily be acquired in practice by able men with a good general education. In the words of J. S. Mill, the object of university education is to make ' capable and cultivated human beings . . . Men are men before they are lawyers or physicians or manufacturers; and if you make them capable and sensible men, they will make themselves capable and sensible lawyers or physicians.'[3] A pertinent illustration of this attitude is afforded by those who enter the teaching profession. Practically all those from ' Redbrick ' have qualified themselves by acquiring the special Teachers' Diploma; in the schools to which they are

---

[1] This is the Harvard Committee's summary of the qualities which a general education should foster (op. cit., p. 65).
[2] Morison, op. cit., p. 287.
[3] Inaugural Address to the students of St. Andrew's, p. 7.

going it is a condition of employment. But at 'Oxbridge,' till lately a majority, and still a substantial proportion, of those who are going to teach—at least if they are men and if they hope to teach in a 'Public School' or university—undergo no such specialized training. They are not led to think it requisite.

Thus Peel and Gladstone went straight from their 'Double Firsts' at Oxford into the House of Commons and, with small delay, to the Front Bench; and they were probably the two Prime Ministers of the nineteenth century who acquired the greatest mastery of finance and administration. But even in their day the practice of the ancient universities was not without its critics. Robert Lowe, for example, cited examples, from his Australian experience, of men who had reason to lament their costly education which made them 'acquainted with the distant events of distant nations, but left them in utter ignorance of the laws of nature and placed them under immense disadvantages in the struggle with her which they had to maintain.'[1] And to-day we are being made far more constantly and painfully aware of the price that has to be paid when, for example, a civil servant goes to the Ministry of Agriculture or the Board of Trade with a First Class in 'Greats' or in the Classical or Mathematical Tripos, but without either practical experience or theoretical training in farming or in commerce.

In the university world to-day opinion is fairly well convinced that both these policies are one-sided and that some combination is needed. Neither the technical expert in blinkers nor the 'gentleman amateur,' neither the journeyman nor the dilettante, is equal to the demands of the times. Thus in 'Redbrick' there is widespread recognition of its present cultural defects and desire to amend them.[2] The grounds of this recognition are the same as those so admirably stated in the Harvard Report. The student is being trained with some success for competence in his special occupation. But that part of his education which looks to his life as a responsible human being and a citizen has fallen behind. Most of the detailed proposals discussed later in this and the following chapter spring from a sense of this need. On the other hand, there is a growing demand in responsible quarters that the universities shall

---

[1] *Life of Lord Sherbrooke II,* p. 22.

[2] It is another question whether this yet amounts to a burning conviction leading to action and guaranteeing a readiness to make the necessary sacrifices.

do more than they have so far done in the way of providing training for particular callings. The Barlow, the Goodenough, the Mc-
Nair and the Percy Reports all testify to this. To determine the
content of such courses is regarded as not being a matter for the
university alone, but for consultation between the university and
the leading practitioners in the professions concerned; and an
apparatus of advisory committees has been developed. Side by side
with this is a conviction that the leaders in our national life require
a more intimate understanding of technical problems. They should
at least be able to foresee, as for instance the protagonists in the
Industrial Revolution did not foresee, the secondary consequences
of their actions. For this they need to have some understanding of
the economic and psychological mechanisms of society and of the
contribution which technics can make. The 'enlightened expert'
must replace the 'gentleman amateur.'[1] So at 'Oxbridge' we now
have Institutes of Engineering, Agriculture, Forestry, etc. The
ancient, as well as the modern, universities are no longer educating
a leisured class. The training they give is assuming a more direct
relation to the world outside and the jobs which undergraduates
are presently to do.

So far there is wide agreement. But there is a further point,
even more serious and less generally appreciated. That is the
failure of each type just where it purports to be strong. Thus the
uncultured technician is crippled as a practical man in his own
calling. Even at the humblest level, the parent, already quoted, who
objected to his son's being taught poetry because the boy was going
to be a grocer, was penny-wise but pound-foolish. To get on with
his customers, his employers or his assistants, the grocer needs a
number of broadly human qualities. At a higher level, the need of
background is much greater. The technician who finds himself in
an administrative position of high responsibility requires much
general knowledge and flexibility of mind, a power of understanding
and getting on terms with all sorts and conditions of men, and a
grasp of the place of his own industry or technique in the whole
map. Perhaps the most successful administrator among modern
statesmen was Lord Haldane, incidentally a foremost exponent of
the theory of the liberal university. Haldane was a great War
Minister and effected a radical re-organization of the Army where
all before him had failed, not because he started with more technical military knowledge than his predecessors; he did not. He

[1] See Adolf Löwe, *The Universities in Transformation, passim.*

succeeded because, in his own phrase, he applied to his problem 'fundamental brainwork.' He first extracted from the Army Council a clear conception of what was to be the British Army's rôle in the event of a European war; and he then proceeded, resolutely and logically, to build up its organization on that principle, sweeping aside all that did not conform to it. Haldane was not a product of 'Oxbridge,' much as, in many ways, he resembled a 'Greats' man; Scotland and Germany were his nursing mothers. But he is an outstanding example of the academic mind at its best, applied to practical affairs.

On the other hand, however steeped in traditional culture, however widely read, versatile, urbane and judicious, a man is still an infra-man and an intellectual barbarian, if he is imperfectly aware of the vital intellectual currents of his own day. That is, he fails in culture as well as in practicality. He is not only ineffective, a child in business matters, (as were in Cecil Rhodes' eyes the Fellows of Oriel); he is also a lop-sided human being. This is one of Ortega's most penetrating insights. He contends that every age has its own system of vital ideas, that the vital system of to-day is based on physical science, that a sinister modern phenomenon is the prevalence of the 'learned barbarian' and that this class includes, not only the narrow specialist, but also the man imbued with the culture of the day before yesterday. Such a man does not really possess the freedom of the city. Ortega quotes from a Chinese thinker, 'How shall I talk of the sea to the frog, if he has never left his pond? How shall I talk of the frost to the bird of the summer land, if it has never left the land of its birth? How shall I talk of life with the sage, if he is the prisoner of his doctrine?'[1] In his view there are five great cultural disciplines, Physics, Biology, History, Sociology and Philosophy, and no one is a cultured person who has not some acquaintance, not so much with the conclusions as with the methods and mental outlook, of them all. The science man is commonly weak in the last three, the arts man in the first two. Only a minority of university teachers to-day satisfy Ortega's criterion of culture; most of us clearly do not.

It is clear then that the university must combine these aims, the occupational and the cultural. In framing its Degree Course, it must have in mind preparation for life. But it must remember that, for the vast majority of its students, life will be life in a job.

---

[1] *Op. cit.*, p. 58.

# 2  CONTENT

## a. Background—Rigidity and Elasticity

The medieval idea of the foundations of knowledge ' rarely went beyond knowing what somebody had said about something.'[1] In the early days of the universities knowledge in every field rested upon a few authoritative texts.  In Theology teachers expounded The Bible and Aristotle, in Medicine Hippocrates and Galen, in Law Justinian's Pandects or, if they were canonists, the Decretum of Gratian.  In Arts there were the classical, or at least the Latin texts.  But at first Arts was the elementary Faculty, the gateway to the others; and instruction consisted in the traditional *Trivium* (Logic, Grammar and Rhetoric) and *Quadrivium* (Arithmetic, Geometry, Music and Astronomy).  Later when for various reasons the higher Faculties had withered and for most purposes the Faculty of Arts had become the university, these became the germ of the modern Faculties of Arts and Pure Science.

By the beginning of the nineteenth century, in Oxford and Cambridge at least, Classics and Mathematics were firmly established as the fundamental and unchallengeable disciplines, the subjects without which you could not get a degree at all, the only subjects in which you could get an honours degree.[2]  Their sovereignty was defended on such grounds as the following.  First, as compared with all other literatures or sciences, they are basic.  No science can get any distance at all without the use of mathematics.  The modern European languages and literatures are largely derivative;[3] and in any case the bony structure of language, its grammar, has been evolved from a study of Latin and Greek and subsequently applied to other languages.  Thus other subjects cannot be understood without reference to Mathematics or Classics, but these can be understood without reference beyond themselves.  Secondly, they are articulated and rigorous as are no others.  Hence mathematical analysis or Latin prose composition provides a unique mental gymnastic.  To acquire information has only an inferior educational value.  Thirdly, they deal with what is objective and certain as opposed to what is subjective and conjectural.  ' 317 is a prime number, not because we think so or because our minds are

---

[1] Rashdall, *op. cit.* I, p. 440.
[2] In Cambridge at first even Classics did not stand on quite the same plane as Mathematics.  Mathematics was compulsory, and this caused much trouble to Macaulay among others.
[3] Non-European languages hardly entered into the picture.

shaped in one way rather than another, but *because it is so,* because mathematical reality is built that way.'[1] In the classics, the canons of excellence have long been fixed and the best models have been recognized. This contrasts with modern literature or philosophy where fashion is constantly changing or with history which is mostly the record of 'one damned thing after another' connected by no clear principle. Fourthly, in them expertise is attainable, recognizable, and communicable. The charlatan has small opportunity to deceive. As Aristotle said, no one will listen to a mathematician attempting to argue plausibly; he must offer exact demonstration or be silent.

By comparison, modern languages and literatures, history and philosophy, the empirical sciences, are either elegant accomplishments or merely hypothetical, uncertain and cloudy. The study of them is regarded as a 'soft option'—'a let-off to easy-going students from the realms of rigorous thought.'[2]

The multiplication of Honours Schools at Oxford and Cambridge during the last hundred years[3] has done away with the monopoly of Classics and Mathematics, and in the modern universities such a monopoly has never arisen. The change is due to a number of causes. An increasing number of the professions have demanded a university training for their recruits. Pressure has come from the schools to provide outlets for the large number of able potential students who have not the background, in Classics or Mathematics, which would enable them to take honours in those subjects, but who are of first-class calibre. The immense development in the scholarly study of other subjects has done much to remove the reproach of dilettantism, though, even so, it is true that many of those who have done the most brilliant work in the sciences or in the modern humanities enjoyed their first academic success by becoming 'Wranglers' or by achieving a First Class in Litt. Hum.

Not only in the universities but in the whole educational field, there has been during the last fifty years a strong and very natural reaction against any 'strait-jacket' conception of education. An obvious example is the modern attitude to the tragi-comedy of the Prince Consort's education of his eldest son. The Prince Consort's error lay in assuming that there was some fixed pattern to which

---

[1] Hardy, *A Mathematician's Apology,* p. 70.

[2] Morison, *op. cit.,* p. 349, cf. Whewell, *op. cit.,* pp. 31–40 and Newman, *op. cit.,* pp. 142ff.

[3] See Winstanley, *Late Victorian Cambridge,* Ch. V, for an account of the Cambridge development.

a Prince of Wales should conform.  When that educational scheme failed to overcome the Prince's passive resistance, no other was available and the Prince remained uneducated.  In the university the alternative scheme of education is deliberately ' student-centred.' The student is not to be fitted to his environment, but rather the environment to the student.  The queen of the sciences is no longer theology or metaphysics, but presumably psychology.  This aim calls for the utmost possible individualization of curriculum.  Each student is encouraged to develop his own tastes and aptitudes.  The primary function of the teacher then will not be to inculcate information; there will be no particular ground which all students ought to cover and no particular books which all students ought to read. Nor will it be to mould the pupil to any particular pre-determined shape.  It will be rather to act as a midwife and to assist the pupil to bring his own intellectual offspring to birth.  Only so, it is felt, can justice be done to his adult status; only so can *Lernfreiheit* be fully attained.

This policy, in its extreme form, has been subject to very damaging criticism.  First, to leave it to a young untrained man when he enters a university to select, without any guidance, from among a vast array of options, is to overburden his judgment.[1]  The policy of emphasizing the adult character and responsibility of the student is, in principle, right, for it is the way to develop capacity for responsibility; in this respect the British tradition has been defective.  But to carry it to an extreme point with students who normally enter at eighteen, fresh from school, is simply a *reductio ad absurdum*. Secondly, it has a devastating effect on the cultural unity of the university.  Those who hardly at all have read the same books or know the same things have little in common and only a slender basis for co-operation.  Lastly, and most important, its presupposition is quite unconvincing.  Human variation is certainly great; ' One man's meat is another man's poison.'  But we know now that, behind all our physical differences, certain ingredients of food in a certain balance are essential to bodily health.  There are dietary laws which we neglect at our peril.  But the ' elective system ' assumes that there are no such things as vitamins of the intellect, no objective principles of mental diet, an assumption with small intrinsic plausibility and much discredited by experience. Under this system the graduate is apt to have acquired nothing but a smattering of unrelated subjects.  He has learned ' less and less

[1] Hutchins, *op. cit.*, p. 71.

about more and more,' and he may end with little notion of what
'knowing' really means.

The United States is the land of extremes. The 'elective
system' was itself a reaction against the extraordinary woodenness
of the traditional curricula;[1] and during the last thirty years there
has been a growing reaction against its own extravagances, and the
tendency has been to restore some measure of intellectual discipline.
In this country, even in the heyday of liberalism, it was never
pushed to similar extremes. An Honours School must necessarily
have a considerable degree of coherence, but even in the Pass
Schools the principle of 'grouping' has been generally observed.
The combinations allowed have not been unlimited, and they have
been dictated by some principle of congruity or balance. To-day
new combinations are being explored, but they are never haphazard
combinations.

From a Christian standpoint, there is one general comment to
be made. For us both extreme rigidity and extreme licence are
ruled out. Any attempt to force students into one or other of a
few, preconceived, narrow moulds conflicts with the high value
which Christianity puts on the individual, its respect for his freedom
and responsibility, its sense of his essential being and destiny as a
child of God. On the other hand, the Christian sense of human
creatureliness and human perversion forbids us to take the idiosyncrasies of the individual, just as he stands, as a sufficient basis for
determining the lines of his education.

### b. The Present Position

At the conclusion of his *History,* Rashdall devotes some space to
reflections on the general character of the university. The main
body of his work is, of course, concerned with its origin and early
history. Universities, he points out, are the creation of the Middle
Ages, though learning in some shape has been pursued throughout
recorded history. At the end of his exhaustive study of the facts
he therefore naturally asks himself what are the distinctive marks
of the 'university,' what exactly is its new and specific contribution
to the world, and obviously he speaks with peculiar authority. In
one of his final sentences he describes the university as 'a place
where the different branches of knowledge are brought into contact
and harmonious combination with one another.'[2] Unfortunately

---

[1] Examples are given in Morison, *op. cit.,* pp. 26off, 344ff.
[2] *Op. cit.* III, p. 464.

the situation in the universities to-day, described in Chapter III (above), is often such as to make a mockery of this dictum. We have already quoted Archbishop William Temple's saying, that there is no relation between different subjects other than simultaneity and juxtaposition. Of course this is intentionally provocative and is not intended to be taken quite literally. But very many members of universities, both senior and junior, will feel painfully that it is less remote from the facts as known to them than is Rashdall's statement made fifty years ago. A growing number of both students and staff are becoming conscious of an undue contraction of intellectual range and a grave lack of intercommunication. We are split into sections, each inhabiting its own watertight compartment. The actuality of the university to-day flagrantly contradicts its ' idea '; the university is failing to be the university.

## (1) Arts and Science

Here is our biggest division. For practical purposes we fall apart into two groups, each living in its own separate intellectual world, and our respective ways of thinking do not overlap. Each group is lop-sided. We need, but do not get, a ' humane ' education, that is an education of the whole man (which must include both ' Humane Studies ' and the study of the Natural World). At the moment our greatest danger is that we should be excessively absorbed in immediate needs and neglect more fundamental ones—*propter vitam vivendi perdere causas.* We need above all things to cultivate our sense of values.

But it must be said emphatically that this does not mean a plea for more ' Arts ' and less ' Science.' Any such plea would be misconceived. Technical narrowness is found among ' Arts men ' at least as frequently as among ' Science men,' and a complacent acquiescence in their own one-sidedness even more often. ' The Science man knows nothing of Arts and regrets it; the Arts man knows nothing of Science and is proud of it.' This saying has gained currency lately, and it has sufficient truth in it to sting. Indeed in recent years, it is from the Science side that any considerable attempts at synthesis have come. The nemesis of an excessive emphasis upon ' Arts ' is seen in some oriental universities, where there is a glut of talkers and lawyers and a dearth of men who can, and will, tackle practical tasks of the utmost urgency. In these universities indeed a great switch-over of students to such subjects

M

as Agriculture, Engineering and Medicine is required not only for practical purposes, but in the interests of health, sanity and realism. The ' Babu ' is not only ineffective, he is a freak.

The ' Arts man ' and the ' Science man ' suffer from opposite limitations. The characteristic failing of the ' Arts man ' is bookishness. He inherits what Rashdall tells us was the supreme defect of the medieval universities, 'a fatal indifference to facts— of external nature, of history and of life. Books are put in the place of things.'[1] He does not rub or stretch or bump—or be bumped— enough. He breathes too exclusively the stagnant air of the study and exposes himself too little to the sting and throb of bumping obstructiveness. The ' Science man ' on his part is apt to develop too little his sensitiveness and appreciation and to have small training in the reflective assessment of values. He is liable to dismiss as illusion, or to belittle as subjective caprice, the difference between Salisbury Cathedral and the Albert Memorial. Concentrating for his own purpose on what is clear and precise, he tends to overlook contexts and nuances. He is blind to that which, being on the fringe of consciousness, is obscure, eludes exact statement and shades away illimitably into the distance, and thus he may miss whole vistas of reality. He may lose the disturbing beauty of the diamond in stating the chemical formula of its composition.

> *Dann hat er die Teile in seiner Hand,*
> *Fehlt leider! nur das geistige Band.*

### (2) ' Subjects '—The Myth of Fixed Species

The list of separate ' subjects ' recognized as such by the universities at any one time is due, in considerable part, to historical accident; and, in any case, ' all lines of demarcation are purely provisional.'[2] But these lines are often regarded as though they were absolute and final. The student who was advised to read some Burke for his course in Political Science, and demurred, saying, ' But I did Burke in my English course,' was the victim of a not uncommon superstition. This sense of boundary lines across which one must not trespass has various causes. One is the short-sighted utilitarianism of students exemplified by the student of Dr. Hutchins's anecdote (quoted above, p. 58) who demurred to being asked to consider the social and economic background of a law. If we are candid, we must admit that another cause is sometimes the inertia of

---

[1] *Op. cit.* III, p. 457. The Renaissance did not mend matters by substituting classical learning for philosophy.
[2] Paulsen, *op. cit.*, p. 322.

teachers, who have, as it were, acquired a vested interest in the *status quo*. They have grown accustomed to existing landmarks and have written their lectures on that basis; and they are reluctant to make a fresh start.

With this goes a somewhat exaggerated suspicion of new and wide subjects, which cut across existing boundaries and are often themselves not very clearly delimited. Education, Psychology, Geography and Sociology are obvious examples. Graham Wallas relates how he advised two Oxford undergraduates of his acquaintance to read some Psychology and later found that each had been discouraged by his tutor from acting on the advice; one tutor had adduced 'the curiously scholastic reason that Psychology was neither Science nor Philosophy..'[1] It was, as it were, a ' gate-crasher' having no right to admission to the university. No doubt fear of the charlatan is a respectable motive, but it sometimes cloaks an obstinate reluctance to move out of accustomed ruts.

This fissiparous tendency is enhanced by the distinction between ' Honours ' and ' Ordinary ' degrees. In England, two-thirds of the students work for Honours and nearly all the abler and more ambitious students are among these. (Scotland has a different tradition and the proportion there is much smaller.) But Honours courses are commonly much more specialized than those for the Ordinary Degree. Hence specialization tends to be a condition of high academic distinction. This has its good side; it is good to have learned one thing so well that you know, and can show others, what knowing means. To know when it is that you don't know, is a valuable fruit of scholarly humility. But here a distinction must be made. ' It is not my subject,' is a justifiable demurrer, if it means ' I cannot speak on it *ex cathedra*.' But it may mean, ' I cannot speak on it at all and disclaim all responsibility concerning it.' Then it is demoralizing, for we are constantly called on to act intelligently in spheres too wide to be known exhaustively.

These factors tend to split up the academic body into sections and to accentuate the tendency of its individual members towards an extremely contracted range of knowledge and interest. Unfortunately there are other reasons for this, some of them outside the control of the university. The ' Oxbridge ' tradition presupposes that undergraduates come from educated homes; that is, from homes where there are plenty of books, where conversation is sometimes on intellectual themes and where interesting people come and

[1] *Human Nature in Politics*, p. 124.

go. To-day, at 'Oxbridge' as well as at 'Redbrick,' the majority of students do not come from homes of that kind, and accordingly labour under a severe handicap. Largely owing to the pressure of examinations, school has for most of them been able to do little to redress the limitations of the home. When they get to the university, they are working under a series of pressures, the weight of which is perhaps not yet fully realized by many of the older teachers. There is pressure to cover the ground of an exhaustive and exhausting syllabus, to make ends meet, to make sure of a job; for many there is the pressure of uncertainty about personal standards and beliefs. Above all is the fact that a whole generation has not got the normal expectation of life. Whatever the actuarial calculations, the normal, healthy young man of university age at ordinary times looks forward confidently to another fifty years of activity; to-day he does not. The psychological effect is pervasive. Most of the older among us have not yet got a full imaginative grasp of what it means to grow up in an age of insecurity. Many a student's life to-day is dominated by *Angst*.

This is inimical both to intellectual adventure and to the impulse to 'stand and stare.' When students get to the university they are not often disposed to push open the doors of subjects other than their own and to gain a nodding acquaintance with them. For such explorations they lack time, opportunity, incentive and encouragement. Though they are more rigorously selected than their predecessors, and on the average more able, their intellectual initiative tends to be smaller and their range of interest to be more circumscribed. An instructive contrast is provided by the experience of Arthur Balfour at Cambridge eighty years ago. ' There was nothing unduly irksome about the discipline. I was never taught anything I did not want to learn. I was not required to produce essays on subjects about which there was nothing I desired to say, nor to attend lectures I did not wish to hear. Yet in spite of this apparent laxity, there was about the place an atmosphere of free interest both in things intellectual and in things athletic which I found infinitely attractive . . . I ministered, as the mood took me, to a very catholic appetite for literature, for science, and for history.'[1] Obviously the happy-go-lucky system, or absence of system, of Mid-Victorian Cambridge can furnish no model for to-day. Balfour was a member of a privileged caste whose circumstances protected them from all need to toil or spin, and he was

[1] *Chapters of Autobiography*, pp. 33-34, 50.

also a man of exceptional mental power. No doubt very many of his contemporaries used their freedom to learn nothing at all. Nevertheless his experience contained an element of great value, which belongs to ' the idea of the university ' and is in danger of being squeezed out.

### (3)  The Influence of Research

Another factor making for concentration of attention on a limited field is the growing part in the work of universities which is taken by research. This affects students as well as staff. In many fields it is now common for the abler students to be expected themselves to have some first-hand experience of research before they leave the university. Either it is a condition of the highest honours, or it is the growing practice for the better men, after taking their first degree, to take a second, research, degree. This is a salutary departure from the older English practice. It has mostly taken place in the present century, and ' Redbrick ' rather than ' Oxbridge ' has been the pioneer. In the nineteenth century indeed the backwardness of our ancient universities in this respect was notorious. Matthew Arnold said that Oxford and Cambridge were essentially glorified *Hauts Lycées,* where men could prolong their school education under admirable conditions. The graduate who wished to go further, and to engage in some systematic advanced study in his own line, must go to Germany to realize his ambition. Oxford and Cambridge did next to nothing to promote such study.[1] In modern American terminology, they were all ' College ' and hardly at all ' University.' In contrast to this, the better students to-day are not only made acquainted with the products of investigation, but are admitted to the workshop and encouraged to lend a hand there. They not only learn about the mental mining and quarrying which is the source of knowledge; in a modest way they participate in it. Up to a point this is thoroughly healthy, and for future teachers it is indispensable.

It can, however, be abused. It is only in some fields that the neophyte can make original contributions of any value. In the search for some task which is both within his compass and has not already been performed, the youthful researcher is driven further and further from the centre to themes which are peripheral and, too often, trivial. But it is a disastrous mistake to turn the promising student, immediately he graduates, out of the main road ' into

[1] *Op. cit.,* p. 286.

some little side-track, to research in some unimportant subject, simply because it has not been done before.'[1]  As usual, America leads the way in extravagances.   Dr. Flexner pillories a large number of these, including M.Sc. theses on 'Trends in Hosiery Advertising,' 'Buying Women's Garments by Mail,' and 'A Time and Motion Comparison of Four Methods of Dishwashing.'   But it is to be feared that the titles of B.Litt theses even at Oxford and Cambridge would show some queer examples.   On the other hand, such researches seem rarely to be concerned with the social effects of technical advances—a type of investigation which might be highly educational.

The result is too often the production of a 'botched scholar' instead of an 'educated man.'[2]  Even for the future scholar or scientist, premature specialization is to be deprecated.   He is liable to be buried under a mass of details and problems at a stage when his real need is a general survey of the field in which he is to work. No doubt it is a great experience for the really outstanding young graduate to be caught up in an exciting investigation directed by an inspiring professor; and this may be some compensation for any restriction of its compass.   But the great majority of those who take the Bachelor's or Master's degree by research, are not going to be lifelong research workers.   Pure learning is not, and should not be, their primary aim.   Also, to train their own successors, though an important, is not the chief, educational task of professors. Professor Bernal indeed goes so far as to say that no student should leave the university without having done one or two years of research.[3]  He points out that, for the future school teacher for instance, it is more important to know how science is done than to amass information which, if required, can be got later from books.   On such a matter he speaks with authority and he may well be right.   But it does not follow that the tyro must aspire to add to the stock of the world's knowledge; his object may reasonably be to educate himself.   He need not search painfully for some problem, which no one has tackled—and which *ex hypothesi* is likely to be unimportant.   For instance, it is part of the regular training of an architectural student that he should produce designs; he does this as an exercise and no one supposes that the buildings are to be put up; nor is he given tasks which are out of the common

[1] E. de Selincourt, quoted in Board of Education Departmental Committee's Report on *The Teaching of English in England*, p. 236.
[2] These terms are Professor Dobrée's.
[3] *Op. cit.*, p. 249.

and which no one else has done. So, both in science and in arts, it is true that ' the beginner has no right to expect any but subjective discoveries.'[1]

The introduction of research into the curriculum of young students, graduate or undergraduate, is only an offshoot of the radical change which has taken place in the whole orientation of the university in this country. The change affects staff even more than students. Investigation, it is now understood, is, equally with education, the duty of every teacher. In the main this change has been beneficent, and even the university's teaching work has been immensely invigorated. But at the moment there is some disproportion which has unfortunate repercussions. For promotion, and for appointment to all posts other than the lowest, scientific productiveness is widely regarded as being, not only of high, but of exclusive importance.[2] By comparison, such things as power of presentation, interest in pupils, contribution to corporate life are hardly taken into account. Or, if in this statement there is some exaggeration, at least it is widely believed by junior staff. The primacy and indispensability of research for purposes of advancement have been successfully instilled into them by the heads of their departments. When they have performed their routine teaching duties, they feel themselves under pressure to give all their energies to this to the exclusion of other things.[3] Those who do give time to other things, e.g., to contacts with students, sometimes complain that this is a barrier to promotion; it is no way to get a chair. Undoubtedly some of this grumbling must be discounted. In any event mediocrity is likely to resent being passed over. But, even so, it is hard to avoid the conclusion that disproportionate weight is often attached to the number and bulk of published papers.

This is not only harmful to the other activities in which members of the staff should engage; it is liable to affect banefully their own long-term contributions to thought and knowledge. Like the students they tend to be deflected into by-ways, where originality can more easily be claimed, to take up lines of study which promise

[1] Sir Oliver Lodge, *The City University*, p. 19.

[2] ' By the careful editing of a text he has qualified himself for senior academic office.' This sentence from a letter of commendation is a straw showing the direction of the wind.

[3] In one Common Room recently it was said : ' All the ones really interested in students have gone now that old X and Y have retired.' This remark is exaggerated, but it has a spice of truth in it.

quick returns, and so to sacrifice quality to quantity and depth to clarity. As Professor Bernal points out in an admirable passage,[1] this is singularly unlike the procedure of the great scientists (such as Darwin) who have often spent many years in preliminary study, meditation, and apparently aimless experiment.

But the worst effects are seen in Arts. As investigators and original thinkers, our Arts Faculties were comparatively late in the field. This may partially explain why they have tended to imitate, somewhat slavishly and with unfortunate consequences, the methods of the natural scientist. They have been inclined to emphasize, and to select for study, just those aspects of things which are quantitative and measurable. In Literature, for instance, they have been preoccupied with linguistic and biographical detail, because that admits of such treatment. But this involves them in a glaring lack of proportion. As one critic has put it, the *raison d'être* of Departments of Literature is, presumably, that poets have some access to truth, different from the purely rational. But the one thing a Professor must not do is to say what contribution to truth this or that poet can make. He may tell you ' how many variants there are between the first and second edition, where the poet got his story from, how his poem suggests that he was once seduced by a dark lady in the Charing Cross Road—in fact anything but what really matters if the presuppositions implied in the existence of Departments of Literature are at all sound.' In this way a faulty sense of values is silently and irresistibly diffused.

' For God's sake, stop researching for a while and begin to think.' This is an adjuration applicable to many scholars. We need—and should encourage and honour—not only discoverers of facts hitherto unknown but explorers of ideas and rethinkers of values. It has been well said that we should speak of the *improvement*, rather than of the *extension* of knowledge. We want more thinking about the importance of things already known. Books like Fisher's *History of Europe*, Trevelyan's *History of England* or *Social History*, Whitehead's *Science and the Modern World* and Bernal's *The Social Function of Science*, do not profess to make known new facts but to throw new light on the significance and interrelations of old facts. In so doing they are performing a function no less important, no less admitting of the highest distinction, no less truly original than that of works of ' research ' in the narrower and more technical sense. They help us to get closer to the heart of

[1] *Op. cit.*, pp. 54-55.

things and to look once again at familiar objects in such a way that they take on a new meaning for us. Fresh and unexpected features make their appearance, and sometimes a whole landscape lights up.

### c. Lines of Advance

A healthy intellectual ferment is beginning to make itself felt in the universities, and it has been much accelerated by the dislocations of the war years. Both objectives and methods are being re-thought. The new *Universities Quarterly*, the *Cambridge Journal*, the Manchester organ *Humanitas,* the Universities Number of the *Political Quarterly*, the longer-standing *Universities Review*, the books of 'Bruce Truscot' and many others, are providing and stimulating constructive thinking. But the ferment is still quite unequal to the occasion. Many of the strictures which we have just made elicit a fairly general, but rather tepid, assent. There is nothing like enough intensity of conviction to overcome the prac-tical difficulties in the way of alteration and that 'impalpable, resistant tradition as difficult to penetrate as a London fog,' which Flexner detected in Oxford and Cambridge, but which is familiar to university reformers everywhere. In practice the transmission of culture in Ortega's sense is still regarded as a luxury rather than a necessity. But this is a gross, and at this time even a catastrophic, error of judgment. Yet nothing adequate will be done without an overpowering conviction that the present one-sidedness is wrong and a general sense of shame and of personal responsibility. This is essential. Given this, there is room for much experiment in method. We are still indeed at the stage of trial and error, but the following are some of the paths which are being explored.

### (1) Single Integrating Courses

A generation ago McTaggart used to give a popular course of lectures in Philosophy to all who cared to come. In quite recent years Professor Hodgson in Oxford and Dr. Whale in Cambridge have given courses in Christian Doctrine. All these were voluntary and the two latter were given in response to a demand. They were given on the personal responsibility of the Professor concerned, but similar courses might be statutory and even be followed by examina-tion, as, till fairly recent years, were Divinity examinations in Oxford and Cambridge. Their common feature is that they pose to students the problem of a philosophy of life, and, it may be, offer a solution. The enormous audiences which attended the lectures of the theologians give significant testimony to the demand. But though such lectures can effect something, they cannot effect much. At best they offer 'a pill for an earthquake.' The hiatus is too great between the lectures and the whole of the remainder of a student's studies and corporate life. In this sense they cannot 'integrate.' They do not knit up John Smith, the engineer, with John Smith, the Christian or Marxist. They may help John Smith to achieve a conscious philosophy of life or to make him a Christian or at least remove obstacles to his being a Christian. What they cannot do is really to integrate his *Weltanschauung* with his specialist working life and its presuppositions. Indeed how few lecturers would be competent even to attempt that! It is not really possible to think imperially for an hour a week, if all the rest of your life is centred on the parish pump. It is generally agreed that democracy has worked in Great Britain better than in most other countries simply because our people have more experience of responsible deliberation in their ordinary lives, in local government, friendly societies, trade unions, in 'their neighbourhoods and familiar provincial connections.' Where these are absent, plebiscites are a sham. So here, one hour's airing will not free minds which are confined to their grooves for the rest of the working week. Ortega indeed avers that the requirement of such a course, where it exists, is a 'miserable residue' of something which once was meaningful (when culture was taken seriously), but has ceased to serve any end at all.[1] To regard such a course as likely to go near to satisfying the need which evokes it, is disastrously to underestimate the tension and painful searching of heart involved in genuine integration.

## (2) Broader-based General Degree Courses

Here the American universities have been the pioneers. There are two principles on which the broadening of courses through the addition of new subjects may be carried out. Such subjects may be selected because of their affinity, or because of their unlikeness, to the main subject of study. It is the latter principle which has been most explored in the United States and is most relevant for our purpose. Within the last year or two valuable reports have been produced at Harvard, Yale and Princeton. These differ instructively in detail, but resemble one another in the general

[1] *Op. cit.,* p. 43.

character of their findings.[1]   Their objective is to provide some
common intellectual experience for all students and to ensure that
they shall all have some understanding of the main different fields,
of the laws they have in common and of the principal differences
in their aims and methods.   Thus the Harvard Report distinguishes
three main fields—the Humanities, the Social Sciences and the
Natural Sciences.   It proposes not to abolish specialization, but to
supplement it.   Out of sixteen courses necessary for the Degree, no
less than six must be in ' General Education '; that is, directly concerned with general relationships and values, with ' what needs to
be done and to what ends ' rather than with ' what can be done
and how to do it.'   Both in Humanities and in Social Science one
particular course is compulsory for all.[2]

In boldness and thoroughness these programmes are much ahead
of anything on similar lines that has yet been proposed in this
country.   They constitute a resolute attempt to provide some common core of knowledge and ideas and some genuine preparation
for life and for citizenship.   But they do not meet the needs of the
British Honours student; and, in a minor degree, they suffer from
some of the same limitations as the single integrating course.

### (3)   Combined Honours Schools

These are devised specially to meet the British or rather the English
predilection for ' Honours.'   They have already been introduced,
perhaps a little timidly, in a number of universities.   They include
many, and are likely to include more, different combinations both
in Science and in Arts.[3]   Theoretically the development of such
Schools should go far to meet the needs of general education, but
in practice there are various drawbacks and there has been no
great rush to enter them.

First, they still lack prestige, in spite of the distinguished example
of the Oxford School of *Literae Humaniores*.   The specialist heresy
dies hard, and there is some suspicion that they are really ' soft
options.'   There is also a good deal of uncertainty about their
market value.   Secondly they are not usually organic growths but

---

[1] Of these the Harvard Report is the fullest and the most accessible to
English readers. (*General Education in a Free Society*, from which we
have already quoted extensively).

[2] Owing to wide differences in mathematical equipment, this was not thought
practicable in Natural Science.

[3] As yet there has been little attempt to combine the two, and the existing
organization of Faculties would present some difficulty.

are pieced together ingeniously from fragments of existing, special Honours Schools. Students who take them attend lectures and laboratories side by side with students of the special Honours Schools. The lectures are primarily designed for specialists, and the students are taught by specialists who are not themselves the product of the General Honours School. They are nobody's child, in the sense that there is ordinarily no professor or dean whose first interest and responsibility they are. In these circumstances they tend not to be coherent wholes in the sense in which ' Greats ' is an coherent whole; and, to fulfil the demands of two or three different sets of specialists, they are liable to be overweighted. No doubt these defects are due in part to shortage of money and staff, and may be temporary.

### (4) Widened Professional Courses

Probably this is the most hopeful line of approach. It is so, *economically,* because the vast majority of students to-day must qualify themselves to earn their living immediately on leaving the university. Peel, Gladstone and Balfour were rich men's sons and did not have to concern themselves about this. It is so, *educationally,* because the teacher starts from the student's, already existing, centre of interest and shows him that he cannot do his own job properly without relating it to many other things and indeed, ultimately, to the universe. It is also the most effective method, in that cultural and occupational education are related from the first and do not require to be brought together at a late stage, when the student's personality may already have been ' split.' Thus the doctor has some concern with the whole lives of his patients, because their mental state affects their physical condition; and the teacher is concerned with the whole lives of his pupils. The scientist cannot disinterest himself in the human effects of the atom bomb, nor the engineer in the economics, psychology and ethics of labour management.

This method can be illustrated a little more fully from the fields of Engineering and Medicine. A method of widening engineering education is sketched by Mr. David Paton.[1] ' We have to find some way of giving " education for citizenship " and more, in an organic relation to engineering and the life of an engineer. One method is to start with the factory. Works visits can be extended to cover matters not of technical interest, but of industrial relations,

---

[1] *Blind Guides?*, pp. 64, 66.

and be followed by discussions with works managers, specialists in industrial hygiene, trade-union leaders, sales managers and so on. This leads on to other subjects—the way in which the freedom of action of a works manager is circumscribed by the higher control (and thence to the organisation of capitalist industry, trusts, holding companies, the place of banks in the system—economics and economic power generally); the place of medicine and psychology; the basis of decisions taken by responsible persons in industry (" efficiency," " the service of the community," or something else— leading on to ethics and philosophy); the clash of interests between manager, worker and consumer, and the ways in which their interests are reconciled and their disputes settled (leading on to a study of politics, and the theory of the class structure of society and thence also to ethics and philosophy); the place of industry in the community (with reference not only to consumers, but also to the effect of an industry on the town in which it is situated and so on).

'These tentative suggestions would involve lectures as well as " field work "; but the subjects are all professed in most universities already, the change involved being no more than what is already admitted on all sides to be urgent, namely the reduction of departmentalization. It is not to be expected that the engineer will acquire any profound knowledge of economics, ethics or industrial hygiene; it is to be hoped that he would not merely be given neat answers to the problems raised. What such courses should do is to indicate the kinds of problems which are raised and the ways in which they are susceptible of solution—not a scheme of technical instruction, but a scheme of instruction in method, with sufficient technical matter to make the method intelligible.'

It is interesting to compare with this proposal an account of work actually done by Professor Aydelotte when Professor of English at the Massachusetts Institute of Technology.[1] He started from the engineer's desire to write a clear business letter or engineering report. This led to a discussion of what is meant by ' Engineering.' Is it a ' trade ' or a ' profession?' What is its function in society? Is it concerned with the direction of human as well as material forces? This leads to the further question, ' What should be the aim of Engineering education?' and to some introduction to writings on all these questions by distinguished engineers. This

[1] Some account of this is given in the Board of Education Departmental Report on *The Teaching of English,* 1921, p. 156.

opens up the question of the relation of Applied to Pure Science, and of the relation of Science to Literature; and here again there are the books of T. H. Huxley, Tyndall and others to be discussed. In this way the young engineer, in pursuit of his own proper business, is led by a continuous path to English Literature, and he is now ready for some industrial and social history. ' We do not ' says Professor Aydelotte, ' ask our students to be ashamed of being engineers, but we do ask them to be ashamed of being narrow, one-sided engineers.'

Another illustration is to be found in the recent Goodenough Report, which is in process of transforming medical education. For our purpose its most significant feature is that, at one and the same time, it is concerned to give medical education a greater cultural width and to relate it more closely to the practical work which most of the students will ultimately have to do. The Committee assert that the doctor should have an outlook beyond the confines of an examination syllabus, a well-disciplined mind, wide human interests, and an intelligence able to move with the progress of human knowledge. He should observe accurately, reason logically, assess the claims of new knowledge, and possess a sympathetic understanding of people and their environment. Therefore his training must be concerned with general principles rather than with a mass of factual information and must stimulate independent thought rather than memory. At the same time the basic training is to be related more closely to what the average G.P. will need in his daily practice. At present the student meets during his clinical training with a number of types of rather unusual disease which occupy the beds and are of interest to his teachers. On the rare occasions when he subsequently comes across these in his practice, he will have to hand them over to the specialist for treatment. But he has little experience of types of case he will meet every day in practice, because they are not usually serious enough to require hospital treatment. The Committee propose a ruthless cutting out, during the basic training, of time-consuming clinical studies remote from the ordinary daily needs. These are relegated to the advanced training of the specialist.

These are only illustrations of a kind of reshaping of curricula which is required in most fields. Above all the student's attention should be drawn to his presuppositions, that is to the judgments, historical, legal, scientific and literary, the tacit assumptions psychological, sociological and philosophical which are involved in

his course of study. If he is a Christian, he should be encouraged
to relate these to the presuppositions of his faith, and, if they are in
conflict, to decide where he stands. This sort of enquiry is almost
entirely neglected at present, largely because most teachers are
themselves unconscious of such implications. Yet they should be
the headstone of the corner.

Before leaving the question of professional courses, it is pertinent
to raise an extremely topical question. For which jobs should a
university offer specific preparation by its degree or diploma
courses? If it is asked to provide a degree in journalism or
librarianship, mining or building, on what principles is it to decide?
Flexner urges that it is only the 'learned professions' for which
universities can make this kind of special provision without lower-
ing their standards and compromising their character; that is, those
professions which have their roots deep in cultural soil and derive
their essential character from intelligence.[1] Another criterion he
suggests is, that they should be professions which are primarily
objective and disinterested rather than actuated and obsessed by
the 'profit motive.' On these principles he would, himself, admit
law and medicine but he would reject most others.

It is likely that a large number of Dr. Flexner's academic readers
will feel that he is setting himself to defend a vital principle, but
they may feel less confident that he has stated it correctly or
applied it rightly. In particular they must ask themselves searchingly whether the operative reason which in the past has caused
the singling out of law and medicine is not social and conventional.
May not the distinctive mark of law and medicine, as compared
for instance with glass technology or industrial fermentation or
sanitary engineering, be less any intellectual superiority than simply
that they are professions which gentlemen have been accustomed
to enter?

The proper criterion is to be found in method of treatment
rather than in subject-matter. There is no subject which, in itself,
is common or unclean. It is not reason enough to turn down any
proposal, that it is directed to training for a job which has hitherto
been regarded as low-grade or 'banausic.' It is not reason enough
to justify acceptance, that there is a vigorous demand and influential support is forthcoming. The right questions to ask are these,
What is the proposed syllabus and what are the qualifications of
the teachers available? Does it confine itself to imparting 'the

[1] *Op. cit.*, p. 30, *cf.* Hutchins, *op. cit.*, p. 40.

tricks of the trade' or does it concern itself with fundamental principles? Cannot the professional training in question be carried on as well anywhere else as in a university? Is the demand a genuine demand for the intellectual improvement of the training available, or is it only a snobbish demand for the right to attach, to a training already in being, a label which is popularly supposed to be superior? Can the university undertake the work without prejudice to existing commitments and standards? In these matters the university must steer a middle course between ' accumulative inertia' and ' spendthrift disassociation.'

## 3    METHODS

### a.    Lectures

Everywhere the lecture, that is, a formal discourse of a teacher to a class, is, and always has been, the chief normal means of instruction.[1] But in this country at least it has recently come under very heavy criticism. It is questioned whether its survival, or at any rate its predominance, is not a particularly harmful example of academic inertia and conservatism.

A number of charges are levelled against the lecture-system. First, it is a form of mass-production, and, as such, it is out of place in a university which must aim at excellence. It is impersonal, a lecture being given to a large number of students at once and admitting of no individual attention. In schools very large classes are admittedly an abuse. Secondly, it does not exercise the mind of the student, whose part is only to be a passive recipient. Worse than this, in a large proportion of lectures, the student is throughout the hour writing for dear life, in a desperate attempt to commit to paper as much as possible of the lecturer's words. During that time he is, in effect, reduced to a recording machine and is quite unable to give his mind to the matter which his ears are absorbing. In theory he will do that ' to-morrow,' but ' to-morrow never comes.' Thirdly, the whole performance is incredibly wasteful of time. The number of man-hours consumed is shocking and is quite disproportionate to the intellectual harvest that is reaped. That could be achieved far more economically if the lecturer were to publish the text of his lectures, or at least to have it multiplied and

---

[1] The only obvious exceptions to this generalization are Oxford and Cambridge, at certain periods in their history, and, in modern times, the Faculties of Science where much of the instruction is given informally in laboratories by demonstrators.

circulated. Fourthly, the effect is positively harmful in so far as students come to expect that the lectures they attend will supply all the material they need; ' and that if only he attends them regularly, records them accurately, studies the record assiduously, and in the day of reckoning reproduces it faithfully, he will be assured of a good degree.'[1] Unfortunately that expectation has sometimes been justified, though more often perhaps in the past than at the present day. Thus accurate memorizing will be set before the student as his goal rather than wide reading and original thought. Lastly, as we all know, a considerable proportion of lectures are bad. In this country, unlike France, little attention has been paid to the technique of lecturing. In general, lecturers are conscientious about the matter of their lectures, but give little thought to their form or their delivery. Professors of European reputation have been known to drone throughout the hour from a dull manuscript in a voice inaudible beyond the front two benches. Also lecturers seldom improve, for they suffer from an almost total lack of criticism. If they write a book, reviewers will tell them of its faults; but students who attend lectures are usually too polite and too tongue-tied to perform this service.

Much of this criticism is valid. But it has now become fashionable to decry lectures indiscriminately; and, like most fashions, it is overdone. In fact, the lecture may be a very fine instrument of education and nothing else can fully take its place. It is quite untrue that it is, always and only, a cumbrous way of doing something which can, equally well and less wastefully, be done otherwise. Even Professor Bernal, who is one of its severest critics, admits the need for a certain type of lecture, that which keeps pace with a growing subject when textbooks quickly get out of date, but we would take wider ground. A lecture is much less impersonal than a book, since it involves a meeting of speaker and hearers. Nothing can replace the stimulus of a great teacher. The real justification for the lecture is that it brings such a man face to face with a far larger number of students than is possible through tutorial hours and seminars alone. Many of us, who look back on our own student days and ask ourselves what we acquired which was of lasting value, will feel that the high lights were the lectures of one or two great men which we were fortunate enough to attend. And what we got from them consisted not mainly in the substance of what they said, most of which we have forgotten. It was rather

[1] U.G.C. Report, 1929-30 to 1934-35.

N

an attitude; some portion of their own faith and fire was com-
municated, something of their profound belief in their own subject
and of the reverent temper in which they approached it. Such
kindling depended entirely on their personal presence, on an actual
'meeting.' Some of the 'Ordinary Classes' of famous Scottish
professors have proved to be the outstanding intellectual impetus
in the life of some of their hearers. But those who have 'sat under'
Edward Caird or Henry Jones or—to name one living example—
Sir Herbert Grierson, will realize that a mere reading of the text
of the lectures they heard, without the presence of the man and
the sound of the living voice, would have given them only a fragment of that which they have in fact received. Further, a lecture
need not be an entirely one-sided affair; it admits of give and take.
The lecturer may watch the faces of his audience. Where they
are perplexed or have not taken his point, he can repeat, elaborate,
or give fresh illustrations to meet their difficulties. Where he sees
response, he may himself gain new inspiration. Gladstone said of
the orator that, what he receives from his audience in vapour, he
gives back in flood. It is true that oratory is not the business of
the lecturer; but with him too, at his best, the two-way exchange
should exist. Because a lecture-audience is not vocal, it is not
necessarily condemned to be passive.[1]

Even so, much of the indictment still holds. The lecture *may*
be an effective instrument of education; but what proportion of
university lectures has in fact the dynamic quality of which we
have been speaking? Though there are brilliant exceptions,
lecturers as a body need to develop a new intellectual conscience
in regard to the art of lecturing. To suppose that this either comes
by nature or does not come at all, and so does not require thought
and trouble, is a groundless superstition. In any event, whatever
the quality of lectures, the crying evil is that the bulk of students
attend far too many of them. 'A student should not be taught
more than he can think about.' To profit from most lectures, a
student needs to go over his notes carefully, to look up the refer-
ences and to read some at least of the books mentioned. That is,
he needs to spend a lot of time on them, other than in simply
memorizing them, and in practice the time is seldom available.
Most students are stuffed with much more mental food than they
are able to digest. It would be better if they were required to

---

[1] A brilliant defence of the lecturing-system is to be found in Paulsen,
*op. cit.*, pp. 191–199.

attend only half of their present number of lectures and were able to spend some of the time thus saved in digesting those they do attend. This would involve a ruthless cutting down of existing requirements. It would mean that both student and tutor must, once for all, abandon the vicious idea that lectures are designed to ' cover the ground.' They may light up brilliantly certain portions of it; but, for covering the necessary ground on which he is going to be examined, the student must learn to rely on private reading under tutorial advice.

### b. Tutorial System

The distinctive mark of the tutorial system is that it is informal and catechetical. The tutor takes a single student, or at the outside two or three together, usually in his own private room. The pupil produces a composition or essay for criticism, or he is asked questions or engaged in discussion. The method is that of dialogue, and the style is conversational. Till recently it has been peculiar to this country and indeed to Oxford and Cambridge.

The origin of this system seems to have been due to the practical lapse of the teaching function from the two Universities to their Colleges; that is, to a large number of small corporations, each having a good many of the characteristics of a family.[1] The undergraduate was normally assigned to a single tutor throughout his career; and thus responsibility for his instruction and for supervising his conduct was in the same hands. The tutor was in an intimate and quasi-parental relation to the student, and apparently he not only arranged for, but actually gave, the whole of the instruction. Thus he acted as a sort of general maid-of-all-work, and for the greater part of any advanced work he would be, almost of necessity, unspecialized and unskilled. For several centuries before the middle of the nineteenth the scholarly standard of the tutors in most colleges was not high.

A hundred years ago there was long and acrimonious public debate about the rival merits of the Tutorial System (in possession) and the Professorial (advocated by many reformers). Hamilton and Halford Vaughan urged the superiority of the expert teacher to the amateur; Whewell and Pusey the superiority of the personal

[1] Sir William Hamilton, in his *Edinburgh Review* attacks on Oxford, ascribes this to a deliberate and insolent usurpation, but he does not seem to have been justified in so doing. See Hamilton *Dissertations and Discussions*, pp. 436-7, Rashdall, *op. cit.* III, pp. 150, 163 and Mallet, *op. cit.* III, p. 291.

approach and the requirement of activity in the student. The debate was complicated by the intrusion of other motives, patriotic and religious; the ' Professorial ' system, being popularly identified with the German universities, was arraigned as un-English and godless. But the discussion was vitiated by the apparent assumption on both sides that the two must needs be alternatives and not complementary. So far as Oxford and Cambridge were concerned, it ended in a draw. A much improved tutorial system, enriched by an inter-collegiate system of lecturing, remained the basis of most of the teaching in most of the Faculties. But university chairs were revived and many new ones were added; and of necessity instruction in Natural Science was organized, in the main, on a university rather than a college basis and on ' professorial ' lines. The modern universities however were from the outset organized on the model of the Scottish universities and of those of other countries and were non-tutorial.

To-day there is wide agreement that, for many of the evils pointed out, the most effective remedy would be a more extensive and intimate contact between teachers and students. It is agreed also that this would involve the introduction into the modern— possibly even into the Scottish—universities of some form of tutorial system. That again involves the provision of a substantially higher ratio of staff to students than has been customary. This is now the declared policy of most of our universities and if it were not for shortage of funds and of personnel, would already have been put into practice. This indicates a dramatic conversion, a new adhesion to the old English, in contrast with a much wider, tradition. For good or evil, it is a movement of high importance; and from the point of view represented in this book, it is necessary to estimate its value.

The great merit claimed for the tutorial system is, of course, the much larger amount of individual attention it makes possible. The tutor can go the particular pace and meet the particular difficulties of the individual student, and, in some subjects, enable him, through discussion, to develop and to test his own ideas. The tutor can give more of himself to, and can elicit more from, the student in these conditions than he can possibly do with a unit in a large class. Against it the critic urges that it is a hot-house system; intellectually, the pupil is being coddled; such treatment is suitable for juveniles but not for adults, for whom it is more bracing to be left to shift for themselves and to make what they can of books and of the lectures of a few high authorities. Also it is urged that, with any staffing at all likely to be practicable, the tutorial system is quite disproportionately expensive in time. The razor is blunted by excessive use. In some of the colleges of our older universities, the convention that every undergraduate, at whatever stage, must be given his hour a week has gone far to sterilize men capable of distinguished contributions to learning.

Certainly it is important to distinguish the work of the tutor from that of a ' coach.' But the final educational test of different teaching techniques must be their success in firing the student. It was once asked whether a famous Victorian statesman was really a man of first-class mind; and it was replied that he was a man of admirable second-class mind in a first-class state of effervescence. To produce such an effervescence in its students should be the university's aim. The same point was made by an engineer who defined the objective as being ' to find the right detonator to explode each individual student.' It is in this respect that the tutorial system has unique opportunities. ' Real life is meeting '; techniques vary, but this is the vital principle. It was expressed by Plato, when he declared that the sole way of acquiring his philosophy was ' by strenuous, intellectual communion and intimate personal inter-course, which kindles it in the soul instantaneously like a light caught from a leaping flame; and, once alight, it feeds its own flame thenceforward.'[1]

### c. Examinations

In this country university examinations may be regarded for practical purposes as a product of the nineteenth century. They are bound up with the evolution of the universities from play-grounds of the upper classes into places for the serious mental training of an intellectual élite and its preparation for its work in life. They were designed to be at once a healthy stimulus to students and a useful test of their fitness, either for advanced academic work or for the more promising openings in the pro-fessions. Their growth resulted from the same movement of opinion as produced the throwing open of Civil Service appointments to examination. It was desired to put an end to the adventitious advantages of the ' gentleman ' and the ' Blue ' and to replace ' influence ' or local connections by a test which should be intellec-tual, objective and democratic. The Victorians indeed were so

[1] *Epistle* VII, 341 c.

well pleased with this system that, at one time, even many teaching posts were filled by examination; and it was a point of honour, just as in an examination for a prize, that the examiners should take no account of any other knowledge of the candidate's fitness which they might possess but should restrict themselves entirely to the papers in front of them.

No one has yet suggested a satisfactory alternative to examinations, but they are regarded with much less complacency to-day. Even so, the full extent and degree of their baneful psychological influence is quite inadequately realized. Some defects indeed have become patent. 'Examination,' says the Goodenough Committee, 'must be the servant and not the master of training.' But far too often, in practice, this relation is notoriously reversed. To some extent even the teachers, and much more the students, become obsessed by 'what pays for the Schools.' Thus the thought of the examination cramps and spoils teaching, and this is far worse when the examination is wholly 'external.' Further, examinations are apt to test memory rather than intelligence; 'the nightingale took no prize at the poultry show.' And so far as they do test intelligence, it is hardly the highest type of intelligence. It may be doubted whether Darwin would have shone conspicuously in tackling a series of three-hour papers, each demanding five or six answers. On the other hand, the more the examiner tries to set questions which are not primarily factual and which will test the student's ability and grasp of principle, the more subjective does the assessment of the answers become.

But our main concern is not with the technique of examination nor with widely recognized difficulties such as the above. It is with a more insidious demoralization, a kind of intellectual poison which is being diffused. This has two aspects, intellectual insincerity and an idolatrous cult of success. Thus, in such subjects as Literature and Philosophy, the candidate is invited to express and to defend aesthetic or moral judgments, at a time when his own genuine personal judgment is still immature. He is constantly tempted, not really to comb out his own mind, but to express opinions which he thinks will 'go down' with the examiners, because he gathers they are correct. He does not develop his own sensitivity; he simulates those feelings and judgments which he fancies are expected of him. Similarly he writes in a style which is not natural to him but which seems to be 'the thing'; the literary art which he chiefly cultivates is the art of pastiche. He is led to pretend to a maturity which he has not got and he thus becomes a cynical window-dresser. Having been accustomed, and indeed incited, to play with values, he is insensibly ' conditioned ' to a scepticism and cynicism concerning all values, which is more profound than any he could have acquired from a conscious philosophy.

He is also ' conditioned ' to another disastrous mental attitude, that which assumes that the master-aim of a university career is success. At every stage, from the primary to the secondary school, from the secondary school to the university, from the university to a job, success in examination is the key which unlocks the gate to personal advancement. The student is like an athlete or race-horse being trained for a series of contests; the training is the means, the race is the end. What matters, is to get success rather than to deserve it. Examination is no longer the servant but the despot. So appearance takes precedence of reality, the sign of the thing signified, window-dressing of the building up of stock. In words used long ago by Whewell, preparation is for the review rather than for the battle.

On these lines a cynical philosophy is absorbed far more effectively and irresistibly than it could ever have been from direct precept. The complex of feeling and behaviour out of which it emerges is one into which each new generation of students is plunged. That is unintended, but its influence is none the less powerful. When it is accompanied by official or unofficial professions of an idealistic philosophy, it is hardly surprising that many of the best students react with something like nausea.

As usual, it is much easier to diagnose than to prescribe. But certainly the first need is that we should realize more clearly the prevalence, the naturalness and the falsity, of the attitude here described. Pharisaical condemnation by persons, in or out of the university, who are not subject to the same stresses will carry us nowhere. Nor can a remedy be found in any obvious institutional action, expressing itself in alterations of regulations, technical improvements in the conduct of examinations, etc. The question is really one of values, and false values can only be resisted or expelled by true ones. The reason why the disease is so extensive is that so many students have no values which they hold with firm conviction. There are no moral values in which they have been so nurtured that these have become a second nature to them. The Christian at any rate ought to be immune; and, if he is not, there is something badly wrong with his Christianity. If serving God, and not personal success, is the context in which he approaches his examinations, they will fall into their proper place.

In regard to most of the points made in this chapter, one dismaying reflection is recurrent. It is easy to get a fairly general assent to them in university circles. But it is very hard to get any effective action; and it is doubtful whether Laodicean friends are not worse even than open enemies. Some of the more sensitive students and teachers are coming to feel that they are involved in a great pretence; the pretence that they are doing work of university quality and temper, when much of it is, in fact, only hackwork. When they talk candidly together of their experiences, we hear of too many lecturers who take up their posts full of keenness and spring and of a spirit of high endeavour, who, in a few years, lapse into a soulless routine, and of third-year students who have less intellectual curiosity and genuine interest in the things of the mind than they had as freshmen. There is one factor in particular which bears much of the responsibility, and that is the general overloading of curricula. The student has already suffered from this in Higher School Certificate and the vicious process is prolonged. Professor Bernal has described its operation in science. The subject-matter, he says, is always increasing while the time available remains the same. There is an undue time-lag before new knowledge is admitted to the curriculum. But 'when at last the new element of knowledge is admitted, it is taken to the end of the syllabus and the rest of the subject is appropriately squashed to make room for it, the whole process resembling the old peasant method of dressing by which a new petticoat is put on every year on top of the others, in the pious expectation that one of the previous ones has now become too ragged to be of any use.'[1] In School after School there is so much ground to cover that it can only be done in a breathless rush and a somewhat mechanical manner. The only remedy is a ruthless application of the knife. But when it is their own subject which is in question academic people find it extraordinarily hard to nerve themselves to this, though the Goodenough Committee have set an example. Yet to delay shows a defective sense of proportion and is to underrate the deadening effect of the treadmill. Here words used by Berdyaev about the tempo of modern life are peculiarly pertinent; ' It exacts from man a continual activity, which once in operation imposes a condition of spiritual inner passivity.'

[1] *Op. cit.*, p. 78.

# VIII

## CORPORATE LIFE

### I THE ENGLISH TRADITION—ITS STRENGTH AND WEAKNESS

The medieval university was a form of guild. The distinctive feature of Oxford and Cambridge has been the high degree to which they have developed one aspect of the guild, namely the fraternity of the guild brothers. Common study has been based on common living. The student, who came in order to acquire learning or a professional qualification, found that he had entered into life-membership of a society possessing a remarkable power to enlist his affection and loyalty.[1] To it henceforth he was attached by silken cords of singular tenacity. So there came into existence a new type of community, having many of the qualities of the family; its members regarded themselves as sons of an *Alma Mater*.

This has two consequences. First the teacher's is a pastoral job; to the student he has a personal, and not merely a business, relation. He has not only contracted to give a certain amount of instruction, but is to be the ' guide, philosopher and friend ' of his pupils. His liability, like a parent's, is unlimited. Secondly the university (or the college) elicits the devotion of a large number of its *alumni*. They not only share ' a number of subjects of common interest, of agreeable retrospect, of endearing recollection,'[2] they have in some measure undergone a ' paradigmatic experience.' That is, their university years have been to them a vivid and compelling experience, making an exceptionally deep impression, indeed going far to mould their minds; and it is in the light of that experience that later experiences are interpreted. They look back on these years as a time of happiness and mental expansion which glows in the memory; a time when stimulating friendships were formed, when some contact was made with one or two great men who

---

[1] In the first instance this effect was a by-product. It was unplanned and unforeseen, either by the scholars who first came together or by the early benefactors, the kings and bishops, who made college life possible. But they proved to have builded better than they knew.

[2] Whewell, *op. cit.*, p. 88.

excited reverence, when the blood ran fast and the mind exulted in a new awareness of its powers. They regard their university, in Newman's words, as 'a second home, not so tender, but more noble and majestic and authoritative.' Of course, the university's power to produce such an effect is bound up with its historic character. Each generation of freshmen enters into a great inheritance. The beauty and dignity of their surroundings, the studious cloisters, the high embowed roof, the storied windows, richly dight, the pealing organ, impart an element of splendour to the quality of the common life and enhance the student's sense that he has become a citizen of no mean city.

Whatever the limitations of this tradition, it is the characteristic English contribution to the whole university world. Just now our own modern universities are keenly conscious of its merits and are striving to incorporate something of it and so are many universities in the United States. There, during the second part of the nineteenth century, German models and German influence were supreme. But more recently the need of a strong corporate life has been realized and the introduction of 'Houses' at Harvard and of 'Colleges' at Yale, is a salient example of a new trend. Our tradition may need to be supplemented, but to jettison it would be calamitous. In its main outline we must hold on to and develop it.

But it is important to distinguish the general character of this tradition, collegiate and family, from the particular form which it has taken in the past. In this there are elements of more dubious and transitory worth. The family has tended to be patriarchal; it has, very markedly, been a society of unequals. The teacher has been regarded as being *in loco parentis,* the student *in statu pupillari.* They have differed as adult and adolescent, superior and subordinate, director and directed. (The *Statuta et Decreta* of the University of Oxford contained a whole chapter, *De Moribus Conformandis,* of which the first section is entitled *De Reverentia Juniorum erga Seniores.* The Statutes of Trinity College, Cambridge, in words almost identical with some of those in the above Section, contained the following passage, 'We decree and ordain that all inferiors behave themselves towards their superiors in a submissive and reverent manner.')[1] 'Discipline' was a major concern both of college and of university, and they set themselves to keep a strict watch over the morals of students. They employed

[1] Whewell, *op. cit.,* p. 80.

an array of disciplinary officers, of Proctors and 'Bulldogs,' of Deans or Censors. Students were required to observe a considerable number of rules and prohibitions concerning freedom of movement, costume, hours and, sometimes, expenditure. Drunkenness, gambling and sexual licence were offences against academic discipline. These rules were supported by sanctions in the shape of 'gatings,' fines and rustications.

The theory behind this exercise of discipline is clear.[1] The 'light mind and impetuous spirit' of the undergraduate is 'not to be uncontrolled.' He is hedged about with rules and authorities so that 'he acts in a little world which is constituted of definite relations and duties, and requires a certain self-restraint and self-regulation at every step.' In this way he is gradually prepared for adult status and responsibility. It follows that he 'cannot act at the university except in the capacity of a pupil,' and so all participation in politics is excluded. This system, says Whewell, works well in practice; 'it leads to the general prevalence of that respectful temper, those good manners and orderly habits at which it aims. Even tempers of great levity and stubbornness are awed and tamed and in a little while moulded to their position.' Now all this is admirable good sense if you are dealing with boys. But, in universities, it is really a relic of the time when the age of entry was much lower than it is now. At a moment when the universities are crowded with ex-service men it is obviously fantastic. But, even in more normal days, does it not tend to prolong immaturity and irresponsibility?

The English tradition has also been prejudiced in the eyes of many by another historical association. During much of the nineteenth century, Oxford and Cambridge, strong in corporate life, were gravely deficient in care for learning. The typical Victorian parent sent his son as a commoner to Oxford or Cambridge as to a combination of an unequalled finishing school and a highly eligible club. He sent him to acquire manners, *savoir-faire,* the ability to mix well with his fellows and to pull his weight as a member of the governing classes; and if a little learning could be thrown in, that would be all to the good. Similarly, in the words of a verse from a Lesson much read on Founders' Days, the college was inclined to look for 'rich men' (no anxiety to the Bursar) 'furnished with ability' (no anxiety to the Tutor) 'living peaceably in their habitations' (no anxiety to the Dean). They

[1] It is very fully stated by Whewell, *op. cit.,* pp. 78-134.

sought to turn out each graduate 'a scholar and a gentleman,' but they were more uniformly successful in the second aim than in the first. There is however no inherent incompatibility between the two, and the old-time scholarly deficiencies of Oxford and Cambridge are things of the past.

It is also an aristocratic tradition. It belongs to a patrician society, free from harsh material cares, able to command the services of others for all menial work, and, in temper, somewhat lordly, gay and irresponsible.

Finally all corporate bodies are liable to suffer from introversion and need to be on their guard against it. In the bad old days before the first Commission the ancient universities certainly did so suffer. A modern writer speaks, not too severely, of 'the walls of sloth, self-satisfaction and exclusiveness behind which the universities conducted their business and their pleasure.'[1]

## 2   OXFORD AND CAMBRIDGE TO-DAY

Before the nineteenth century the atmosphere of Oxford and Cambridge was masculine, celibate and clerical. But it was not highly intellectual and abuses and sinecures abounded. In Victorian and Edwardian times, at least after the first Commission, these universities were at their strongest. The abuses had largely disappeared. The teachers were probably as highly selected as any university teachers in the world. As a body, they were scholarly, and markedly conscientious in the performance of their duties. Their mode of living was gracious, dignified and ritualistic. It had in it a good deal of state and something of luxury.[2] Hall and Common Room often produced sparkling examples of 'the feast of reason and the flow of soul.' Many Fellows of Colleges were married, but there was still a strong nucleus living in college and easily accessible to undergraduates. Eminent visitors of various kinds were to be met at High Table and would accept invitations to address student societies or public meetings.

[1] Addison, *Religious Equality in Modern England,* p. 68.

[2] Macaulay speaks of 'the spacious and stately mansions of the heads of houses, the commodious chambers of the fellows and scholars, the refectories, the combination rooms, the bowling greens, the stabling, the state and luxury of the great feast days, the piles of old plate on the tables, the savoury steam of the kitchens, the multitudes of geese and capons which turn at once on the spits, the oceans of excellent ale in the butteries' (in his speech on the Maynooth Grant, reprinted in *Miscellaneous Writings* III, p. 296). This was a hundred years ago, and few colleges can boast quite the splendours of Trinity College, Cambridge. But even if the picture is impressionistic, it is not untrue.

But there has always been a debit as well as a credit account. Such a style of living in such an environment is very attractive, but in its very absence of provinciality it is provincial. Whatever the standard of excellence, to mix always and exclusively with 'the best people' is to fail in catholicity. What in moderate doses is highly stimulating, may fail as a staple diet. However select, the Senior Common Room cannot afford to be self-sufficient; it is too small and too uniform a world for that. It can be trivial. A certain cleverness and verbal facility and polished, esoteric wit can be a snare. They can serve as a disguise for second-rate comment on matters of first-rate importance. 'Beware, beware, beware the S.C.R.,' were the very pertinent concluding words of a letter of congratulation to a young man just elected to a Fellowship.

Certainly dons as a class are not, in any ordinary sense, 'remote and ineffectual.' But it may be doubted whether, for most men, a lifetime of continuous service in Oxford or Cambridge is healthy. In the main the young graduates who stay on as dons are, at that stage, the intellectual pick of their contemporaries, and it is those whose academic record is a shade less outstanding who go out into the world. But, though there are conspicuous exceptions, a comparison of the same men thirty or forty years on is liable to be disturbing to academic complacency.

In any case the Victorian and Edwardian era is past. Life in Oxford and Cambridge has changed and is changing to a degree not yet generally recognized. The family atmosphere has diminished and in some respects there has been an approximation to 'Redbrick.' This is due to a number of causes. A much larger proportion of undergraduates than formerly comes from uncultured homes. They are not 'geared to absorb easily a taste for civilized living.'[1] They are conscious of social awkwardness and ignorance. In these respects they are unsure of themselves; and this puts them on the defensive and interposes a barrier. This can only be overcome through the exercise of a good deal of social skill and at the cost of patient effort. But dons, like undergraduates, are less leisured and carefree than of old. For the present at any rate both universities are much overcrowded, and this means that teachers are working under pressure and their relation to their pupils is inevitably less personal and intimate and rather more stereotyped than it used to be. Also new social and economic conditions compel

---

[1] See a valuable article by Mrs. Proudfoot in the *Nineteenth Century,* April, 1947, 'The Rôle of Oxford in the Post-War World.'

many married men to find time for domestic ' chores.' ' The scholar in the scullery' is much handicapped in the performance of other than routine duties. Again the growth of Science, particularly in Cambridge, and of some of the newer Honour Schools in the Faculty of Arts, such as Modern Languages and English Literature, has radically altered teaching organization, and this has important social repercussions. The organization of these studies is not based on the colleges, and many of the teaching staff are not Fellows and have no college rooms in which to see pupils. With the larger numbers of undergraduates a larger proportion must live in lodgings and both dons and undergraduates must go further and further afield to find accommodation. At the same time they are less pocket-easy than formerly and 'reading-parties' and other common expeditions in vacation are less possible. All this hinders any very close or free and easy relation between S.C.R. and J.C.R. In Oxford particularly, a rapid and inordinate growth in the size of the city and the ceaseless and insistent noise of traffic have much impaired the traditional atmosphere of peace. Further, there is beginning to be some uneasy self-questioning about a certain element of luxury which has been associated with the life of the S.C.R. To-day that element is not, in fact, very marked. College life is a curious mixture of splendour and squalor. If it has something of Capua, it has also a good deal of Sparta, particularly for the older men. Guest-nights and occasional ' Feasts' are a warm-hearted exercise of the art of hospitality; and for any who have enjoyed that hospitality, to criticise it would seem singularly ungracious and repugnant. Yet the question will not be silenced, whether to do oneself well is not a little incongruous and anachronistic in a stricken world. It behoves Christians at least to ask themselves seriously how far they can combine the atmosphere of the High Table on a guest-night with the ethos of the New Testament.

## 3 'REDBRICK'S' PRESENT INSPIRATIONAL POVERTY

In any comment on the ' Redbrick' universities, it is necessary to remember that they are still very young. In the main their growth has been the affair of the last half-century; and that period has seen two world-wars and one world-slump. Throughout they have had to struggle with extremely restricted means. What they have done is what they could rather than what they would. An examination of Oxford and Cambridge at the same age would have disclosed little of the wealth of collegiate and corporate life in which those universities now excel. In what follows we are not imputing blame. We are only recording facts of which most 'Redbrick' teachers and administrators are already ruefully conscious and impressions which we believe they share.

Students do not 'go up' to Liverpool or Leeds as men 'go up' to Oxford or Cambridge. This is symbolic. The majority of the 'Redbrick' students are not uprooted from their everyday environment. They have not the stimulus of a wholly fresh start in new, spacious and exhilarating surroundings. Few of them have been at boarding schools, and the 'Public Schools' are almost entirely unrepresented. Their next-door neighbours in the lecture-room or at the laboratory bench may only be their own doubles. In their student days, very few of the alumni of modern universities have undergone any 'paradigmatic' experience. They do not commonly look back to them as a time of expansion and exhilaration, of happiness and of friendships, which stands out in their memory. They have not experienced any vivid sense of well-being and touch with reality, of new insight and release of energies, of wonder and 'wild surmise.' Their life has not been glamorous but rather drab. 'Know you her secret none can utter?' is not a question which springs naturally to their lips. The Honours student may indeed have been brought into fairly close contact with his Professor or with one or two members of the staff of his Department. But there is no *genius loci,* no 'atmosphere' which is almost 'foolproof' in the sense that it continues for a long time almost independent of the vagaries of the individual teacher. If Oxford and Cambridge suffer from a surfeit of cream, 'Redbrick' too often has to put up with skimmed milk. For this there are a number of causes.

### a. Failure of Students to form a Community

Space and time are the great obstacles. The 'Redbrick' freshman does not commonly enter a new and exciting society which will dominate his life in term time for several years. For five days in the week he arrives at the University, often from a considerable distance, at 9.30. From then till 4.30, except for an hour's luncheon interval, he is at lectures or in laboratory; or, if he is an Arts man and has an hour or two between lectures, he may spend it in the Library. At 4.30 a very large proportion of students hurry away to catch the bus or train to their homes, which may be at any point within a radius of thirty miles. On Saturday and Sunday they are not seen at all. Such a timetable leaves little opportunity for social life. In Oxford and Cambridge students of the same College meet one another at meals three times a day, and small groups can gather in private rooms at almost any hour of day or night. The evenings are available for the meetings of societies in rich profusion and the early afternoons for games. The distances are manageable. There are also the Sundays which are free of routine duties. In 'Redbrick' on the other hand, the meetings of societies have to be crowded into a part of the luncheon hour, or to be held immediately after the end of lectures in the afternoon. Even then students are tired, only some will delay their return home, and those only for a limited time.

It is true of course that all these universities make considerable provision for the encouragement of corporate life. They have 'Unions' to which, in England, all students must belong and whose fees are collected for them by the university. These student bodies have their own club premises, in some cases very good; and, within fairly wide limits, they manage their own affairs. They elect 'Student Representative Councils' which speak for the whole body of students in their relations with the authorities and with the world outside, or else the Union Committee perform this function. They have refectories in which students congregate for luncheon and to some extent also for 'elevenses' or for tea. They have playing fields which vary in their quality but in general are not gravely inadequate to the existing demand. In the immediate neighbourhood of the universities gymnasia, swimming-baths, 'squash' and fives courts are beginning to appear. Within each Union have sprung up a large number of voluntary 'societies.' Some of these are cultural, e.g. dramatic or musical societies. Some are political, representing different party points of view. Some are religious, mostly local branches of inter-university organizations. There are also a number of purely social functions which usually take the form of dances.[1]

But though the skeleton exists, it has little clothing of flesh. In practice the timetable difficulties described above prevent most

[1] In one respect the social life of the 'Redbrick' universities is richer than that of Oxford and Cambridge. They are genuinely 'mixed' universities, whereas Oxford and Cambridge are still primarily masculine institutions which, in recent years, have made certain concessions. At 'Redbrick' women were admitted at a very early stage in its history; they were admitted on equal terms and consequently in much larger numbers.

students from taking advantage of the opportunities which, theoretically, they possess. For instance a very much smaller proportion of students than at Oxford and Cambridge takes any part in athletics. Playing fields are usually too distant from the university to be used except on Saturday or Wednesday afternoon, and possibly on summer evenings. But a more formidable obstacle is lack of enthusiasm. A considerable number even of the athletes may prefer to play nearer their homes, for local or 'Old Boys' teams with which they were connected before they came to the university. This is symptomatic. Also, within the university, such social and athletic life as there is tends to be organized on faculty or departmental lines and provides no cross-section of the community. A student plays football on Saturday afternoon or dances on Saturday evening only with just those students by whose side he worked in laboratory or lecture room the previous day. The refectory is, in fact, the place where the ordinary student most often meets any large number of his fellows. But its atmosphere commonly resembles that of a noisy and overcrowded City restaurant rather than that of a College Hall. He may have to stand in a queue for anything up to half an hour before he gets a seat, and he has then every inducement to hurry through his meal and get outside again.

The result is that only a small minority of the whole student body takes any real part in corporate life. In one typical university where a careful survey was made, the proportion was reckoned as being as low as twelve per cent. For the remainder, entry to the university has involved no epoch-making change or mental enlargement. The centre of their interests, social, athletic, religious—even cultural outside the limits of their degree course—remains just what, and where, it was before. Also the social functions which draw numbers, the occasional dance and the annual 'Rag' may do something to promote good fellowship, but such meeting is on a trivial plane and does little to inspire. Even with the few who take a larger part, there is some deduction to be made. It will often be found that the main weight is carried by a nucleus of students who are already in Halls, so that the proportion of the others who contribute to, and get stimulus from, the common life is even smaller than appears. Also there is not unknown a type of office-seeker who gives too much time to student politics. He is seldom a serious student academically and he does not really command the respect of his fellows.

o

### b.   Separation of Students and Staff

Students and staff are sundered partly by the sheer physical difficulty of meeting outside classroom or laboratory. The necessary time and place are not available. Within the university the student is fully occupied in working hours; at any other time he is not there. Very few universities have joint Common Rooms where students and staff can mix informally. A Fellow of a College at Oxford or Cambridge has normally a room in college to which he can at any time invite undergraduates. But at 'Redbrick' a teacher, particularly if he is young, has rarely a room at his personal disposal to which he can invite a student informally. Outside the walls of the university, once students and staff have gone home or to their lodgings, they are scattered over an enormous area. They could only meet by careful prearrangement and by the expenditure of a good deal of time and trouble, and so, in practice, they do not. Casual and informal contacts on a free and easy basis, the seed out of which so much may grow, simply do not occur.

There are also psychological causes of the separation. On the side of the staff there is sometimes a measure of indifference and boredom. We are told of Harvard eighty years ago that the staff were distinguished but their educational effort was small. In the words of a student of those days, 'These competent and learned instructors did not give us of their best, but having listened to our stumbling recitations and inscribed an estimate of our blunders, would then withdraw to the congenial companionship of erudite neighbours, contented if collegiate discipline had been reasonably secured . . . We realized that we were in the presence of distinguished men, but they moved in a higher sphere and tolerated undergraduates as the unruly subjects of official discipline.'[1] Similarly 'Redbrick' lecturers often feel that their duty is to their subject rather than to their students. 'Out-of-school' attention to these they regard as a form of wet-nursing, and, in any case, as an 'extra' and not as the activity in consideration of which they were originally chosen or are paid or are likely to be promoted. Even where there is goodwill, it is not easy to befriend a student in such a way as to be really useful to him. Students, on their side are apt to be embarrassed and tongue-tied. Without social ease or experience, they are on the defensive and irresponsive in face of the unfamiliar. They are apt to alternate between two extremes. They

---

[1] Quoted Morison, *op. cit.*, p. 307.

regard members of staff either as distant Olympians, to whom they sign themselves, 'Yours respectfully,' or as enemies in a class-war, any advances from whom are to be received with suspicion as of Greeks bringing gifts. On neither side is there often found that skill in the art of conversation which, starting from simple and trivial things like the weather and minor personal happenings, can achieve a real contact between persons;[1] or, better still and less sophisticated, the instinctive tact which is the result of imaginative caring.

### c. Separation of Staff from One Another

Here again the causes are partly physical and partly psychological. Homes are very widely dispersed. There is seldom any 'university quarter,' such as North Oxford or Old Aberdeen. Within the university, the refectory at lunch-time is the main meeting ground. But accommodation both in refectory and in the common room is often quite inadequate; and the extreme dearth of private rooms has the effect that many lecturers curtail the time they actually spend in the university to the minimum necessary for fulfilling formal duties. But, over and above this, there are psychological barriers. The old classical background, which once was shared by all, no longer exists, and nothing has taken its place. There is no common cultural basis or community of interest. This is due to specialization; but it is aggravated by an instinctive shrinking, characteristically British, from deep personal relations. For lecturers of different Faculties, bridge or golf may be the only easy meeting ground. Departmentalism is also fostered by a peculiar brand of arrogance to which academic persons are liable, a contemptuous lack of interest in, or respect for, distant fields. 'What I know not, is not knowledge,' 'What I am not interested in, is not interesting.' Hence the absence of communication described in an earlier chapter. Finally there has developed an unfortunate estrangement between teachers and administrators. Administration tends to become a whole-time, specialized job. The Registrar, the Bursar, sometimes the Dean, and even the Vice-Chancellor are less and less teachers who are found to stand out in practical capacity and more and more members of a separate profession. They may easily lose intimate touch with their colleagues and lose sight of major problems under the pressure of day to day necessities. Yet it is they who represent the university, as such, to the mass of students. On

[1] See *General Education in a Free Society*, p. 69.

the other hand teachers are apt to have a deep suspicion of ' bureau-cracy.' In most Senates or Faculties a resolution would be carried with acclamation : ' That the power of the Office has increased, is increasing and ought to be diminished.'

## 4  REMEDIES (OTHER THAN HALLS OF RESIDENCE)

The personal side of university life, the experience of fellowship and of bracing contact and comradeship, is being crowded out. This is the result of drift rather than of any deliberate policy. But we have been acting on the tacit assumption that these things, however desirable, are yet of the second, rather than the first, order of importance. To amass knowledge and to pass examina-tions, has been regarded as the student's primary business. But this is an inversion of values, not only for the Christian, but for all those for whom the real ' challenge of our time ' is found in the personal relation between individuals and groups. But, if so, the trouble cannot be put right simply by improvements in machin-ery and organization, requisite though these are. Something more fundamental is needed. That is a new attitude of mind, a change of heart, both among staff and among students, but especially among staff, since it is normally from them that an initiative must come. We must acquire a new imaginative awareness of our real situation and a new sense of responsibility concerning it. In plain language, we need to repent. For, however unwittingly, we have allowed ourselves in practice to become isolationists; and isolation-ism as a policy for any section within the university is wholly damn-able. To regard with benevolent approval projects for enhancing corporate life, will take us very little way. What is needed is a missionary fervour which puts this aim in the forefront and is strong enough to overcome physical obstacles and the more subtle difficulties of shyness and embarrassment. This involves, among other things, genuine and lively concern in the interests of colleagues in departments remote from our own. For practical purposes the enemy to be feared is not the man who denies openly the value of social contacts, for such a man is seldom found; it is the man who relegates them tacitly to the status of ' extras.'

The physical obstacles to the common life call for the urgent attention of university authorities. Staff Houses, Common Rooms, private rooms for members of the teaching staff of all grades, should be provided on a liberal scale. Also, as is now generally recognized, a considerably higher ratio of staff to students is needed if they are to be free for other than routine duties. There has been another valuable development in one or two universities which might well be extended. That is the assignment of students, at least in their earlier years, to 'moral tutors' or 'regents.' Thus each student has some one member of staff to whom he can confidently look as 'guide, philosopher and friend,' and to whom he can go for personal counsel on any matter. A good deal might also be done to promote various forms of joint activity by staff and students at week-ends or in vacation. These might take the form of 'reading parties' such as used to be common among Oxford and Cambridge men, or they might be primarily recreational, as with Alpine Clubs, hiking expeditions, etc. It has been suggested that universities should acquire country houses which could be used as centres for such purposes. One university has recently tried the extremely interesting experiment of a 'Freshmen's Week-end.' This was held immediately before the beginning of the session. Freshmen were invited to meet socially some senior members of the staff, and to hear talks and enter into discussion on the purpose of the university and the ways in which to make the best use of it. These are only a few among a large number of possible experiments. For the moment what is essential is to recognize the need and to be ready to make experiments. It is not amenity but something far more fundamental that is at stake, and in this field defeatism is inexcusable.

## 5 HALLS OF RESIDENCE

In the medieval universities, 'Halls' were originally only 'eleemosynary institutions for the help of poor students, boarding-houses and not places of education.'[1] They were private ventures of individual masters who took a few students into their own houses or possibly even of a group of students who clubbed together, though some of them eventually grew into 'Colleges' through endowment by prelates or princes. Something like this is broadly true of the earlier Halls in the modern English universities. Where the majority of students could live at home, the problem of residence was less acute than at Paris, Oxford or Cambridge to which students flocked from all parts. But a not inconsiderable minority came from a distance, and especially when women were admitted,

[1] Rashdall, op. cit. I, pp. 197-198; cf. p. 500.

parents often felt some uneasiness at letting them go into lodgings under no sort of supervision or protection. A certain number of 'Hostels' were set up either by religious bodies or by groups of philanthropic persons in the area. At first these were recognized rather than actively sponsored by the universities concerned. But, later, the universities provided a certain number of Halls of their own; the pioneers being naturally those universities or university colleges, not situated in large centres of population, which could not attract students without making some provision for their residence. Such Halls, built out of university funds and directly controlled by the universities, were usually larger and better provided than others and enjoyed more prestige. But, even so, the total provision has been small, owing in large measure to financial stringency. Lectures have been compulsory for all; residence has been optional and indeed only available for a minority. On the whole it has not been regarded by the authorities as being a matter of the first importance, while students have fought shy of it as relatively expensive and restrictive of liberty.

Recently there has been a widespread conversion. This is partly due to the growing intolerableness of the alternative. With the increase in their own number on the one hand and on the other the acute housing shortage, it has become much harder for students to find lodgings. To do so, they have to go further and further afield and to pay more and more. Too often the lodgings, when found, are cramped and gloomy, and life in them is lonely, drab and joyless. But still more, the change of view is due to a growing sense of the educative and civilizing possibilities of residential life and of its power to stimulate and to enlarge the mind. In England, and even to some extent in Scotland, there is now a strong student demand for a liberal provision of Halls. On their side the 'Redbrick' university authorities are now including in the forefront of their programmes of development a multiplication of Halls on a scale which should transform the character of the common life. Many of them indeed contemplate making a period of residence compulsory for all students. If anyone asks what these universities are doing to provide for students that element of inspiration in which they have been lacking, the shortest answer is that they propose to make themselves residential.

Hence at this moment Halls are in fashion. Let 'Redbrick' redress its cultural inadequacy by making itself, as it were, semi-collegiate! Halls are now seen to be, not only a desirable adjunct but, an indispensable medium of the highest education. In the main that seems to be the view of the university authorities and of the students. But it is held with something less than full conviction by a number of university teachers, and even its advocates have not yet fully adjusted themselves to the new conception. So it is important to press the question, ' What degree of educational importance really belongs to Hall life ' ?

The devil's advocate has a good deal to say. First, he urges, the present emphasis on Halls is the wrong kind of imitation of Oxford and Cambridge; it copies their faults rather than their virtues. To those universities, the colleges have often been a curse, diverting attention from the real end of the university to what is irrelevant or at, most, secondary. The university itself, says Sir William Hamilton, exists for learning, but its colleges and halls only ' for aliment and habitation.' The training they give and the excellence they impart is social rather than intellectual. Instead of stimulating a disinterested intellectual enthusiasm, they provide a pleasant and unexacting society and they minister to physical and intellectual comfort. They have been the charming classrooms and playgrounds of the upper classes. It is college life that has given point to the severity of the eminent German critic who contrasted the contribution to culture made by Halle in all its poverty with ' Oxford spending its inherited millions in hereditary indolence.'[1] We are told that President Eliot was too busy increasing the intellectual opportunities of Harvard to care much for its social life; and does not that witness to the soundness of his sense of values?[2]

Secondly, it is said, the pastoral approach to the student which Halls embody is grandmotherly and ' personal ' in a bad sense. It is intrusive, fussy, patronizing and retarding. (Perhaps this is specially true of some halls for women). It conflicts sharply with the sentiment expressed in a letter of the late Sir Walter Raleigh, written in his own student days, ' To escape the eternal personal judgments which made school a place of torment is to walk upon air. The schoolmaster looks at you; the college-professor looks the way you are looking.' Life in hall is cloistered, sheltered and irresponsible. The student is unduly shielded from the rubs and jars and responsibilities of ordinary life.

Thirdly, some Halls in fact are mere boarding houses, devoid of

[1] Paulsen, *op. cit.*, p. 131.
[2] Morison, *op. cit.*, p. 418.

any cultural influence, their tone boorish and philistine, hostile to sensitiveness and originality. In their daily life there is much dull routine varied by horseplay. In what is probably the best known passage in *The Idea of a University* Newman describes the automatic effect of bringing together ' a multitude of young men, keen, open-hearted, sympathetic and observant, as young men are; . . . . they gain for themselves new ideas and views, fresh matter of thought, and distinct principles for judging and acting, day by day.'[1] But this description is ludicrously inapplicable to some existing Halls, of which it is true that, in the words of experienced observers, ' Undeniably, the whole atmosphere of these Halls militates against a full student life and the development of personality.'

Fourthly—and alternatively—the successful Halls, which do genuinely exert a fine cultural influence, are liable to produce a divided loyalty and to usurp the university's place in the affections of its students and alumni. In the older universities, the don who is primarily ' a college man ' is a familiar figure; and the affection of the alumnus is often given to Balliol or to King's rather than to Oxford or Cambridge. At times the colleges have usurped the powers of the university and have reduced it to little more than a federation. In his *Edinburgh Review* attack on Oxford, Sir William Hamilton traced its defects to college usurpations and compared the colleges to a fungoid growth.[2] In short the inferior Hall does little good and may do positive harm to the students, while the good Hall threatens to disrupt the university.

Finally, it is urged, Halls are in any case disproportionately expensive. Any large expenditure upon them involves the diversion of university funds from general purposes for the benefit of a small and privileged minority. The universities of the world get on without them and have always done so. Even if they are desirable in themselves, it is absurd to put them in the first order of priority. If a university has to choose between a hall and a laboratory, it should choose the laboratory every time.

Such misgivings should be expressed trenchantly and faced candidly. Nevertheless the cumulative case for the institution of Halls in the modern universities is overwhelmingly strong. There, and there alone, is found a mixture of all sorts of students. People of widely different interests, social backgrounds—and, where there is

[1] *Op. cit.*, p. 146.
[2] *Dissertations and Discussions*, p. 415.

a senior common room, of different ages—are brought into easy, intimate and continuous contact, with leisure and opportunity to cultivate one another. 'As compared with lodgings or with many homes, a hall affords an environment where intellectual interests are strong. It offers students exceptionally favourable opportunities for the stimulating interplay of mind with mind, for the formation of friendships, and for learning the art of understanding and living with others of outlook and temperament unlike their own. It can be, and it often is, a great humanising force.'[1] It is impossible to visit a good Hall without noticing a marked contrast between the third and the first year students. The seniors have passed through a civilizing process, which, while expressing itself in the externals of manners, is no mere veneer but a genuine mental enlargement. It is specially valuable for those who have never been to boarding schools or away from their home surroundings. For the future administrator or statesman or industrial leader, or indeed for the future citizen, the setting in which he lives and the quality of the common life in which he takes part determine his mental development at least as much as the knowledge he acquires. This is one more example of the familiar truth that the most effective education for community is through actual experience of the challenges, stimuli, responsibilities and necessary adjustments of community-life.

As compared with lodgings and with most homes, Halls provide conditions exceptionally favourable to study. Space, quiet, warmth, a sufficiency of wholesome food, freedom from distraction, periods of silence, a suitable rhythm of life, the presence of books, an atmosphere of respect for the things of the mind, are available for the student. He needs, and in Hall he has, ample opportunity both of solitude and of society.

Again, criticisms on the ground of privilege or exclusiveness are relics of the days when Halls were few and exceptional. Once they become the general rule, for a certain period at least, in the student's life, there is no reason to object to expenditure on them any more than on lecture rooms or laboratories. But, in general, neither critics nor defenders have yet adjusted their minds to this change.

There are two opposite errors to be avoided. One is to regard 'Halls' as mere 'frills' or luxuries. The other is to regard their provision as being itself a panacea; irrespective of conditions, the

[1] U.G.C. Report 1929-30 to 1934-35, p. 17.

mere congregation of students under one roof and under some sort
of rule may be worse than useless. All depends on the character
of the Hall and the degree to which it attains certain desiderata;
and, in practice, this will depend on whether the university is
thoroughly in earnest with its hall-policy and on the degree of
weight it attaches to it.

What are these ' desiderata '?

### (1) General

The Hall must be a real community, diffusing a distinctive atmosphere which is morally and intellectually stimulating. The lesser
loyalty is not to be jealously circumscribed but rather to be regarded
as an elemental training in the larger. ' The love to the whole is
not extinguished by this subordinate partiality.'[1] On the other hand
the Hall should not aspire to become a college. It would be a mistaken policy to develop it as a primary teaching centre. At Oxford
and Cambridge the university's one-time virtual abdication of its
teaching function in favour of the colleges was a misfortune; in
this respect those universities serve as a warning and not as a
pattern.

### (2) Buildings

Secondly, the buildings must be well designed. This is a matter
not only of technical efficiency but of considerable spiritual significance. From Plato downwards educators have recognized the
powerful indirect influence of physical surroundings. Notoriously
much of the impact of Oxford and Cambridge on their students
has been mediated through a certain architectural magnificence.
This is the product of a lordlier and less democratic age than ours,
and the ' Redbrick ' halls cannot and should not vie with it; but
they should have a modest dignity of their own and should give
satisfaction to the eye. A barrack or a mean and dingy building
defeats its own purpose.[2] The public rooms should have ample
space and furniture of reasonable comfort and shapeliness; and the
provision of ' a room of one's own ' for every student is of extreme
importance, though it has often not been forthcoming. The
student's rights should include the management during many hours
of the day of his own timetable and the means of seeing friends

---

[1] Burke *Works*, Vol. III, p. 228.

[2] This is partly a question of finance. Halls should no longer be the
Cinderella in any university household.

or of refusing to see them. The business of visiting and of being visited is an essential ingredient in student life, and so is the ability, at need, to ' sport one's oak.'

What is the proper size of a Hall? On this there is no clear consensus of opinion. The size of a large proportion of the existing Halls has been determined by necessity rather than by choice, by the amount of money available rather than by any considered educational policy. But, generally speaking, a Hall of twenty or thirty students is not only uneconomic but the range of its students is too restricted and it lends itself to excessive domination by the personality of a strong Warden. On the other hand a Hall can easily be too large to be a genuine community; it becomes impossible for the warden to know all the students in any significant way and the students themselves are likely to split into a number of small cliques. The best social unit is probably somewhat smaller than the best economic unit. But in a world of personal relations any doctrinaire regulation is exceptionally maladroit. ' Not less than seventy nor more, at the outside, than a hundred and fifty,' may serve as a rough general rule. But within these wide limits there is ample room for experiment.

## (3) Warden

More than any other factor, the personality of the Warden makes or mars a hall. A good Warden in a hovel will produce better results than a mediocre Warden in a palace. But this is not yet adequately recognized in the university world. For instance, the appointment seldom receives the same quantity and quality of attention as does the appointment of a professor. As a rule the whole-time Warden's salary and status are not comparable with those of a professor, and they are in sharp contrast with those of the ' Head of a House ' at Oxford or Cambridge. Again a whole-time Warden is seldom a member of the Senate. He may only learn indirectly, and much too late to influence decisions, of changes of regulation vitally important to his students and to their corporate life. In effect the Hall tends still to be tacitly regarded as a backwater, not in the main stream of university life, and the Warden as an auxiliary rather than as one of the university's most responsible officers. But if hall-life is regarded not merely as a convenience but as a fundamental part of university education, a Warden's responsibility is no less than a professor's and expenditure on him from university funds is no less legitimate. In this instance most universities have not yet readjusted their minds to the new policy.

Should a wardenship be regarded as a whole or a part-time job? Here the university authorities are in a dilemma. Sometimes they appoint as Warden one of their lecturers, or even a professor, who retains his teaching post. This ensures for the Warden status in the university and fellowship with the teaching staff; but he is liable to be overburdened, to be faced with a conflict of duties, and—particularly in a large Hall—to have too little time to give to the students. On the other hand the whole-time Warden can devote himself to the job, but it is difficult to pick the right man or woman, since the qualifications are nondescript; he is not learned, except *per accidens*; and, only too often, he is not really regarded by the teaching staff as one of, or on a par with, themselves. On the whole, opinion seems to be moving towards appointments which are mainly full-time, but with the addition of slight academic duties to give status and a link with the teaching staff. That is, the wardenship itself is a Warden's primary job.

What are the attributes of a good Warden? In addition to being a reasonably efficient administrator, he must be able to get on terms with, and to inspire, students without overpowering them. He must be a good delegator. He, or she, must be neither a ' dryasdust ' nor a ' governess,' neither a mere ' hearty ' nor a mere ' quartermaster.' He must himself care passionately for the things of the mind. If possible he should have a high academic qualification, and it is extremely desirable that he should have outside contacts which may help him to open windows and to correct the natural tendency of any small community to contraction of interests. A Hall in which there is frequent coming and going of visitors from the great world and from the civic community can contribute notably to the real education of its students. The married Warden who keeps open house has a great opportunity; but, in his case, it is well to take account of the wife as well as of the husband.

### (4) Senior Common Room

A Hall should not be regarded simply as an institution which provides accommodation for students and is administered by one or two officials. It is rather a community consisting of senior and junior members who seek together an intelligent organization and use of their time outside the lecture room and laboratory. Hence the residence in Hall of a number of the teaching staff, over and above Warden, Subwarden or Bursar, is valuable. It gives an opportunity for the free and unfettered intercourse of seniors and juniors which has played so large a part in the older English universities. In some instances such members of staff might undertake a special personal responsibility towards a small number of students as 'moral tutors' or 'regents,' but this is not essential. Members of staff naturally require slightly more extensive accommodation than students, and provision for them should be made when the Hall is being planned. It may well be worth sacrificing room for even a dozen extra students in order to include half a dozen dons.

(5) Students' Self-Government

The only way to train for responsibility is to give opportunity for exercising responsibility. This is one of those truisms which are often neglected, but, in dealing with persons of the student age, to neglect it is inexcusable. All communal living entails some rules, but these should be confined to what is necessary for the general convenience. Rules for the sake of 'uplift' are reported still to linger in a few women's Halls, but they are relics of an outmoded and unduly juvenile conception of education and it is high time they were ended. In every Hall the Students' Committee should have real power and should be entrusted with as much as possible of the organization of the common life. If a Hall is to be an effective instrument of education, it is essential to break down on both sides the last remains of fear and suspicion. The disciplinarian Warden, or Hall Committee, which grudges all 'concessions' to students lest they may be abused, is matched by the mentality of certain students who subconsciously regard the university staff as 'the bosses,' only to be dealt with along the lines of collective bargaining. The remedy for both is a sufficiency of free and easy personal contact and experience of friendly and informal co-operation. 'The students' representative committee should be given real responsibility within certain clearly-defined limits. Obviously there are certain major decisions of policy which cannot be taken by students. But this does not mean that they can be entrusted with no responsibility at all. In no university is the power given to students to run their Union wholly illusory, and neither administrative breakdowns nor irresponsible acts are of frequent occurrence. That similar powers are not granted to the same students within Hall must be due to the failure to see Halls as potential centres of a common life.'

### (6) Cultural Activities

Halls need, though not very many yet possess, good working libraries, where students can have easy access to the reference books and textbooks most in demand. These should be not only book-stores, but reasonably comfortable and dignified reading-rooms, where students can work in, and draw inspiration from, the atmos-phere of a library. But they should also be centres of a lively cultural life, of which the aim is simply mental enrichment with-out any *arrière pensée*. For this they need good recreational libraries, supplied both with current fiction and with literary classics of many kinds, in which students can relax and can browse, at leisure and carefree, on a variety of fare. They should also provide opportunities for music and for a dramatic society. In many a Hall production of an annual play is one of the most stimulating experiences which its members undergo. Above all there should be places where students become alive to the main problems of the day and develop their own philosophy of life. In Hall students should be able to discuss these problems with a greater intimacy and fullness than elsewhere and to give some thought to their own future task in society in relation to them. For the creation of an atmosphere in which such developments are likely, a heavy responsibility rests on the Warden and the senior residents.

### (7) Selection of Students

The selection of entrants should rest mainly with the Warden. Variety is highly important; the Hall should be a fair cross-section of the university. To admit a disproportionate number of students of any one type, to allow a large majority to consist of intending teachers or doctors or engineers, is to impoverish the common life and to run the risk of a dull monotony. Students should be drawn from different Faculties, different parts of the country, different types of school and of home. Further, the inclusion of a certain number of overseas students is specially desirable. This needs emphasis, since, at a time like this when there is great pressure on accommodation, they are liable to be crowded out. But any narrow nationalism must be sternly repudiated. Universities are, and always have been, cosmopolitan. When civilization is plainly

endangered by national estrangements, the dull, unimaginative
selfishness which excludes all foreigners till every qualified Briton
has found a place is not only unneighbourly but disastrous. It
is true that a somewhat greater maturity may reasonably be
required in a would-be student from overseas, particularly if he
represents a civilization remote from our own. But on all grounds
our universities must welcome some foreign element; and if foreign
students are to be here at all, it is particularly important for many
of them to be in Halls. Otherwise they find it hard to make any
personal contacts, and too often they are lonely and embittered.
In Hall they are made welcome and are speedily at home; and,
on their side, they contribute an invaluable element to the life
of the Hall and to the education of their British fellow-students.
One or two university colleges have gone out of their way to
welcome and to incorporate such students in their Halls, and they
have been richly rewarded. Obviously the proportion of overseas
students in a Hall cannot be high if its essential character is to be
preserved, but a small number of places might well be reserved
for them.

## (8) Relation to the University

This needs to be strengthened. At present Halls are often at a
great distance from the university and from one another and this
is a misfortune. Few British universities have anything resembling
a ' Campus.' But if parochialism is to be avoided and the university is genuinely to be a community, new Halls should be built near
together and, where it is physically possible, near the university.
To some extent a Hall can serve and enrich the whole university
as well as its own members. For this purpose new ways should be
explored of bringing outside students into Hall on particular occasions and for particular purposes, as some of them already come in
for dances or for the Play. Again if residence for a limited period
is made compulsory for most students—as several universities propose to make it when building progress admits—those students who
have gone out of Hall into lodgings or have returned to their
homes should retain their membership of the Junior Common
Room. Like the senior undergraduates at Oxford and Cambridge
they might be required to dine in Hall a certain number of times
each term. The same principle holds good for the staff. In some
Halls a number of non-resident members of the university staff
are elected to membership of the Senior Common Room. They are

encouraged to dine in Hall on certain evenings, and in this way the social circle is widened. This again is an example which might profitably be imitated.

# IX

## THE UNIVERSITY AND THE WORLD

### I GENERAL PRINCIPLES

Wisdom consists in keeping a balance between two or three general principles which, at first sight, seem to contradict one another. First, no social institution can be a law to itself. In the last resort the university must be judged by its service to the whole human family. Secondly, the university is not merely a means to any end other than itself. Mary's worth is not to be assessed by her contribution to Martha's efficiency or the *raison d'être* of the Church by its utility in maintaining morale. Similarly, the university has a character and a value of its own which must be safeguarded; and since its members are in the best position to appreciate these, the duty of guardianship falls specially on them. Thirdly, ceaseless criticism, from without as well as from within, is necessary to the university's health. For the plea of trusteeship, however true in itself, is constantly used in practice to palliate and to perpetuate evil things like privilege, preciosity, blind conservatism, social indifference and irresponsibility. It has been truly said that we, in the universities, must carry very far the examination of what we and our present activities are worth to society; and in doing so, we must make opportunities to see ourselves as others see us.

These principles are universally valid. But their application must vary with time and place. 'Now and in England,' our society is conscious both of instability—and of a furious increase in the pace of events—and also of the urgency and the possibilities of social planning. Certainly the university must never suffer itself to become simply the handmaid of Church or State. But it requires to-day a steadily growing awareness of the needs of the outside world and a strong sense of responsibility in regard to them.

### 2 THE UNIVERSITY AND THE STATE

Here and now we are at a critical growing-point in the relation between universities and the State. There has recently been a notable increase in public interest in the universities, owing to realization of their war-services and of the part they may play in reconstruction. Public opinion is inclined to do more for them and to demand more of them than has been customary. For practical purposes and irrespective of their precise legal status, it is coming to regard them as national institutions rather than as private corporations, however august and venerable.

## a.  The Past

In the past, any external control of universities has taken one of three main forms. The first of these is, to lay down fundamental laws for a university in its charter of foundation. It is true that two or three of the earliest universities, Bologna, Paris and Oxford, came into existence without any formal charter. They were customary societies rather than legal corporations; they were not made but grew.[1] But since the middle of the thirteenth century, the legal existence of any university and the validity of its degrees have depended on the grant of a charter by the powers that be, whether ecclesiastical or temporal; and the conditions laid down in the charter cannot be varied by the university but only by the power that granted it.[2] The essential mark of a university is the power to grant degrees which will be recognized in the world at large. But a degree was, originally, itself a licence to teach—the *jus ubique docendi,* and it was a principle generally recognized in the Middle Ages that ' nobody should set up as a teacher without having been himself for an adequate period taught by some duly authorized master.'[3] There was thus, among authorized teachers, a kind of apostolic succession.

The second is the exercise by the sovereign of a quasi-visitatorial power. The Pope frequently intervened dictatorially in the affairs of the University of Paris. In the thirteenth century, for instance, he restrained the University from enforcing its own regulations against the Friars. In the fifteenth century, orthodox king and archbishop together trampled on the University of Oxford, in order to extirpate the Lollardy favoured by the university, and Louis XI reduced the University of Paris to an ignominious subjection from which it did not recover. On the other hand, James II's despotic and ill-judged treatment of Oxford and Cambridge, and in parti-

---

[1] Rashdall, *op. cit.* I, pp. 143, 283, III, p. 49.

[2] In the early centuries this was the Pope and later the King.

[3] Rashdall, *op. cit.* I, p. 283.

cular his violation of Magdalen College, was one of the causes of his downfall. Like the earlier Marian persecution, if in a lesser degree, it left a permanent imprint on the British mind. 'Hands off the universities' has become a sentiment that will not easily be dislodged. During the nineteenth and twentieth centuries university constitutions have frequently been remodelled by legislative action, following on enquiries by government-appointed Commissions. This has happened to Oxford and Cambridge (three times), to the Scottish universities, to London, Durham and the University of Wales. But in all these cases such Royal Commissions have only been set on foot in response to strong demands for reform from within the universities concerned, though they have sometimes been highly distasteful to the university authorities.

The third method is control of major university appointments. This is widely used in other countries, but extremely sparingly in Great Britain. It is true there are some 'Regius Chairs' of considerable dignity and antiquity, and in Scotland three out of four Principalships are Crown appointments. But these seem to be rather relics of earlier activities of the Crown as 'pious founder' than to be due to any general principle. They are relatively few in number and they are confined to the older universities. In practice the Crown has long exercised this responsibility with a good deal of regard for university opinion and a scrupulous abstention from political bias.

## b. The Present and the Future

The new factor to-day is the enormously increased financial support which the Treasury is giving to the universities. At the beginning of the century such support was negligible in amount. In the years between the wars it grew till it represented, on an average, about one-third of their total income. It is now being quadrupled and, in future, is likely to be not less than two-thirds of the whole. Obviously this has given the Government an irresistible weapon for establishing control of university policy, *if it were minded to use it and were supported by public opinion in so doing*. It could then exercise pressure without recourse to the cumbrous, and necessarily occasional, action of the Legislature. Hitherto the power of the purse has been exercised with extreme restraint. It has been an accepted maxim that any serious infringement of university autonomy would be too high a price to pay for increased co-ordination and efficiency. In this respect, Great Britain appears

to be unique.  Elsewhere universities fall into one of two classes—
that which is both subsidized and controlled or that which is neither
controlled nor subsidized.  Here alone they are heavily subsidized
but ordinarily uncontrolled.  Should such governmental abstinence
continue?

In this situation there are those who cry ' Ichabod.'  They hold
indeed that the universities have sold their birthright for a mess of
pottage.  At the close of the Middle Ages universities lost much
of their independence concurrently with a great accession of endowment from royal patrons; ' in their poverty had been their strength.'[1]
So, it is argued, the civil power, bringing gifts, should always be
suspect.  On the other hand there are those who regard the same
facts as giving an opportunity for forming and executing a comprehensive national policy over the whole university field, which it
would be cowardly and irresponsible to shirk.

At the outset we must repudiate each of two extreme views.
According to the one, universities are sluggish corporations, complacent and selfish, which require to be re-directed and galvanized
by central authority, in the spirit in which Napoleon rationalized
so many French institutions.  ' Universities,' said Lord Melbourne,
' never reform themselves.  Everyone knows that.'[2]  Hence, by
implication, reform must be imposed upon them.

> Afar will Democracy chase it,
>     That gang of impenitent dons,
> Who drowned the soft murmur of *Placet*
>     By bawling their truculent *Nons*.

But this is based on the ' hubristic ' and precarious assumption that
Westminster and Whitehall know better what is good for the
universities than do the universities themselves.  According to the
other view, the right of the universities to be master in their own
house is so indefeasible that it is in all circumstances morally *ultra
vires* and almost impious to lay a hand on them.  ' Spoliation ' and
' totalitarianism ' are charges freely made against every form of
external regulation.  But this attitude rests on the equally presumptuous and implausible assumption that, in university affairs,
a monopoly of wisdom and of a sound judgment of values rests
with the S.C.R.  Such doctrinaire guild-socialism would have made
impossible the reform of Oxford and Cambridge which resulted

[1] Rashdall, *op. cit.* III, p. 167.
[2] Quoted by Winstanley, *Unreformed Cambridge*, p. 187.

from the first Commission, and would have left them still the homes of flesh-pots and sinecures, of dead languages and lost causes. It was in fact, the main basis of the contemporary opposition, but fortunately that was defeated.

That all state-intervention is to be welcomed, and that all is sacrilegious, are equally untenable propositions. But, short of such fantasies, there is a running debate between the upholders of more moderate positions, each of which is worthy of respect. Without denying the ultimate overriding authority of the State, and hence its right to intervene, a large body of university opinion would urge that such authority should only be exercised with extreme circum-spection and in the last resort. To act otherwise, would be, in Burke's phrase, to take the extreme medicine of the constitution for its daily bread. On the other hand it is urged that universities left to themselves are slow-moving bodies, having little cohesion with one another, that they require to be kept up to the mark and that there is small prospect of any coherent university policy for the country as a whole without some direction by central authority.

These are views maintained on such grounds as the following.

## (1) The Case for Autonomy

(i) *Cuique in sua arte credendum.* ' Academic freedom is simply a way of saying that we get the best results in education and research if we leave their management to people who know some-thing about them.'[1] Otherwise we are likely to get unintelligent criticism and the ' philistine' in the saddle. The criterion of methods, organization and results is likely to be what ' the low world' with ' coarse thumb and finger' finds straightway to its mind and values in a trice. The proper way of doing a job can only be determined from within. It is true that this is less obvious when the question is, ' *What* job shall the expert do?' For example, it is less obvious when the question is, ' For which occupations shall vocational preparation be provided?' or ' What classes of student shall be admitted to the university and on what conditions?' than when it is concerned with methods of teaching, hours of work, or the value of residence. ' He who pays the piper calls the tune'; but even so the cogency of this maxim varies with the piper. If you are engaging Toscanini and his orchestra, you will do well to leave to him the major voice in deciding the programme.

(ii) University autonomy is in line with the British tradition of

---

[1] Hutchins, *op. cit.*, p. 21.

spontaneous cohesion.  The national genius has shown itself in a rich profusion of corporate bodies of voluntary origin, and often of high prestige and great longevity, such as the Inns of Court, the Royal Colleges of Physicians and Surgeons, the Royal Society and the British Academy, the Public Schools, the Boy Scouts, the Friendly Societies and the Trade Unions.  In all these the normally operative force is custom rather than precise regulation.  Local and functional freedom, in contrast to bureaucratic centralization, has been the source of much in our history that is most characteristic and is most prized.  To respect the autonomy of the universities is in tune with this tradition; that is, to respect their freedom to make their own rules of admission, to determine their own subjects and methods of teaching, to publish what they think fit without let or hindrance.  Government should no more think of dictating these things than of dictating the rules of the Athenæum or the M.C.C.  Theoretically it can do so, but it should have sense enough to refrain.  To exercise its full effect, a university must have an individuality which can be known and loved.  This condition is fulfilled in an eminent degree by the older universities, and the younger members of the family shine with a reflected lustre.  ' The universities are bodies of the highest rank and dignity in the kingdom, and, whatever you do with regard to them, you must do with the most scrupulous respect not only for their position but even for their prejudices, and above all with a scrupulous respect for the fond and fervent affection of the community for them.'  So Gladstone argued in 1850.[1]  Hence reformation should come from within and not from without, even if it comes somewhat slowly.  We should trust to ' that power of self-development which is the happy peculiarity of English institutions,'[2] by which, for instance during the nineteenth century, the college buildings and the college system silently adapted themselves to the altered needs of the time.

(iii)  Any sort of regimentation is unfavourable to the creative thinking which is the highest task of the university.  This depends indeed much on co-operation.  But it is on a type of co-operation involving sensitive, uninhibited and immediate response between fellow-workers steeped in a common scholarly or scientific tradition.  It requires free and constantly renewed personal volition, to which any kind of stereotyping is an obstacle.[3]

[1] *Hansard,* Third Series, Vol. 112, pp. 1495 ff.
[2] Rashdall, *op. cit.* I, p. 533.
[3] See Graham Wallas, *The Art of Thought,* ch. 12, and Michael Polanyi, *The Foundations of Academic Thinking.*

(iv)  The risk of political interference is great and the experience of other countries should be a danger signal.  Even fifty years ago, in the heyday of *Wissenschaft,* it was hard for an avowed Social Democrat to get, or to retain, an academic post in Germany.  But more recently National Socialist Germany, Fascist Italy and Communist Russia have afforded glaring examples of politically-dominated universities.  Against this, as Mr. Attlee has recently said, it is vital to preserve the liberty of disputation, the freedom of the instructed to question and to challenge the instructor.  Also universities are to some extent supernational.  The failure of the German universities to offer any effective spiritual resistance to Hitlerism is rightly felt to have ' let down ' the university community dispersed throughout the world.  Bodies such as the Institute of Cultural Relations or International Student Service bear witness to a recognition by university people of ties and obligations which transcend national frontiers and are not to be dissolved or suspended by the fiat of any national government.  Indeed the health of society requires a certain balance between different ' Orders '— political, economic, cultural, religious, rather than the absorption of all the rest by a single one, the political.  Society needs the university, not only as an agent but sometimes as a mentor.  For that purpose a certain independence is necessary; just as the Crown appoints the judges and they act in its name, but one of their duties is to do justice, if need be, between the Crown and its subjects.  So, for the due performance of its function, the university must be recognized as an independent spiritual organ of the community.

(2)  The Case Against Complete Autonomy

' The university does not at present fulfil all the purposes for which she is designed as a national institution.'  When Lord John Russell, as Prime Minister, introduced his Bill for the better government of the University of Oxford, it was on that premise that he based his argument.  Naturally its validity was hotly disputed.  It was argued that the university was not ' a national institution,' but was founded by Churchmen for Churchmen; and that a large part of the endowments of university and colleges were given, for the benefit, not of all and sundry, but of particular sets of people, coming from particular localities, belonging to particular families (e.g., Founders' Kin), holding particular beliefs or preparing for particular callings.  To divert these endowments to other purposes, to throw open the foundations to other classes than those contemplated by the founders, was robbery. But, sincerely and even passionately as it was urged, that argument would not do a hundred years ago, and it will do still less to-day. It is true that the British universities are not State-universities. But the nation cannot regard them simply as private and voluntary societies, free without question to make their own rules, to go their own way, to conduct—and possibly to wind up—their own affairs. In certain, highly important, respects at least they are national institutions, in as much as they powerfully affect the national life at a hundred points and are vital to its well-being, they depend increasingly on the financial support of the Treasury, and they recognize obligations not only to a section but to the whole community. Hence the State as 'the operative criticism of institutions' has a certain responsibility for keeping universities like other institutions up to the mark.

The argument against all intervention is apt to take two inconsistent forms. The one, much used at the time of the original Oxford and Cambridge Royal Commission, stresses the wrongfulness of any interference with the intentions of founders and benefactors. In the university, it is suggested, this would be a breach of trust, in Government it would be confiscation. The other stresses the character of the university as a living community and not merely a piece of governmental machinery. It asserts the university's right to grow and develop in its own way and not only in accordance with some formal specification; that is, its right, as against any external prohibition, to outgrow its own past. The one is based on rigidity, the other on flexibility. But the academic purist cannot have it both ways. In any case the former of these lines of argument is generally dishonest; it certainly was so in the mouths of the diehards of a hundred years ago. By a kind of tacit conspiracy many original statutes had long fallen into abeyance. In Cambridge a number of the Elizabethan statutes were flagrantly disregarded from the first.[1] On this head Oxford was equally vulnerable to attack.[2] In effect the real contention amounted to this : insiders may quietly discard constitutional rules but outsiders must not openly abrogate them. But it is not legitimate to arrogate to the life-tenants of a corporation an exclusive right to the management of its affairs against the Legislature.[3] In any case, now that

[1] Winstanley, *Unreformed Cambridge,* p. 4 ff.
[2] See Sir W. Hamilton's indictment in the *Edinburgh Review.*
[3] See Gladstone in the House of Commons. *Hansard,* 3rd Series, Vol. 131, pp. 892 ff.

endowments count for so much less, the argument is much less plausible than in the nineteenth century.

The case for autonomy really rests on the other basis, i.e., on the inherent right of associations in a free country to conduct their own affairs in their own way and to develop spontaneously according to the inner necessities of their own nature. But, from the point of view of public policy, this claim is subject to serious deductions. In the first place universities are guilds. Left to themselves, they are subject to the common faults of guilds and other corporate bodies, to lethargy, ' the pleasant torpor of too fixed a tradition '; to a prejudiced conservatism, intolerant of the innovator, who is liable to be hampered, proscribed and regarded as guilty of infamous conduct in his professional capacity; to self-centredness issuing in an obstinate defence of its accustomed privileges and monopolies. Thus an appeal to the sacredness of the freedom of associations was made about the same time, with equal indefensibility and fortunately with equal ill-success, on behalf of the unreformed universities and of the corrupt municipal corporations of the eighteenth and early nineteenth centuries. That is, ' Liberty ' was invoked on behalf of an essentially illiberal régime. Further, an academic guild is liable to a special bias of its own which accentuates these defects. It often suffers from a morbid hypertrophy of the critical, in comparison with the creative, faculty. ' Donnishness ' is injurious to progress. It sees the objections to any particular action as it were through a magnifying glass; it sees the objections to inaction with no such clearness. Dr. Flexner is, in general, warmly eulogistic of Oxford and Cambridge, but he was not without warrant when he wrote, ' Progressive efforts are likely to encounter an impalpable, resistant tradition as difficult to penetrate as a London fog.' A clever satirical analysis of types of argument current in university politics forty years ago arrives at the triumphant conclusion that ' Nothing must ever be done for the first time.' Also the university is liable to be insulated. ' A philosophy, a mode of thought, a habit of mind, may live on in the lecture-rooms of professors for a century after it had been abandoned by the thinkers, the men of letters, and the men of the world.'[1]

The case against complete non-interference is strengthened when account is taken of the time-factor. The processes of ' reform from within ' are excessively slow-moving. Thus at the time of the

[1] Rashdall, *op. cit.* I, p. 266.

first Royal Commission, the Vice-Chancellor of Cambridge wrote
to his Chancellor (Prince Albert) to deprecate interference with the
university's 'gradual course of improvement.'[1] But it was all-too-
gradual.  Agitation had already been going on for twenty years,
and it would probably have continued, with small result, for twenty
or forty more if the Legislature had not intervened.  Few would
now dispute that surgery was then imperative.  But to-day the argument for haste is far stronger amidst the startling, and indeed
terrifying, acceleration of social change.  Academic constitutional
machinery is, too often, funereal in its rate of movement.  If the
university is to be thought of as a living organism, its psycho-
physical processes seem sometimes to resemble those of the mastodon
or the dinosaur.  Indeed the *status quo* is defended in depth by a
whole series, as it were, of barbed-wire entanglements; committees,
delegacies, syndicates, boards of faculty, senates, councils, courts.
But in the critical world of to-day there is simply no time for
'muddling through'; that method belongs to the leisurely days
that are no more.

Further, in academic circles, the bogy of State-interference has
been much overworked.  There are other forms of interference
more sinister, and, in Great Britain and America at least, more
common; and these are often tolerated by academic tories.  Indeed
the State may approach a university as rescuer rather than a
dragon.  There is the tyranny, and sometimes the stranglehold, of
the dead hand, of the millionaire benefactor, of alumni, of munici-
palities, of vulgar opinion expressed shrilly by the cheap press, in
the old bad days even of the 'noble patron.'  Indeed the dogma
of freedom from external interference may be, and in the past often
has been, used to deny internal freedom.  Against such tyrannies
occasional State-intervention may come as emancipation.  Without
such intervention in the past, it is hard to see how in Oxford and
Cambridge nonconformists or unbelievers could have been admitted
to full academic citizenship, how democracy could have been established against the oligarchy of the 'heads of houses,' how the
university itself could have been emancipated from the domination
of the colleges.  State-action on such lines is truly 'a hindrance of
hindrances.'  It does not stifle, but augments or even creates,
freedom.  To raise the standard of 'autonomy' against such
intervention would be hypocrisy.

[1] Winstanley, *Early Victorian Cambridge*, p. 271.

### (3)  Restatement of the Question

So far our picture is grossly over-simplified.  So long as we think merely in terms of a sharp antithesis—' either-or '—between university autonomy and State control, we shall never get beyond the debating-society level of understanding.  In the abstract, autonomy and State-control are contrary and incompatible; in real life so sharp an antithesis is crude and doctrinaire.  In Great Britain the actual relation between State and universities is far more subtle and less clear-cut.  In any case, to be confined to such a choice of alternatives, either no planning or no freedom, would in practice be intolerable.  On the one hand we *must* have more national planning than we have been accustomed to, in view of the crisis in which we now live and of the sheer pace of events.  ' Let them rip !' is an impossible slogan for to-day.  Also the universities are institutions of such significance for the national life that it is out of the question for government to disinterest itself in their development, at least to the extent of ensuring that it is going forward and that it is responsive to major national needs.  On the other hand we *must* have freedom for the universities to develop according to the dictates of their own nature, as that is understood by those who have the ' feel ' of them which comes only from long inside experience.  Rigidity is death to the university, death from arteriosclerosis, but we have had lurid examples in totalitarian countries of the effect of political interference, that is death from violence.  We must have both freedom and planning.  Our practical problem is not whether, but how, we are to combine them.  Whoever the planners are, whether Ministers of the Crown and civil servants, or Vice-Chancellors, professors and lecturers, their job is to plan in such a way as to preserve, and even to enhance, the university's vital freedoms.  On the other hand, in this country government has found a technique which enables it to give a very large financial support to universities, while leaving them a measure of elbow-room unexampled elsewhere.  It is the job of the universities to use this autonomy not for selfish isolation and contraction out of social responsibilities, but so as to rise to the height of the times and to give the maximum of public service compatible with their primary mission.

For an adequate understanding of these tasks, certain preliminaries are essential.  (1) On both sides some familiar caricatures or stock-figures must be got rid of.  The statesmen or civil servants who represent the British Government in its dealings with universities are not in the least like Prussian drill-sergeants or Russian commissars. They are not even like the stock figure of a British bureaucrat—rigid, philistine, conventional, a patron of mediocrity and a foe to originality. University teachers and administrators to-day are equally removed from the College Fellows of the eighteenth or early nineteenth century—lazy, socially irresponsible, and stubbornly retentive of their accustomed routines and privileges. To ignore this change is to repeat the mistake of 'Big Bill Thompson' of Chicago, who could not distinguish George V from George III. (2) The relation between government departments and universities is not like a tug-of-war. It is not a tussle or collision of wills between two opposing groups, the one set to direct and dominate and the other to resist. (3) If there were such a collision, the British universities have, for some centuries now, been far from merely helpless victims of superior force, as James II found to his cost. They can be formidable antagonists. 'At the universities had been formed the minds of almost all the eminent clergymen, lawyers, physicians, wits, poets and orators of the land, and of a large proportion of the nobility and opulent gentry . . . There was no corner of England in which both universities had not grateful and zealous sons. Any attack on the honour or interests of either Cambridge or Oxford was certain to excite the resistance of a powerful, active, and intelligent class, scattered over every county from Northumberland to Cornwall.'[1] (4) What was true at the end of the seventeenth century has been no less true in the eighteenth and early nineteenth centuries. Indeed the position of the universities became even stronger, for if military terms are to be used, they have had an effective fifth column operating within the enemy's lines and occupying many of his key positions. Statesmen and higher civil servants have generally themselves been graduates, warmly sharing in that 'scrupulous respect and fond and fervid affection' for the universities which Gladstone ascribed to the whole community. For instance, out of twenty-three Prime Ministers between 1800 and 1915, twenty-one were university men and twenty had been at Oxford or Cambridge.[2] In the last hundred years, six Prime Ministers have been most prominently identified with individual universities as their Chancellors, and two others had served their university in Parliament as its Burgesses.

[1] Macaulay, *History of England* II, p. 278.
[2] The only exceptions were Wellington and Disraeli.

There has thus been a psychological atmosphere of understanding and friendliness which contrasts sharply with what has prevailed in many other countries and in some British Dominions.  On the other hand, the university authorities in recent years have commonly possessed a keen sense of duty to the nation.  They have not resented, but have invited, guidance from government and its representatives concerning public needs which the universities might help to meet; e.g., the varying demands for men with different types of specialized training, such as chemical engineers, agricultural biologists, school teachers..  They have consistently been anxious to understand and to satisfy such demands, though they have properly been watchful lest fulfilment of a large number of immediate, short-term needs should be at the expense of the universities' most distinctive functions and their long-term usefulness to the world.

At this point, no doubt, certain doubts and questions may legitimately be raised.  It may be said : ' Your picture applies to Oxford and Cambridge, but how far does it apply to Sheffield or Bristol?  Even with Oxford and Cambridge, while it has been and in large measure still is true, will it last?  Is it not beginning to pass away, and is it not likely to do so at an increasing rate?  There are fewer graduates in the present Cabinet than has been usual, and may not the higher ranks of the Civil Service well be less monopolized by university-trained men in the coming era?  In any case, ought it to last?  Is not the dethronement of ' the old school tie ' overdue?  Perhaps it is no accident that Lord John Russell, who set up the first Oxford and Cambridge Commission, was himself the one university-trained Prime Minister of the nineteenth century who was not an Oxford or Cambridge man.  Perhaps it is as well that he did not see these illustrious universities ' through a happy mist of youthful memories but in the cold light of reason.'[1]  From the other side, university stalwarts sometimes fear that Vice-Chancellors and such like have too much spiritual kinship with administrators in government service and may too easily ' sell the pass.'

The answer to such queries seems to be, first, that the reputation of the older universities is so high and so firmly established that the younger universities reap the benefit.  A certain prestige has come to inhere in the very name, ' University.'  Secondly, a close liaison and sympathy between representatives of universities and those of government departments or ministers is in the main

_____
[1] Winstanley, *Early Victorian Cambridge*, p. 220.

healthy, though no doubt it needs to be democratized and not to be an esoteric understanding between the privileged.

The crucial point is this. The proper relation between government, in all its grades, and the universities is not that of master and servant, still less that of artificer and tool. It is not even that of superior and subordinate officer. It is that of partners in a common enterprise. They do not meet as diplomats representing rival Powers, each striving to extort as much, and to make as little, concession as possible. They meet as allies, for consultation rather than debate; as Churchill and Roosevelt used to meet in wartime rather than as Bevin and Molotov meet to-day. Except in a physical sense they are not on opposite sides of the table. They are united by a common purpose, though they have different angles of approach, different intellectual contributions to make, and hence are likely to do a better job by pooling their ideas. The technique of such contact is, not only to eliminate, but often to capitalize friction.

Sir Oliver Franks has lately given an illuminating account of the relation between the Service Departments and Industry in wartime, as mediated through the Ministry of Supply.[1] It was far from consisting in the issue of orders by the Departments and their execution by the industrialists. As Sir Oliver puts it, it was ' dialectical.' That is, there was a constant intellectual cross-fertilization, which often resulted in solutions to problems more ingenious and successful than either party could have attained by themselves. Sometimes, under the stimulus of national demand, industrialists found ways of making possible the hitherto impossible. But sometimes, under the comment and criticism of the industrialists, the departments radically modified their original demands. This analogy is valuable for our purpose, since the relation between State (as represented by ministers and government departments) and universities is certainly dialectical. But there are two points of difference between the two cases, both of which emphasize the special importance of the university's initiative. First, as Sir Oliver points out, in wartime the common end of the joint enterprise was crystal-clear and undisputed—to win the war. In peacetime this situation is not reproduced. To some extent the partners are feeling their way as they go along; they are gradually modifying and enriching a conception of their common purpose, which is at first rather nebulous. Secondly, in wartime, political considerations are

[1] *Central Planning and Control in Peace and War.*

dominant and the last word is always with the final political authority, the War Cabinet. In peacetime the proper relation between politics and culture is less simple and obvious. Legally it is true, a government supported by Parliament can always enforce its will; it can remodel or even close down a recalcitrant university. Short of this, it can apply almost irresistible pressure by cutting off supplies. But what is legally allowable may easily be morally wrong or politically inept; and there are weighty reasons for allowing to universities a very high degree of autonomy, as is the tradition in this country. If all is to go well, the predominant rôle in the ordinary management of any concern must be with the partner who supplies the knowledge and experience rather than the partner who supplies most of the capital.

Indeed the relation between the universities and the government resembles less that between producer and consumer or between tradesman and customer than that between artist and patron. Execution the patron must obviously leave to the artist. Choice of theme he need not so leave; he may entrust the artist with specific commissions. But the greatest achievements in painting, or music or poetry, are likely to occur when the artist chooses his own subject and is not harassed by a demand for quick results, easily appreciable by the layman. Government control means lay control. There is always the danger that the layman, employing criteria which he can understand and seeking to satisfy the felt need of the moment, will impair or destroy the university's most precious, but intangible, assets. He will use a razor to sharpen a pencil. It is only the insider, soaked in a tradition of craftmanship, who is likely to have the trained flair and the sense of perspective, which will enable him to say, ' You can't do that there 'ere,' when it is vital to say it.[1] Such ' autonomy ' does not imply anarchy. To repudiate government control, which would probably have been somewhat rigid and insufficiently informed, is to keep room for the elastic control of a constantly developing professional tradition, to which scholars and scientists are sensitive and which is the criterion whose authority they recognize.

Here two observations of Professor Jaspers are relevant. ' The genuinely human State achieves along with power a simultaneous limitation of power, *because it aims at realizing Justice*'; and again, ' The university claims freedom of teaching and learning as the

[1] See Michael Oakeshott, ' Rationalism in Politics,' *Cambridge Journal,* vol. 2, no. 2.

condition of the *responsible* independence of teachers and lecturers.'[1] That is, the State is not morally free to mould the university to its will, nor is the university morally free to go its own way at its own pleasure. Their relation will only be healthy when both recognize a higher loyalty. Similarly Professor Michael Polanyi has pointed out that the basis of the intellectual conscience of the scholar or the scientist is his sense, in discovery, of making contact with a spiritual reality by which he is controlled. Professional tradition may be corrupt. But it is properly rooted in access to spiritual reality and in a consequent moral compulsion. *Hier stehe ich und kann nicht anders.* His claim to freedom is in the name of this, more funda-mental, allegiance. He makes it, not as a gifted or privileged, but as a dedicated, person. The university must be free, as the Church must be free, to obey God rather than man.

To-day in Great Britain, it is broadly true that the contacts of State and universities are governed by an understanding of this kind. When their representatives sit down at a table together, both parties recognize the special function and character of the university and are determined to preserve it. So as their discussions go forward, mind is stimulated by mind and ideas flash to and fro. When a conclusion is reached, the question where it first originated is usually unanswerable. Where this spirit prevails, the precise machinery of co-operation is of secondary importance.

At this point we may well be challenged. It may be said, ' Your picture is highly idealized and utopian. Can you seriously suggest it is photographic ? Are not government and its servants on the one hand and university spokesmen on the other less dis-interested and enlightened than you have painted them or than they like to suppose themselves ? Are not ministers sometimes obsessed with vote-catching and amenable to political pressure; and do they not play for safety and for easy popularity ? Are not civil servants liable to be philistine and power-loving, disposed to tame and standardize what they do not quite understand ? On the side of the pundits, is there not sometimes a limpet-like clinging to privilege and a shrinking from facing radical criticism and change ? In their personal composition is there no tincture, here of the complacency of Bumble, there of the opportunism of the Vicar of Bray, and elsewhere of the artfulness of the Heathen Chinee ? Finally, if there is concord, may it not simply betoken

---

[1] In his deeply moving rectorial address at the re-opening of Heidelberg University in 1945, C.N.L. No. 247 (the italics are mine).

an unholy alliance of the two types of panjandrum to keep in their
places the plebeian and the rebel?' In such charges there is,
undeniably, some element of truth. It must be borne constantly
in mind so that we may be on our guard against the snare. In
particular the Christian should remember how constantly idealization has led to idolization of the ephemeral and to a flight from
reality. But, when all deductions are made, it remains true that
the prevailing type of relation between our universities and our
public authorities is a fruitful one. Indeed our tradition in this
respect is the envy of many other countries; it is something to hold
on to and to develop.

What is the practical moral? First, in an age both of crisis and
of planning, some increase of planning in the university world is
inevitable. A somewhat quicker adjustment of universities to
major social needs is imperative. Secondly, government has some
responsibility for seeing that this is done, and it can give some help
in the doing of it. Encroachment on the one side and suspicion
on the other are misconceived and a little out of date. The chief
danger to our universities to-day does not come from probable
government interference nor are their gravest defects due to this.
They are due rather to the pervasive influence of the mass mind,
and it is this which is the most formidable menace. Against this
the State may even be an ally, since the level of enlightenment in
government circles and government offices is commonly much in
advance of the man in the street. Thirdly, universities need, nevertheless, the maximum of autonomy and inner flexibility. Reform
is far more effective and is likely to be more wisely conceived if it
comes from within and takes full account of the intangible factors
which outsiders will almost certainly ignore or underestimate,
because they cannot easily be formulated but can only be recognized
by the trained eye. Direct State-action, like surgery, should be
occasional and rare; its function is negative rather than positive,
it is to remove otherwise immovable obstacles. It is, at its best,
only a necessary evil. Fourthly, the condition of university
autonomy is responsibility. It is only by a quick and sensitive
responsiveness to what is really going on in the world, and by a
readiness to undertake even drastic reforms without undue delay
when the situation calls for them, that freedom can be maintained.
Freedom simply to go on in accustomed ruts will, and ought to,
be unattainable. Finally, the only guarantee either of reform or
of freedom that is worth much rests, not on the law, but on the

Q

convention of the constitution.  It consists in the education of public opinion both inside and outside the universities.  Among the general public, there must be more widely diffused some understanding of the true character and purpose of universities and of the conditions in which alone they can do their best work.  What is wanted, is a growing reverence for learning and scientific enquiry and for their values.  Within the universities we need a more lively understanding of major communal needs and of the significance of communal changes actually occurring.  We need, too, to practise regular and searching self-examination in regard to the university's fulfilment of its responsibilities to the nation.

## 3   THE UNIVERSITY AND THE LOCAL COMMUNITY

The relationship here discussed affects different universities in very different degrees, since Oxford and Cambridge are almost entirely national rather than local in character and so, in most respects, are the Scottish universities.  London again is metropolitan and its local affiliations, though they exist, are not strongly marked.  But for the ' Redbrick ' group of universities, designated sometimes as ' civic ' and sometimes as ' provincial,' it is of primary importance, and any estimate of their worth must take it into account.  These universities are regional not only by hard necessity but by deliberate choice.  They came into existence for two reasons.  The first was to extend the opportunity of university education to a wider social circle, Oxford and Cambridge being then confined to the few and to the specially privileged.  To effect this, as Matthew Arnold wrote eighty years ago, ' We must take the instruction to the students and not hope to bring the students to the instruction.'[1] The ' Redbrick ' universities have put into practice what Arnold preached.  Secondly, they embody the aspiration of the great seats of population to become intellectual centres as well as mere places of business, and so to continue the tradition and to emulate the glories of Athens and Alexandria, of Rome, Florence and Venice.[2] Thus there is, by deliberate intention and almost by definition, an

[1] *Op. cit.*, p. 290.
[2] Perhaps this might be expressed rather more precisely and less grandiloquently as follows.  Our great industrial centres came into existence, as it were overnight, with little coherent planning or civic consciousness.  At their outset these universities represented the effort of a few enlightened and public-spirited men to convince their fellow-citizens that there are other essential elements in civic greatness than commercial success and to stimulate them to aspire to such things.

organic connection between these universities and the cities or districts in which they are set. They are not only *in,* but *of,* their regions. Such a university 'meets the desire of the people for it, and it is strong according as they take interest and pride in the extension of its influence and in the distinction of its members.'[1]

For this local connection there is a heavy price to be paid, or, at least, there are formidable dangers to be surmounted. First, there is an obvious risk of parochialism and philistinism. 'Redbrick' university is liable to be 'provincial' in a qualitative as well as in a geographical sense. It has not been founded in Canterbury or York, Winchester or Salisbury, cities rich in historic buildings and traditions, but in 'Drabtown.' It may too easily take colour from, rather than irradiate, its surroundings and be drab inwardly in its soul as well as outwardly in its body. 'Can any good thing come out of Nazareth?' was the cry of critics at its foundation. 'Anyone educated in Manchester,' said the *Saturday Review,* 'would certainly be dull and probably vicious.'[2] Even the first Principal of Owens College, in his inaugural address, spoke of 'the prodigious, antagonist forces' to be encountered in an industrial metropolis. That it would have low intellectual standards, that its degrees would therefore be fraudulent trademarks, that it would recognize no values other than those of Mr. Gradgrind or Mr. Podsnap, were prophecies freely hazarded at its outset. Happily these forecasts have been belied, owing, in large measure, to the outstanding ability and idealism of many of the early teachers. But a certain cultural penury remains, as of a pasturage irrigated from too few sources.

Secondly, there is insufficient variety among the students. Two-thirds of these come from the immediate neighbourhood of their university; and, of these two-thirds, not less than ninety per cent. continue to live at home. It has been said that the 'Redbrick' student meets only his own double. He is liable to be inbred and unawakened, and to remain in *statu quo* mentally as well as physically.

Thirdly, an industrial city is an uninspiring physical setting for a university. Instead of spacious and stately buildings, green lawns, and the glamour of a historic tradition splendidly embodied, you have buildings frequently dingy and cramped and sometimes sordid, set in an environment of smoke and slums.

[1] S. Alexander, *A Plea for an Independent University in Manchester,* p. 5.
[2] Quoted in Fiddes, *Chapters in the History of Owens College and of Manchester University* 1851–1914, p. 73.

But there is also a rich compensation. For instance, many forms of study, now recognized as suitable for a university, can only be carried on satisfactorily in the immediate neighbourhood of large centres of population. Engineering and clinical medicine are obvious examples, in which the co-operation of industry or of hospitals is needful. But the same is true, in large measure, of training for commerce, social services, or the practice of law; for such studies the great city is the laboratory. Again, the students of 'Redbrick' have had, on the whole, a greater strenuousness and seriousness of purpose than those of 'Oxbridge.' Life at 'Oxbridge' has been described as 'a serious and studious picnic,' with the accent on the word 'picnic.' But a 'home student' at Manchester or Leeds or Birmingham is under small temptation to forget that life is real and earnest. Most important of all, there are many kinds of 'Hubris,' and academic 'Hubris' is one of them. In large cities academic people more easily find their level and are less exposed to self-sufficiency and complacency. Professors and lecturers are not *ex-officio,* much regarded; self-importance is not a temptation into which they are commonly led. The relation of 'Town' and 'Gown' is healthier where 'Town' is in no way parasitic upon 'Gown.'

Finally the contribution of the lay mind to the management of university affairs, on Court and Council, is a valuable asset, though this is by no means universally admitted. In the early days of the university colleges out of which the 'Redbrick' universities have grown, their government was wholly lay; the teachers were only employees of the Council. Constitutional development has consisted largely in the gradual achievement by the academic element of a substantial share in government. It has been a necessary and beneficent development, and it is not, in all cases, yet complete. But some teachers to-day regard the present as only an unsatisfactory and transitional stage. They regard the participation of the lay element as appropriate only to the infancy of the university and they look forward to its elimination. On this view Councils and Courts should ultimately disappear and Senates should be left in undisputed control. That is the ideal of the guild-socialist but we do not share it. An academic is only a few degrees less harmful than a lay monopoly of power. For the most part the universities have been singularly fortunate in the type of layman whose service they have elicited and in the quality of that service. Not only does he focus the interest of the regional community in its university;

he brings to practical questions a robust commonsense, a financial experience, and in facing any problem a disposition to concentrate on essentials, which supplement the academic mind just where it is liable to be weak. In this respect 'Redbrick' has the advantage of 'Oxbridge.'

The local universities not only derive great benefits from the locality, they can also confer much benefit upon it. Thus they often carry out special investigations of great importance to local industries, e.g., in textiles at Leeds and Manchester, in metallurgy at Sheffield, in naval architecture at Glasgow, Liverpool and Newcastle. It is the opportunity of continuous, personal, intercourse between university staff and industrialists which makes these possible. Some of the 'Redbrick' universities have made substantial contributions to the betterment of life in their own regions by the production of first-rate 'Social Surveys.' Others have done much to promote new knowledge of local history or local geology. Of more fundamental importance, however, is the informal and unsought influence which university people may acquire in these cities and their neighbourhoods simply by being there. Most of these universities have had on their staffs at least two or three outstanding men who, by living unpretentiously among their neighbours the life of the scholar and the sage, have powerfully commended values other than those of Mammon.

What then are the proper lines of advance for 'Redbrick'? On the one hand, it has much to learn from 'Oxbridge.' In its first phase, no doubt, this was too little recognized; it embodied an almost angry reaction from the defects, real or fancied, of the Isis and the Cam. It regarded them as homes of the idle rich, snobbish in standards, narrowly ecclesiastical, and antiquated and escapist in curricula; as designed by gentlemen, for the sons of gentlemen and to perpetuate the ascendancy of gentlemen, and as suited only to a society which was stable, aristocratic and leisured. By contrast they set themselves to be honest and practical, homespun and unadorned, unashamedly provincial in outlook as in speech. They despised what they regard as 'airs and graces,' and they took Scotland and Germany for their model rather than Oxford and Cambridge. That stage has passed. They have become increasingly aware of cultural impoverishment. The importance, not merely for decoration but for mental health, of intangible assets, of personal relations and of corporate life, is better understood. So the 'Redbrick,' and, to a lesser extent, the Scottish, universities

THE CRISIS IN THE UNIVERSITY

are rightly putting the provision of a tutorial system and of halls
of residence in the forefront of their programmes. They recognize
the educational importance of a certain dignity and comeliness in
their main buildings. To some extent, though not yet quite
adequately, they seek to correct any narrowness and undue
uniformity which may result from the predominantly local recruitment of their students by ensuring that their staff is of varied
origin. In a local university, excessive inbreeding of staff is specially
dangerous. But there is need of more circulation between universities and particularly between 'Oxbridge' and 'Redbrick.' Any
tendency of 'Oxbridge' staff to 'stay put' is bad for 'Redbrick';
it is also bad for 'Oxbridge.' Students are less mobile than staff,
but the development of a residential system can and should somewhat reduce the present preponderance of students from the
immediate neighbourhood, without destroying the native character
of the universities of Yorkshire and Lancashire, for example, or of
the University of Wales.

But the modern universities would never grow to their full
stature if they confined themselves to imitation, for in the nature
of the case they will never do quite so well as Oxford and Cambridge the precise things in which those great universities excel.
They would remain 'poor relations' or 'counterfeit presentments,'
and the most brilliant teachers and students would continue to pass
them by or to quit them. Sometimes those steeped in the Oxford
and Cambridge tradition seem to be saying to them, in the words
of the old musical comedy:

'Of course you can never be like us,
But be as like us as you are able to be.'

Many of those who first recognized the obligations of the ancient
universities to the great cities, Jowett, Matthew Arnold, Pattison,
envisaged a condition of perpetual tutelage. But that all the leading ideas should come from two out of the twelve universities in
England and Wales—to say nothing of Scotland—and that the
others should acquiesce in a position of permanent inferiority,
would be thoroughly unhealthy. In fact the modern universities
do not acquiesce. Their attitude is like that of a young man,
vigorous and promising but still a little crude and unsure of himself, towards an elderly acquaintance of high distinction. He
admires and envies the other's accomplishments and particularly

his *savoir faire,* and is eager to learn from him. But he would not, if he could, surrender his own individuality; and he feels in his bones that he has it in him to become something which his eminent senior is not.

In practice this means that the ' organic connection ' with the local community needs to be developed and made real. At present it is sometimes rather formal and theoretical; the local community knows little of the university and cares little for it, and the university is not greatly interested in the local community. Few citizens have penetrated within the walls of the university, or have any concern or interest in what goes on there. Any sense of possession or of pride in the university's achievement is lacking; though physically near, the university seems spiritually remote. As was said in the early days of Owens College, Manchester, ' The crowd rolls along Deansgate heedless of the proximity of Plato and Aristotle.' The university should be spiritually—as the university college of North Wales is physically—a city set on a hill, and it should constantly impinge on the consciousness of all and sundry. It should embody ' the sense that academic work, the life of the teacher, learner and investigator is not something remote from daily life but a form of citizenship.'[1] For this purpose two things are required. The first is more and better publicity. The university must find ways, which will fire the imagination, of explaining to its neighbours what it is doing, why it is doing it, and what it essentially is. Otherwise it cannot gain, as it should, ' the fond and fervid affection ' of the people of its area.[2] Secondly, as a matter of course, the members of universities must develop personal relations with members of the civic and industrial community and a genuine interest in their affairs. In some university centres there is still too little significant intercourse between ' Town ' and ' Gown.' Since, in practice, University Councils are largely self-perpetuating bodies, there is a risk that they may be composed too exclusively of a particular clique and be insufficiently representative. On the side of the ' Town ' there may be, in some circles, a purse-proud contempt for those who do not command a high price in the money-market, and in other circles, a proletarian suspicion of an institution supposed—mistakenly—to cater mainly for the privileged. On the side of the ' Gown ' there is sometimes a certain cultural snobbishness. University teachers in ' Redbrick '

[1] S. Alexander, *op. cit.,* p. 5.
[2] Perhaps the University of Wales comes nearest to achieving this.

are occasionally guilty of a rather supercilious attitude towards townsmen whose foibles they readily perceive and whose un-scholarly mental habits and modes of speech jar on them, but whose practical capacity, robust good sense and fundamental decency they are liable to overlook.

It is in this direction that much of 'Redbrick's' further development must lie; and here it has opportunities as well as difficulties which are all its own.

# 4 THE UNIVERSITY AND OTHER EDUCATIONAL INSTITUTIONS

The universities are the natural apex of the educational system. In this respect a regional university has a special responsibility for service to other educational bodies. This was indeed one of the chief grounds on which enlightened citizens originally based their demands for a university of their own. At the turn of the century for instance, the promoters of the proposal for an independent University of Liverpool put in the forefront of their campaign a claim that the best way to re-organize education was 'by so strengthening in each great city the necessary centre and heart of intellectual energy that it may be able to revivify all grades of education.' In order to irrigate the lower levels, large and full reservoirs were needed at the highest level. So the work of every teacher in a primary or secondary school, in a training or technical college, in a school of art or of commerce, should be enriched and invigorated by the presence of a university in his neighbourhood. As yet, this noble ideal has been only very partially realized.[1] In scientific societies, or in classical, historical, English and modern language associations, as in more informal ways, there is already a good deal of personal contact, and there should be even more. Obviously the university members should do much to keep enquiry alive in such associations. 'He who learns from one occupied in learning, drinks of a running stream. He who learns from one who has learned all he is to teach drinks "the green mantle of the stagnant pool".'[2] This is true for all teachers and not only for university lecturers. Indeed there is a two-way traffic on such canals. The university teacher

---

[1] The University of Leeds under Sir Michael Sadler is understood to have attained a position of cultural leadership in the West Riding which is a brilliant example of what might be done.

[2] *Introductory Lectures on the Opening of Owens College*, p. 22.

can learn much from other types of teacher; his contact with them may keep his own interests wide and fresh and in some fields may keep his speculations in touch with practical reality.

In particular the university has a responsibility to those secondary schools which are its own source of recruitment, and it has the strongest interest in discharging it. In recent years complaints of the quality of entrants from schools have been widespread. Freshmen, it is said, know a lot more but are noticeably less promising than the freshmen of an earlier generation; they have been overpressed, and they are often stereotyped and lacking in intellectual energy and initiative. ' Dons ' and ' Beaks ' unite in deploring this, but each class is apt to cast the blame on the other. Since the universities (or their colleges) set their own scholarship papers and, in co-operation with school teachers, conduct the School and Higher School Certificate examinations, they have the remedy, to some extent at least, in their own hands and action is urgent. But behind all such formal changes, some change of heart is required of teachers generally, and this can only be brought about by university and school teachers acting in combination and influencing one another.

Another way in which university teachers can help and influence the schools is by service on their governing bodies or as co-opted members of Local Education Authorities. In practice this liaison is both valued and valuable, though it is, immediately, with lay governors rather than with staff and pupils. In addition Vice-Chancellors and Principals and some of the senior staff are much in request at School Speech Days. In these ways a large amount of unostentatious voluntary service is already being given. But it cannot be said that the massive effect on the schools, on their general policy and on the fundamental character of the training they give, has been as great as it ought to have been. Probably the reason is that there has, so far, been too little critical discussion inside the universities, and hence too little considered agreement and depth of conviction, about major educational questions such as those discussed in earlier chapters. Once that has been remedied, ' Redbrick ' already has at its disposal the necessary channels of communication.

By far the greatest influence of universities on schools is exercised through their contribution to the training of teachers. On the Two-year (soon to be Three-year) Training Colleges such influence is only indirect. But the supervision of examinations which they have undertaken during the last twenty years is now developing into a closer association. The 'Institutes of Education' which are now being set up as a result of the McNair Report will open a new and promising chapter. In the nature of the case, the colleges have often been segregated, their intellectual standards have been sub-university, and in some instances their conception of discipline has been antiquated. In these ways they have much to gain from closer association with universities. On the other hand, they are nearly all residential, in quality of corporate life they often excel the universities, and many of them have a coherence due to a strong and living religious tradition. So the universities stand to get as well as to give.

But practically all grammar-school teachers and a substantial proportion of those in other post-primary schools are graduates; and, in England and Wales, they receive their technical training directly from the university, during a fourth year spent in a 'University Training Department.' Indeed it is mainly these students, during their earlier years, who fill the 'Redbrick' Arts Faculties. Yet the University Training Departments and Faculties or Departments of Education have been in a radically false position. For, till lately at least, the bulk of academic opinion has had no real belief in teacher-training and has been half-ashamed of the university's part in it. It has been like a shopkeeper who feels that convention compels him to put in his window some types of article which he would never think of using himself or of recommending to his personal friends or to his most valued customers. The course purports to be a combination of theory and practice. But in university circles it is widely felt that, within the limits of a single session, neither the theory nor the practice can amount to more than a smattering. For universities to deal in smatterings, and on such a basis to attest qualifications, is to debase the intellectual currency and to blunt the intellectual conscience of those who are thus attested. Members of other Faculties tend to be sceptical of any attempt, e.g., to teach students how to teach history when the teacher himself has no profound knowledge of history; and, at its best, they regard it as being of a sub-university grade. They have an impression that the curriculum consists of potted psychology and of practical 'tips' of a rather rudimentary and humourless kind, 'a mixture of *Schwärmerei* and psycho-analysis.' They suspect that much of it represents an effort of mediocre minds to standardize what does not lend itself to standardization and to reduce to three or four the ' nine and ninety ways of constructing tribal lays.' They pity their recent Honours men for being subjected to a régime adapted to a much younger mental age. Naturally, they do not talk in this way in public about their Education Departments, but they very commonly do so in private. In any case, their practice reveals their real opinion. Very few teachers at Oxford and Cambridge have themselves undergone such a training, nor have the great majority of the teachers in modern universities. They do not feel themselves to be at a disadvantage through this omission or believe that they have lost anything of value. ' Training ' in their eyes is not for the aristocracy of the teaching profession. So the universities are in the equivocal position of doctors who prescribe and administer medicines which in no circumstances have they any intention of taking themselves.

' Those who can, do; those who can't, teach.' This is a popular adage, and it is invoked *a fortiori* when teaching is the form of ' doing ' in question. To teach teaching, seems doubly removed from any practical grappling with reality. There is in the universities a good deal of scarcely concealed doubt as to whether the credentials of the staff of training departments and the quality of their work have the university hall-mark. In recruiting their staffs, these departments labour under a serious practical difficulty. In principle, Training Departments and colleges should be staffed by the cream of the teaching profession, but no one would contend that, in general, this has yet been attained. Able and ambitious teachers are not attracted into this work because the prospects are poor. Chairs are few and only a small proportion of the staff are likely to get one. The remainder, who join the staff with perhaps five years' teaching experience while still under thirty, must look forward to serving in the lecturing grade for the rest of their active lives, and to being somewhat less fresh and efficient at fifty than at thirty-five, as well as less intimately in touch with the schools. It would be far better if most of them served the university for only five or ten years and were then regarded as strong candidates for headships of important post-primary schools or, possibly, for directorships of education. But that does not happen now and there is a vicious circle.

Finally, it is widely believed that, as a field of study, ' Education ' resembles Mrs. Harris, and that there is really no such subject. The field which ' Education ' Departments or Faculties attempt to cover in their original work is often regarded as having no natural coherence but as consisting of a miscellaneous assortment of bits and pieces culled from other Departments which treat them more scientifically. It is supposed to afford a happy hunting-ground for the cloudy, the pretentious and the second-rate.

Here then is a nettle which ought to be grasped more firmly than it has been. Either universities should cease to do work which they do half-heartedly, because they suspect it is unworthy of them; or they should face and resolve their doubts and should set about the training of teachers and the study of education with full conviction and an unstinted use of their intellectual resources. In fact, there are strong reasons for choosing the second alternative. First, teachers have at least as strong a *prima facie* claim to receive their professional training from the university as have the members of any other profession. Few serious thinkers doubt that, as a nation, we are still ill-equipped mentally for the tremendous tasks with which we are confronted. Eighty years of compulsory education have not yet produced results at all commensurate with the need. If so, teachers are in a key position. As the example of Scotland shows, it is possible to remit all their professional training to other institutions. But, in their approach to their work and their understanding of its aims and methods, they need acutely just those qualities which a university should impart—breadth of outlook, finely disciplined precision of thought and a sensitiveness to the significance of the changing scene.

Secondly, the university needs its Education Department for its own purposes. If its contribution to the whole educational system through this Department has not yet been on a high enough level or wholly convincing to itself, the fundamental reason is that the teachers trained and the educational aims and methods investigated have been those of the schools and not of the universities. It has offered a service to the schools of which it felt no need itself. But that involves a complacency that is no longer plausible.

Much university teaching is notoriously bad. In every university there are some members of staff of high ability who make valuable contributions to knowledge in their publications, but who go through life as incompetent tutors and lecturers, simply because they have never realized that there is an art of teaching or taken the trouble to acquire it. It is true that Training Departments do not now cater for university teaching, and it may be that, as at present constituted, they are not competent to do so. It is also true that in teaching, as in most crafts, the rules of method which can most easily be formulated and taught and tested are not the whole of the story. For instance there is much in proficiency in cooking which cannot be acquired by the most assiduous study of Mrs. Beeton.[1] It is got from prolonged experience and from association in their work with acknowledged experts, and it is transmitted indirectly by professional tradition and is 'caught rather than taught.' The practising teacher has some ground for anxiety lest an undue stress on rules of technique should lead to neglect of this, more elusive but at least equally essential, aspect. But if something is not being done very well, the moral may not be that it should be abandoned but that it should be done better. Taking thought about method may not necessarily carry us very far, but to take no thought at all is really indefensible. To rely wholly on unwritten, professional, tradition may result merely in torpor as it did in eighteenth-century Oxford and Cambridge.

But the need extends far beyond the question of teaching methods. Unless the whole debate—the 'grand inquest' to which this book is designed to be a contribution—is misplaced, the university's aim and basis require more continuous and systematic investigation than they have received. Its traditional unself-consciousness and lack of planning are excessive. They are responsible for grave defects, and they are doubly disastrous in these critical days. To 'rise to the height of the times,' universities must ask themselves fundamental questions and must go on asking them. Here Faculties or Departments of Education have a pre-eminent, though not an exclusive, responsibility. They are the natural centres round which such enquiries will cluster. To dispute the existence of such a subject as 'Education' becomes singularly futile; there is a unity of interest and serious purpose which binds together the diverse material and which is vital to the university. When the university undertakes such investigation in its own sphere and for its own sake, its work in the school sphere will take on a new reality and its attitude to its own Training Department will be revolutionized. Its work for schools will no longer be *de haut en bas*, since it will share many of their concerns.

But it may still be asked, 'Who is sufficient for these things? Is not the rôle we have assigned to the Education Department one which it is ludicrously unequal to performing? And will not the

[1] See Michael Oakeshott on 'Rationalism in Politics' in *Cambridge Journal*, Vol. I, No. 2.

vicious circle, described above, prevent its overcoming this inequality?' The answer is that the circle must be broken, as, in some instances, it has already been. The way to break it is, that a sufficient proportion of our very best graduates and younger teachers (university as well as school) should join the staff of these Departments, with their eyes open, not as a *pis aller* but because they appreciate that these are key positions in which the greatest service can be rendered. To do so at present, involves risk and sacrifice, because the prospects of high promotion are poor. It is therefore an interim measure, for no institution can go on for a long period relying on the self-sacrifice of idealists, since there are never enough of these to go round. Later on, there must be a reasonable prospect of a career such as will appeal to normal motives, 'not too bright and good for human nature's daily food.' But such altruism seems to be required in order to break the vicious circle in the first instance. Here perhaps is a special call to Christian teachers who may find a vocation in such work.

## 5   EXTRA-MURAL WORK

### a.   *How It Has Developed*

The last thirty years of the nineteenth century saw the rise of ' University Extension.' It was originally the affair of Oxford and Cambridge, some of whose most influential teachers felt a growing sense of obligation to carry university education to the less privileged and to use some portion of their large revenues for this purpose. In the words of Professor James Stuart of Cambridge, who was the pioneer, it was ' desirable that the country at large should become part-heir of the immense educational tradition of the two universities.'[1] It took the form of a provision of courses of first-rate popular lectures which were given by teachers from Oxford and Cambridge in a number of the large centres of population. In some places these courses and the interest they aroused were the germ out of which ' Redbrick ' universities or university colleges subsequently developed.[2] Such universities have thus a special moral obligation to pass on to others what they have themselves received.

---

[1] *Reminiscences*, p. 165, cf. *Life of Benjamin Jowett* II, pp. 128-129 and M. Arnold, *op. cit.*, pp. 290 ff.

[2] E.g., Sheffield, Reading, Nottingham, Exeter and the ' Arts ' side of Leeds which began as ' The Yorkshire College of Science.'

The next step came in the first decade of the present century with the institution of ' Tutorial Classes.' Here the initiative came from the working-class movement. The universities acted in response to a demand, and the action was joint-action. These classes have two distinctive marks. First they are intensive; university standards are aimed at in the quality, not only of the teacher, but of the work of the students. They meet twenty-four times a year during three consecutive winters. The second half of each meeting is devoted to discussion in which the students take part, and written work is expected. Secondly they are democratic. The students through their own organizations, generally the Workers' Educational Association, have their full share in the choice of subject and in the organization and direction of the classes. In each area the university and the voluntary organizations are partners, co-operating on a basis of equality. This movement established itself very quickly and with considerable prestige. In its early days there was a strong spiritual impulse behind it. No less a judge than H. A. L. Fisher coupled its central figure, Albert Mansbridge, with Baden Powell as one of the two or three men of our time who have effected something really constructive in education. Particularly in Oxford it enlisted the whole-hearted support and service of some of the outstanding figures among the younger men, William Temple being a notable example. Various authoritative reports have laid it down that extra-mural work of this kind is no mere appendage to the normal work of universities but an integral part of it.[1]

In the years between the wars there was a substantial, though not a spectacular, advance in the number of classes and students. The work was better organized and financed. But, as was probably inevitable, the original spiritual impulse had largely spent itself; within the universities and among their intra-mural staffs there was less of missionary spirit and prophetic fervour. In each university's area a large proportion of those employed as tutors for single classes were not ordinary members of the university staff. The mainstay of the work came to be a small corps of whole-time extra-mural teachers, employed by the Joint Committee, and thus a new branch of the teaching profession has come into existence. More recently still there has been a large development of more informal and elementary types of work, sponsored by Local

[1] E.g., the Reports of the Royal Commissions on Oxford and Cambridge, London, and Wales, and the Final Report in 1919 of the Adult Education Committee of the Ministry of Reconstruction.

Education Authorities, Women's Institutes, etc., and much stimulated by Broadcasting and also by wartime experience of education in the Forces, e.g., A.B.C.A.

### b.  The Problem To-day

Dr. Flexner, after scourging the American universities for shameless commercialized vulgarization, ('helping third-rate book-keepers to become second-rate book-keepers') debasement of standards and playing to the gallery in much of their extra-mural work, goes on to consider the extra-mural record of the English universities. In effect his verdict is, 'Not guilty; but don't do it again.' He points out that ours have never sunk to the depths of many of those of his own country, and that they have nursed the early stages of a socially useful movement which might not otherwise have survived infancy. But he scarcely conceals his opinion that such work is really 'sub-university' in grade, and he suggests that such guardianship is at best a temporary device and that these services should eventually be undertaken by other, and more appropriate, agencies. Is he right in this? Should the universities now seek to draw out? Or, on the other hand, should they take this work more seriously than they are now doing?

### (1)  The case for drawing out

In early days, opposition was based mainly on the presumed controversial and propagandist character of the work. The Workers' Educational Association was regarded as 'red,' and as being likely to produce agitators rather than genuine students. But such criticism is no longer serious. Much more plausibly, however, it is now argued that, whatever its merit at its own level, this work cannot be of true university quality. To equate the standards reached in the evening by tired people without academic training with those of whole-time internal students, is sentimental and unreal. It is to indulge heart at the expense of head and it is intellectually dishonest. Further, the university's extra-mural work is not integrated with its normal work. 'Staff Tutors,' 'Resident Tutors,' etc., are not really, and are not felt to be, members of one community with the internal staff. They are a set of outsiders, recruited *ad hoc,* and generally of slightly lower academic qualifications; and they are often unknown, even by sight, to the great majority of their reputed colleagues. In most universities it is only a small minority of the internal staff who ever take a tutorial class; and to those who do, it may be, primarily, a convenient means of supplementing their income. The position has totally changed since the Ministry of Reconstruction Committee in 1919 based much of their defence of the academic quality of tutorial class work on the fact that, outside London, almost all of it was conducted by tutors who were also occupied in intra-mural university work. The responsibility of the university as a whole for its extra-mural work is mostly only nominal. Hence the presumed guarantee of standards and policies is really a fraud, and its continuance can have only a snobbish value. On the other hand, internal teachers should not be encouraged to take more part, since that would distract them from their proper work and would destroy or cripple their possible contribution to the advancement of knowledge.

From the other side the working-man is told (e.g., by Professor Hogben) that he has nothing to gain from the association of his studies with the university, for it is irremediably bourgeois and unrealistic.

(2) The case for continuing and developing the work

Admittedly, the work of part-time adult students in evening classes is more uneven than the work of the ordinary undergraduate. But, at least in the social studies which they mostly pursue, economic, political, ethical—and to some extent also in literature and history—their greater maturity, and often their first-hand experience, more than compensates for any deficiencies in formal education. Sir Richard Livingstone has recently opened our eyes to the degree to which, in these fields, some maturity of experience is a condition of appreciation. If some of the work of tutorial class students falls below, a good deal of it surpasses, that of the average undergraduate. It is more likely to ' stretch ' the tutor's mind and to enlarge his ideas. There is often indeed a genuine intellectual partnership; the tutor gets as well as gives.

Further, there is present in tutorial-class discussion, in a high degree, just that element of intellectual integrity and of full personal engagement which, from our Christian standpoint, we have insisted is most needful, and which as a rule is quite inadequately present, in all university work. There is the impact of person on person, the combination of respectful attention to the other man's view with candour in criticism of it and sincerity in the statement of one's own. Here encounter is genuine and fruitful, and interest is

R

centred not in diplomas but in knowledge. The student only attends at all because of his keen, and often passionate, concern for the subject of study. He seeks no private advantage for himself. To him the course is not merely one more hurdle to be surmounted in the race for economic security and social status, whose prizes are symbolized by the 'villa at Surbiton.' In such work the university may find an antidote for its endemic faults. Here, if anywhere, it comes out from its ivory tower and is in touch with real life.

Again, it is untrue that the work could now be handed over without serious loss to the Local Education Authorities or to the Ministry of Education or to any other body. The university's own contribution to it is distinctive and invaluable; patience and thoroughness, insistence on facing all and not only some of the relevant facts, a readiness to revise the most cherished conclusions in the light of new data, a temper that is judicial rather than propagandist. Of course the university has no monopoly of these qualities, nor is it itself impeccable. But nowhere else are they so deeply entrenched or so integral to the whole *raison d'être* of the institution. Again and again tutorial class students, looking back on their experience, have affirmed that these lessons have come to them as a revelation. The participation of the universities is also indispensable as a bulwark of freedom. Without them, the voluntary bodies would be very unequally yoked to the public authorities who now find the greater part of the funds required. The fields of study are, in a high degree, controversial. However enlightened their intentions, if the authorities had virtual control of the organization of classes and the appointment of tutors, full freedom of discussion would be precarious. It is only when the immense prestige of the universities is allied with the voluntary bodies that some equilibrium can be maintained.

It is hard to exaggerate the importance of adult education for the future of democracy. If democracy is to be anything but a sham, there must be a sufficient number of people who have an active concern in public affairs and have formed a habit of thinking about them honestly, responsibly and intelligently. From the beginning, a sense of this need has been a principal motive in the working-class demand for such education; and the hazards are to-day more obvious than they have ever been. It is true that the total number of tutorial class students is statistically unimpressive. It does not amount to more than about fifteen thousand in all.

But they are key-people, containing among them a considerable proportion of the natural leaders of democracy, in trade unions, etc., and they influence many others. The universities have, as it were, thrown a pebble into a pond, and the ripples spread in widening circles across the water. In this way a 'Redbrick' university can do much to fertilize the whole region.

In short, the argument for continuing and strengthening the university's extra-mural work is three-fold. (a) Much of the work is of high quality. It includes in large measure an ingredient in which, as we have seen, universities to-day tend to be deficient, an imponderable, but stimulating, corporate influence. In this field the university is genuinely giving education and not mere instruction. (b) Its potential social importance is very great. In it the university is making a momentous contribution to national life. (c) Though it is a joint work, the university's particular contribution to it is irreplaceable. A great deal of adult education is necessarily 'sub-university' in grade, but, through the Tutorial Classes, the university sets a standard which is constantly operating to draw the whole mass upwards.

## (3)   Conclusion

As with the training of teachers, universities are at present in a false position. They are doing half-heartedly what they ought to do either whole-heartedly or not at all.[1] They ought frankly to recognize this situation and to make their choice. But to withdraw—or, as university teachers so often do—to regard extra-mural work as only a casual and marginal activity, would be calamitous and retrograde. The alternative is to take it more seriously.

This would entail a keener interest and sense of responsibility in the university as a whole. This work should no longer be, in practice, the affair only of a semi-detached and outlying Department. The majority of teachers must no longer be content to regard it with a hazy awareness and a perfunctory benevolence. It is extremely desirable that there should be more integration between internal and external work. More intra-mural teachers should take a tutorial class, and more staff-tutors should take some part in the normal work of the appropriate Department. Assignment to the one or the other category need not, perhaps, be lifelong. While there are practical, administrative difficulties

---

[1] Perhaps there is here rather less active criticism and superciliousness and rather more ignorance and indifference.

in some of these suggestions, something must be done to break down the present wall of partition, if the university is really to play its part.

Most needful of all is something which cannot be attained by taking thought. That is a flaming up again of the spiritual impulse which was so strong thirty or forty years ago. But, as with the Education Departments, that can only happen as a by-product of a new imaginative realization both of the need and of the opportunity.

One final question may naturally be raised concerning a large part of the present chapter. It may be said, ' This is all very well. Very likely each of the activities which you commend is, singly, valuable. But, collectively, they are crushing. If contacts are to be maintained with city and county councillors, municipal officials, business men and industrialists, trade unionists, school teachers and governors, a forty-eight hour day would hardly suffice. However desirable in themselves, these activities will in practice be carried on at the expense of the one thing needful. If university teachers are to serve so many tables, they will have no leisure to prophesy. The world will have been too much with them, and they will have " laid waste their powers ".'

To this protest there is no single, clinching, answer, but certain things can be said. First, universities ought to be staffed on a scale which allows for a wider circle of activities than has been customary. Secondly, both for the university and for the individual teacher, some compromise is always likely to be necessary. Thirdly, in deciding on this compromise in the individual case, it is the insiders, the university and its officers, who should have the last word. Fourthly, they should exercise this prerogative with a more acute sensitiveness to outside claims and a fuller recognition of their relevance than heretofore. In short, no formula can be found which will indicate clearly what is the right compromise in every case. But, certainly, there should be more outgoing than there has been; and equally certainly, there is a limit to the outgoing that is compatible with performance of the university's primary task.

# X
# RELIGION AND THEOLOGY

I RELIGION—THE TASK OF
    CHRISTIANS IN A POST-CHRISTIAN
    UNIVERSITY

As Christian members of staff or Christian students, what should we now be seeking to do? What may reasonably be expected of us by other people? In fact we can do little till we are, or at least are on the way to becoming, something that most of us are not now. Our real problem is not how—in the modern vernacular—' to put our stuff across '; it is how to widen and deepen our Christian obedience so that ' our stuff ' is really worth putting across. If, in the university, we are to act as a ' creative minority,' our first task must be to become a ' community of Christians.'

### a. To Become a ' Community of Christians '

A ' Community of Christians ' is a term used by Mr. T. S. Eliot in contradistinction to a ' Christian Community ' or ' Christian Society ' or ' Christian Civilization.' It signifies the nucleus of consciously and thoughtfully practising Christians which should play the part of a creative minority within the wider body. Unless such a leaven exists within the lump, even a ' Christian Society '— if we can attain it—will not long remain a Christian society, for the rulers will become cynical manipulators and the masses will lapse into mental lethargy and superstition.[1] Further, the only way in which a neutral society can become a Christian society is through the activity within it of a genuine ' community of Christians.'

But the term ' Christian ' is itself ambiguous since it is used in a diluted as well as in an undiluted sense. The diluted use itself takes two forms. On the one hand there are very large numbers, in the universities as in the nation, who are detached from the Churches and from any regular religious observance, but who yet may be called ' Christian ' in view of their moral code and their

[1] *The Idea of a Christian Society*, p. 35.

261

prevailing sentiment. The moral principles which they approve and by which they try to direct their lives are largely based on the 'Ten Commandments' and, somewhat more distantly, on the Sermon on the Mount. The repetition of the Lord's Prayer or the singing of 'Abide with me' before a Cup-tie Final evoke in them collective emotion similar to 'God Save the King,' or 'Home Sweet Home' or 'For Auld Lang Syne.' Such a man venerates 'the temples of his gods' along with 'the ashes of his fathers' as part of the cement which holds society together. Like the worship of the emperor to the educated ancient Roman or modern Japanese, these things are felt by him to be a symbolic assertion of oneness with his kind. They are regarded as being at least 'good myth.' But if you ask whether they are more than this and, if so, how much more, you will be tacitly requested not to press the question. For to do so—as he instinctively feels rather than consciously thinks—would only involve him in mental discomfort and would lead nowhere.

The second type of diluted Christianity belongs to those who have still the habit of attending church or chapel. These are not as numerous as once they were, but they are still many; and a very fair proportion are to be found among the senior and the junior members of universities. They have probably been brought up in Christian surroundings, and they maintain a decent participation in communal religious observances. They are not consciously insincere. Christian worship does mean something to them and they would feel impoverished without it. But they are less ready for a spiritual 'Dunkirk' than are, for example, very many Communists. If our own 'Christianity' is of this order, we shall have little that is distinctive to contribute to the university. Our strong words will come to other people as 'a tale of little meaning,' because in truth they have no depth in our own minds. 'If one tenth of what you say is true,' objects one critic quite legitimately, 'you ought to be ten times as excited as you are.' Or, in the words of another commentator, 'From what you know of Christianity would it ever occur to you that it was to kindle a fire that the founder of Christianity came into the world?'[1] In that case we can make no Christian contribution to the university until we have faced for ourselves the paradoxical question, 'How can a man become a Christian when he already is one?' Kierkegaard says explicitly that the transition to a living Christianity is harder

---

[1] T. S. Gregory in *The Listener,* Vol. XXXVI, No. 932.

for a Christian—that is for one who is generally acco
Christian and who is accustomed so to account himself—
one who has made no Christian profession. The former I
were, been inoculated against Christianity. 'The cunning ᴜᴘᴜᴜ
of the World takes the ferment which has worked such radical
changes in the constitution of the human soul, and by inoculating
Society at large with a very dilute and attenuated serum secures
for it a measure of immunity from violent and inconvenient
attacks.'[1]

In sharp contrast with both these classes are those whose
Christianity is undiluted because their commitment is unlimited.
They may not yet have attained any high degree of moral or
spiritual achievement, much less of holiness. But their religion
does not consist primarily in a code, a sentiment or a cultus. Its
distinctive mark is threefold. First they have at least some
imaginative apprehension of the real dimensions of the Divine. It
has been said of a great Cambridge teacher that his pupils felt
they were witnessing a titanic struggle, like a ship with the wind
blowing, going out to sea. He would read a passage from the
Bible and then say, 'Suppose this were true!' It was something
infinitely more powerful than he which was blowing him along;
it was the only time when you saw an idea as something infinitely
more powerful than a man. The idea of God might be something
objective which had escaped control of all the prophets and blew
them where they did not want to go. The type of Christian
wanted, in the university as elsewhere, is a man who does not know
he is anywhere, but is prepared to allow the wind to blow and to
show you what a wrestling for truth means. Secondly, they are
consciously attempting to draw the strength of their daily lives
from God's grace. They are not only set on obedience to God,
they are also feeding on Him. Thirdly, however lowly their
natural stature, mental or moral, that does not preclude in them
a certain recklessness and whole-heartedness in self-giving. In this
sense they are 'pure in heart' or single-minded; they keep nothing
back. It is their genuine purpose to bring every thought and action
into captivity to Christ and, day by day, to live by grace. They
speak to one another 'from faith to faith.' It is only in so far as
we become as these that we can be 'a community of Christians.'

But, quite apart from our various personal faults and failings,
there is a common disability in which the best Christians in our

[1] J. H. F. Peile, *The Reproach of the Gospel*, pp. 155-156.

universities are involved along with the worst. We have all par-
taken as a matter of course in the prevailing ways of organizing
work and of using leisure, and these simply leave God out of
account. In a large proportion of our time we ourselves are thus
involuntary atheists. Yet we know in our bones that 'However
generous the feelings of an atheist, atheism turns to stone certain
deep inner fibres of his being.'[1] Thus the salt has lost much of its
savour. Until this disability is removed, Christians cannot hope to
exert any very significant influence on university development.

To a large extent we all are, and must be, creatures of our social
environment. In the university to-day that environment is anti-
Christian, in the sense that it takes small practical account of
Christ or even of God. Here the university is in tune with the
world outside it. A generation has grown up in which the pre-
conditions of religion are absent, because it is a stranger to the
experiences and emotions which are its natural soil. It has had
small stimulus to a sense of awe, of wonder and enchantment, of
a context to its immediate field of consciousness shading off into
infinity, of moving about in worlds not realized or of abasement
in presence of the sublime. Its mortal nature has never 'trembled
like a guilty thing surprised' and, for it, adoration is not only absent
but meaningless. But that is not all. To dwell on such aridity would
be odiously pharisaical if it were not accompanied by an overwhelming sense that we, professing Christians, are in the same
condemnation. We share the same routine of life with our non-
Christian fellows, and, like them, we have been at home in it. We
have breathed the exhausted air with little more sense of strain
than they. In lecture-room or laboratory, in common room or
committee room, our motives, our objectives and our methods, have
not been noticeably different from theirs. We are only now beginning to wake to the contradiction between our creed and many
of the tacit, communal, assumptions which govern our working
lives.

We can see the general character of this sort of contradiction
most easily by considering some earlier example which is now
beyond dispute. For instance, we have outgrown the institution of
slavery and its moral character is now revealed beyond dispute.
We can see that a Christian slave-owner, or still more a Christian
slave-dealer like John Newton, was involved, however unconsciously, in nauseous hypocrisy. In denying elementary human

---

[1] Maritain, *op. cit.*, p. 83.

rights to the least of Christ's brethren, he denied them to Christ. But he and his contemporaries were blind to this, for they did not really see that they had any alternative. 'That the behaviour of the slave-holders resulted from the circumstances in which they were placed and not from any innate devilry is a fact now conceded by all impartial men.'[1] So it is in the university. It is 'the system' which rules. The personal responsibility of the individual teacher or administrator for the examination system or the non-residential system or for the specialist character of the curriculum is so tenuous as to be almost invisible. These things seem to him to be like laws of nature, which he does not much think about, but takes for granted in 'accepting the universe.' Or else he laments them but averts his attention from an uncomfortable topic as soon as possible, because he does not see anything he can do about it. But such reasoning exempts us from responsibility no more than the slave-dealer if, professing belief in God, we are absorbed in communal activities which effectively ignore Him. 'All things must speak of God, refer to God, or they are atheistic. History, without God, is a chaos without design or end or aim. Political Economy, without God, would be a selfish teaching about the acquisition of wealth, making the larger portion of mankind animate machines for its production; Physics, without God, would be but a dull enquiry into certain meaningless phenomena; Ethics, without God, would be a varying rule without principle, or substance, or centre, or ruling hand; Metaphysics, without God, would make man his own temporary god, to be resolved, after his brief hour here, into the nothingness out of which he proceeded. All sciences . . . will tend to exclude the thought of God if they are not cultivated with reference to Him. History will become an account of man's passions and brute strength, instead of the ordering of God's providence for His creatures' good; Physics will materialize man, and Metaphysics God.'[2] When this passage was written ninety years ago it probably seemed to Pusey's 'liberal' contemporaries to be the height of bigotry. But actual experience of universities with a secular atmosphere has terribly emphasized its relevance and its cogency. It has given a pungent meaning to the question, 'When is neutrality not neutrality?'

In these circumstances the first thing Christians in the university have to do is, to get together. At present colleagues may serve for

[1] Horace White, quoted by G. H. Putnam, *Abraham Lincoln*, p. 41.
[2] Pusey, *Collegiate and Professional Teaching and Discipline*, p. 25.

years on the staff of a modern university without knowing that they are fellow-Christians, unless they happen to attend the same place of worship. It does not often come to light through their action in Senate, or Faculty, or their conversation in Refectory or Common Room. We must, together, evolve a more self-conscious attitude to our task and a clearer and more unified policy than we have yet had. ' To exert influence upon a mass,' says Ortega truly, ' you must yourselves be more than a mass.' The chief obstacle to this, he adds, is ' slovenliness '; and the opposite of slovenliness is ' to be in form.'[1] Mentally as well as physically, this requires continuous self-discipline, concentration and training, in the light of a clear purpose kept constantly in view. Only so can Christians hope to act as a ' creative minority ' within the university.

But if this is to be our policy, two common and insidious perversions of it must be utterly repudiated and vigilantly guarded against. The first perversion would be to become a superior clique, self-righteous and self-important, looking down on our fellow-intellectuals as unchristian and on our fellow-christians as unintellectual. That would be without excuse. The most terrible denunciations in the New Testament are reserved for those who account themselves righteous or—as a modern theologian put it—who claim to be ' the boys.' In any Christian enterprise, humility and humour are vital. The other, and slightly more plausible, perversion would be to become a Christian pressure group, using the ordinary methods of such groups or surreptitiously infiltrating into key positions as Communist ' cells ' are reputed to do. It would be to employ astute tactics, to play adroitly on the passions, prejudices, and above all on the inertia, of other persons or groups; here to utilise the fear which persons in authority may have of the spread of ' subversive influences,' there to appeal to the reformer's zeal for social welfare; and so to inveigle people into courses whose upshot they do not foresee and from which, if they did, they might easily recoil. Now it must be said with the utmost possible emphasis that, for Christians, this would be treason. It would be to betray the cause in an effort to hasten victory, for it involves manipulation of men as opposed to genuine ' meeting.' It is the sin of human pride, as exemplified in an extreme form by Dostoievsky's Grand Inquisitor. To rely on sleight of hand is no more legitimate than to rely on the strong arm. To use for a Christian end the art of

[1] Ortega regards ' slovenliness ' as the besetting sin of his own fellow-countrymen. But in fact it is very widely distributed, and his moral has a general application.

Metternich or Cavour or Bismarck would be blasphemy. Once again a minority which had sought, and conceivably had attained, 'dominance' would have ceased to be 'creative.'

Our real object should be twofold. First it should be, through discussing and praying together, to learn what is our Christian duty in our working lives. This does not mean that we should deduce it from some body of 'Christian principles,' but that we should try together to recognize and to obey the will of God, here and now, for ourselves and for our universities. As Christian citizens of the academic commonwealth, what should we be about? What should be our contribution to its right ordering? For those who take part in discussions in Senate or Faculty or Union Committees, what does Christian obedience entail? What patterns of academic organization, and what types of communal living, are congenial or inimical to Christian values? Judged by Christian standards, what is the status of the various operative ideals or archetypes; the gentleman, the scholar, the 'cricketer,' the go-getter, the sahib, the good comrade, the captain of industry? If on such questions, there is to be an informed and responsible Christian opinion, we need the immense stimulus of sustained discussion. We need to be used by God to help one another in this way, 'lending our minds out.' For that purpose we must learn to understand better the Christian tradition itself which is the source of renewal. We need to see the existing conditions of life and work in the university with some measure of the insight of a prophet.

Our other object requires similar thought and prayer, but it requires also a great deal of quiet experimentation, which may well be prolonged. 'A vitally Christian social renewal will be a work of sanctity or it will be nothing.'[1] No doubt this is 'a hard saying,' and, to speak truth, for most of us not only daunting but somewhat forbidding. 'Sanctity' seems something which we regard with awe and reverence indeed, but also with some shrinking as remote and a little eerie, something that is wholly beyond, not only our attainment but, even our aspiration. But in face of the storms and the secular heroisms of to-day, our faith is likely to be impotent unless it is of a much higher voltage of power than it has yet been. We need, however, a new, lay, pattern of sanctity. The traditional, withdrawn, ecclesiastical type, in the cloister or the desert, will not serve us here. To find a relevant standard, we must know what would be sanctity within the hurly-burly, and for the

[1] Maritain, *op. cit.*, p. 115.

participant in a mixed society such as the university to-day. That is, we must attain some apprehension, however dim, of a new pattern of sanctity which could suffuse the whole of our official and professional lives.

What could such ' a community of Christians ' hope to effect in any university? Granted the leaven, how amenable is the lump? In the main the influence of any such Christian group must needs depend on the quality of insight and energy which it brings to the common tasks. Any commending of the Christian outlook to those who do not already share it will be indirect rather than direct. But, as we have seen, the intellectual situation to-day is utterly different from that of any earlier time, and our methods of presentation of our convictions must be correspondingly different. The mentality of the younger generation, that is, of the students and the younger teachers, has been radically affected by the two World-Wars and the production of the atom-bomb. These men are sophisticated and disillusioned, having been through a searing experience. They are allergic to any form of piety which is at all conventional, secondhand and imitative. They are suspicious of their own motives and doubly suspicions of anyone approaching them with an edifying purpose. They have stripped off whole layers of conventional habit and sentiment. They are as far as possible removed from any form of *Schwärmerei*, and it is now the younger men who listen with a pitying smile to the innocent, and rather pathetic, utopianism of the seniors. In some degree they can make their own an expression of the experience of German university men who have been through even deeper waters, ' We have had glimpses into the reality of the world and of man and of ourselves which we cannot forget.'[1] They have often a sense, however unjustified, of having met Christianity before and of having seen through it. They are far indeed from that docile attitude towards the wisdom of their elders which is attributed to undergraduates by Whewell. Both physically and mentally, they have been ' up against it ' to a degree which the older among us have seldom experienced. Yet their potentialities are enormous. T. E. Lawrence in the first, and Richard Hillary in the second, World-War are examples of the heroic devotion and achievement of which they are capable in the service of any cause which really enlists their loyalty.

Any approach to them on behalf of a Christian scheme and way

[1] Jaspers, *op. cit.*, p. 6.

of life must take nothing for granted. It must explore ' the concrete actualities of experience below the conceptual currency '; and in so doing, it must exercise a ' discipline of continence ' in the use of familiar terms and concepts. Fresh, first-hand and personal, experience is the only basis of belief which is really convincing to them. They will attach a Christian meaning to such experience only so far as it seems to issue from what they can recognize as a genuinely truthful and undistorted description of the experience.[1] ' The only value remaining to us in the collapse of values is sincerity.' That is the background against which all work of the Christian community in the university must be done to-day.

### b. To Become Lay Theologians

All Christians in universities should be, or at least should set themselves to become, lay theologians. That means that they must fulfil the following minimum conditions.

(1) They must be able to read the Bible intelligently. If they had only a vague and woolly understanding of it, on a par intellectually with the jumbled recollections of history satirized in *1066 and All That,* they would be guilty of a peculiarly heinous form of the treason of the intellectuals. They must know the Bible as a record of progressive revelation to minds at varying degrees of crudity or discernment, culminating in a climax up to which everything before it leads and from which everything after it springs. They must also have an educated man's understanding of the broad outline of the results of biblical scholarship.

(2) They must have a general understanding of what Christian doctrine is and why they believe it, an understanding not merely childish but at the level of an educated and scholarly adult. They must not be the sort of people who are reduced to purple embarrassment if challenged on a railway journey by a militant atheist.

[1] See a penetrating analysis by Mr. F. R. Leavis of the difference between the use of imagery in a Christian poet of older days such as Dante and a Christian poet to-day such as Mr. T. S. Eliot. Dante can use the traditional Christian symbols with confidence ; Mr. Eliot, no less orthodox in his own dogmatic belief, cannot. The traditional symbols have gone dead on the minds of most people to-day. New symbols have to be found and given currency, even if they are symbols for the same things. They will be convincing in proportion as they are close to experienced reality. Only if they can feel that this has been explored intrepidly and described faithfully, will men to-day give serious attention to any interpretation of it that may be offered them. F. R. Leavis, *Education and the University,* pp. 87–104, cf. p. 24.

(3) They must have some understanding of what is really going on in the world to-day and of what Christian responsibility in public affairs involves. This entails a sense of perspective far removed from that of the popular newspaper; it is to read the signs of the times with Christian eyes.

(4) They must have devoted some thought to the Christian implications and demands of their own profession, actual or prospective. This must include an honest facing of the question whether it has a right to exist at all.

This duty has special implications for Christian members of the university staff. First, they must bring their Christian faith to bear upon their work and upon its organization. This should be a truism, but it is not. To all appearances many do not do so, and it has never occurred to them to do so. There are professors and lecturers who are churchgoers and even church-officers, but whose contribution to university affairs seems wholly unillumined by their churchmanship. The heritage of western civilization is no part of their stock in trade. Yet it is not only for our private and personal lives but for the university system under which we work, shaped by it and ever so slightly shaping it, that we stand under God's judgment. As officers of the university, or as members of some of the bodies which in aggregate shape its policy, or merely as units helping to constitute the public opinion within the university by which the action of such bodies is ultimately influenced, we have responsibility for the university. In so far as the system is faulty, all Christians should be university reformers. In saying this, we are only applying to the university and to the Christians in it a principle of much wider extent. A besetting sin of the day is fatalism, arising from an increase in the scale of social operations so immense that individual responsibility disappears from sight. ' What is everybody's business, is nobody's business '; that is the familiar tag. There is no escape from social ruin until it is reversed and there is substituted, ' What is everybody's business is *everybody's* business.' As a beginning, all Christians at least should recognize it as *their* business.

Secondly, they should promote discussions of various kinds in their own universities where their own immediate responsibilities lie. ' If the present social situation is to be controlled by Christian principles, thoughts will be necessary which have not yet been thought.'[1] These words are as true to-day as when they were written forty years ago; they are as true within the university as in the world outside it. To this process the group-thinking which has grown into this book is at best one of a number of tiny beginnings. For instance, there should be discussions between Christian teachers in different departments and faculties. In the light of their common faith, they should examine together their several specialisms and the relation of these to one another. That is, they should discuss the kind of issues raised in the chapters of this book; but they should do so with special reference to the immediate situation in their own university and to the question, what they themselves can do about it. They might well take as a basis Professor Hildebrand's distinctions quoted above (Ch. III). They might consider what can be done, in their own university and in the present or the next academic year, to reduce indolence, pride, resentment and distrust and to promote winged alertness, wonder, docility and the power to make intellectual commitments. Such discussions should not be theoretical but thoroughly ' existential.' Other discussions should be held between Christians and other teachers who have a humanistic outlook, are awake to the present crisis, and share the view that ' the challenge of our time ' is primarily personal rather than technical. The object should be to see how far they can evolve a common programme, and the Christians should go as far as they can with such non-Christian colleagues. Alone they are a minority; with such allies they may often be a majority. Finally, they should seek to enter into informal discussion with those colleagues who are, doctrinally, most opposed to them, e.g. the ' aggressive scientists.' They should do so, first, in order to understand and to assimilate the element of truth for which such people almost certainly stand and to hear God speaking through them; and secondly, in order to present to them, as clearly and persuasively as possible, a Christian view of the university problems of the moment. That is, the Christians should expect to be learners as well as witnesses. Of course this implies that, however profound the doctrinal differences, they recognize a bond of unity with the colleagues from whom in creed they are most remote. Whatever theories those colleagues may hold and whatever their logical consequences, the Christians feel themselves still in fellowship with them. Subconsciously, if not always consciously, the two parties recognize common, moral and intellectual, canons of truth, and therefore

Troeltsch, *The Social Teaching of the Christian Churches* II, p. 1012.

frank discussion can still be fruitful. The Christians would not, if
they could, 'liquidate' or banish the 'aggressive scientists'; and
whatever the theoretical implications of 'scientific humanism,' or
its practice in Eastern Europe, they do not believe that, in real
life, they themselves would be silenced by its representatives in
British universities.

Thirdly, they must deepen their sense of pastoral responsibility
towards their students and abjure all notions of limited liability.
They must do so particularly towards the less attractive—the dull,
the gauche, or the conceited. They must show persistence and
ingenuity in finding new ways of making this effective. This does
not entail any revival of patronizing and meddlesome supervision
or infringement of privacy and independence; it is only the friendly,
man-to-man, interest and helpfulness of the more mature towards
the less mature student.

There are also special implications for Christian students, who
should organize their academic life around their faith. First, they
should form a clear conception of what it is that they want to
acquire from their time at the university. That should, in any case,
include some equipment for living responsibly as Christian citizens
and, in particular, the 'lay theologian's' knowledge of the faith
and of the world. Where they have an option, this conception
should guide them in their choice of lectures and courses. It should
guide them too when they decide in which of the many competing
unofficial activities they will take part. Such choices should be
responsible and not merely random and capricious. Next, they
must 'pull their weight' in the communal life, and so, in their
turn, contribute to the university what in them lies. Too often the
communal tone is cheap, and shoddy and second-rate students, not
really respected by their fellows, gain office, because those of more
sense and weight are content to mind their own business and to let
these things go by default. In Christian students such an attitude
is indefensible. Again their faith should affect their attitude to the
staff and to the university authorities. Co-operation rather than the
waging of a kind of class-war, cordiality towards all advances
rather than suspicion, a readiness, and even a determination, to
make the most of opportunities of contact with more experienced
minds—at the student stage these are natural interpretations of
man's duty to his neighbour. That 'we are none of us infallible,
not even the youngest of us,' is a reminder that never loses its time-
liness in an academic environment. The apparent assumption in

some circles that *vox studentium* is *vox Dei* is at least as silly as anything which the despised elders have ever perpetrated.

Further the Christian faith should control a student's attitude towards his work and towards examinations. Feverish overwork, an obsession with the prospects of success, an anxiety often approaching, as the ordeal draws near, to hysteria, are not uncommon but are radically unchristian. They imply a wrong sense of values and a self-centred attitude. Dr. Streeter used to issue to his pupils two leaflets on ' The Gentle Art of Being Examined.' They contained a number of shrewd practical hints, expressed in racy language, about the final stage of preparation and the way to set about things in the examination room. But behind these is a distinctively Christian philosophy. ' If Christianity has anything whatever to do with life, there must be a characteristically Christian way in which to prepare for and to face an approaching examination.' Do your best quietly and then leave results to God. A Christian trust in God gives security, not that you will get a high class, but that you will get the class which He wills you to get. *Me merimnate*—' Don't worry.' This is an injunction constantly disregarded, but it is a plain Christian duty, and it is the natural outcome of genuine belief in God.

Finally, the Christian student, as ' a lay theologian,' must understand his responsibility in choosing a profession, and often in choosing his course of study while still at the university. He should not necessarily choose that career which will give him the greatest security or the best chance of earning good money, or which offers the most likelihood of his making some splash in the world or the greatest scope for expressing his individuality. As a Christian, he is responsible rather for choosing that in which, given his natural aptitudes and previous training, he has the best chance of being of some use. Ambition is not a Christian motive.

## c.  *Their Relation to Official Religion*

### (1)  The Ancient Universities

Here corporate religious observance has still an honoured position. Also ' the genius of the place,' with its traditions, customs and habitual ritual, is imbued with Christian influence. The College Chapels with their daily services, the University Churches which, week by week, Vice-Chancellor, Doctor and Proctors, enter in solemn procession, the stately Bidding Prayers, the formulas for

s

the conferment of degrees, the saying of grace in Hall, even the distant sound of the pealing organ as you cross the Quadrangle; all these serve as threads to connect twentieth-century dons and undergraduates with the faith of founders and benefactors, with Queen Philippa and the Lady Margaret and Henry the Sixth, with William of Wykeham and William of Waynefleet, with Archbishop Whitgift and Archbishop Laud. No doubt any sense of this affiliation is commonly in the background rather than the foreground of consciousness, but it is part of the ' ampler ether ' which students breathe. It is a standing witness to a world beyond the visible world and to a worship which is shared with angels and archangels and with all the company of heaven. In these older universities outward and visible signs of the Christian faith are all about us. We may be little aware of them at the time. But anyone who goes straight from ' Oxbridge,' where they are, to ' Redbrick,' where they are not, must be conscious of impoverishment.

On the other hand much of this is superficial. Beneath the surface, secularization may be as fundamental as at ' Redbrick.' The college chapels are often attended only by a tiny handful of dons or of undergraduates; or, if they are full, it is with visitors who have come to hear the choir. Any definite, Christian, faith or practice is the affair only of a minority. In quality too much of the religion in ' Oxbridge ' is decorous, faintly aesthetic and mildly uplifting. It has small kinship with the elemental force far stronger than men, that turns their lives upside down, that is the religion of the New Testament, of martyrs and Jesuits and Covenanters, and that sent ' the Cambridge seven ' to the ends of the earth. Further it is divorced from the general life of the university. People are as subject to the disintegrating influences of the day in ' Oxbridge ' as elsewhere. There is little resemblance between the normal atmosphere or presuppositions of study or recreation or social life and that of the Litany or the General Confession. In view of these things, it is often asked whether the university's continued use of the forms of religion, where there is so little real life or conviction, is not positively harmful to religion, acting as a kind of inoculation against it; and whether an open secularism would not be the lesser evil.

But, whatever the shortcomings of official religious observances such as a university or a college chapel service, members of ' the community of Christians '—both senior and junior—should throw themselves into whatever there is and should do their part to give it life and reality. They should not boycott it because it seems to them formal and arid and because they can find more spiritual refreshment for themselves elsewhere. Here and nowhere else is worship offered by the college or the university as such, and participation in this is the duty of its loyal members. To contract out of it through spiritual fastidiousness is tacitly to claim special status as one of a spiritual élite; and that is itself a symptom of the most deadly of spiritual diseases.

## (2)  The Newer Universities

With few exceptions (e.g. the Durham Colleges and, in London, King's College and Westfield College) the tradition of these universities has been thoroughly secular. Religion was regarded as a field productive of exclusiveness and contention. Let it therefore be left to the individual or to the home; the university was no place for it. But, in several of these universities, there have recently been signs of aspiration to some form of corporate, religious, observance; and there have been tentative, if rather timid, experiments. In some universities a terminal university service and sermon have been instituted. This has been held either in the university hall or in some neighbouring church or chapel by arrangement with the local clergyman or minister. Here and there the appointment of a university chaplain has been mooted. These developments are due, partly to a sense of cultural thinness and poverty, partly to a sense, sharpened by the war and by the convulsions of our day, that by contrast with Nazism or Communism our own national tradition links goodness inseparably with godliness.

But such developments have a dubious side to them. The new-found interest in religion among members of university councils and other university authorities may resemble too much the attitude of Gibbon's 'magistrate,' and the Christian religion may be welcomed as a useful social cement, which is calculated to preserve continuity and to counteract unsettlement. The 'Christianity' of observances so sponsored is likely to be highly diluted. Here again it is a mistake to be purist, priggish and doctrinaire, and to quench smoking flax. Where such beginnings have been made, it is normally right for Christian staff and students to co-operate with them cordially. But to secure such observances should certainly not be a primary object of Christian policy. In default of a complete re-orientation of university life, their adoption may not even be desirable. It is no use, and it may be less than no use, to put a Christian top-dressing on a thoroughly secularized university. In this matter Christians should not be too naïve and should remember that ' all that glitters is not gold.' We are told that the Portuguese representatives at the Versailles Conference concentrated all their efforts upon one end. They were determined that, in accordance with tradition, the name of God should be invoked in the Treaty of peace. By pertinacious adherence to the methods of the importunate widow they ultimately secured their aim, and thereafter they rested happily upon their oars. But all the other delegates were cynically amused by the incongruity between the piety of the wording and the intrigues of hard-boiled diplomatists which the Treaty, in substance, embodies. It may be doubted whether the Portuguese pietists achieved anything more than a breach of the Third Commandment, and we must beware of imitating them.

At a number of the ' Redbrick ' universities there are one or more Halls of residence which are designed to have a definitely religious complexion. These have been provided by religious bodies or groups and the university has no direct control, though they must fulfil the conditions it lays down for recognition. Most of them are Church of England, some Roman Catholic, one at least is under the auspices of the Society of Friends. A considerable proportion, but by no means all, of their students are members of the denomination concerned. The Warden always is so, and in an Anglican or Roman Hall for men he is in holy orders. Such Halls possess a chapel or at least a quiet room with daily and weekly services. Their *raison d'être* is to do something for the spiritual upbuilding of their students. What does this amount to in practice?

It does not always or of necessity amount to anything. Their religious basis can degenerate into a formality. There have been such Halls where, at times, the relation between Warden and students has been as unsatisfactory, the general tone as boorish, the intellectual and spiritual stimulus as faint as in any others. But this has not been normal. In the midst of the secularized and rather chaotic university, many of these Halls have provided something of the atmosphere of a Christian home. According to Professor Hildebrand, ' A Catholic university . . . requires the conscious production of an atmosphere filled by Christ, an environment imbued with prayer.'[1] Such a description cannot be true of a modern university of the British type, but it may in some measure

[1] Kotschnig, *op. cit.*, p. 220.

be true of a Hall within the university. Much depends on the Warden for the time being. Such Halls can be, and have been, effective centres of corporate, Christian, life. But the ground they cover is small, and it cannot easily be increased. Like the non-provided schools, they tend to be small and ill-found. There was an opportunity for them, when the university itself did little to provide residence or communal life for its students. But with the development of the university's own hall-policy the gap which they once filled will gradually disappear; and the university authorities tend naturally to prefer those Halls which the university itself has planned and over which it exercises full control. It seems unlikely that Halls conducted under the aegis of Churches can play any large part in the years ahead.

### d. Their Relation to Unofficial Religion

Our supreme need is for converted and dedicated Christians who understand their various callings and their citizenship in the light of their faith in God, and who are determined, so far as in them lies, to be agents of God in the reintegration of our disintegrated world. At present the most effective agencies for producing such people are the unofficial societies which from time to time spring up among students. By now, some of these have attained a respectable age and have a considerable record of achievement and world-wide affiliations. Prominent among them are such bodies as the Student Christian Movement, and the Inter-Varsity Fellowship of Evangelical Unions. Also there are a number of denominational societies and notably the Roman Catholic society in each university. Most of these societies do their work by the organization of study-groups and of daily or weekly prayer-meetings. In the vacations they have inter-university camps and conferences, at which they often have the assistance of outstanding Christian leaders and theologians. They set themselves both to deepen and to broaden the religious life of their members. They seek in concert to see and know more clearly what things they ought to do and to receive ' grace and power faithfully to fulfil the same '; they seek to enlarge and deepen their understanding of the Bible and also of the contemporary world, that is of the social and international situation in relation to which the Christian life has to be lived. Inevitably there is in their members some froth and some crudity. They are liable to swing between the extremes of a socially irresponsible pietism on the one hand and, on the other, a Martha-like concern about many things which misses the one thing needful. Yet during the last two generations, with all their shortcomings, they have been a great, Christian, power-house. For instance they have been a chief field of recruitment for the mission-field, and they have been the nursing-house of a large proportion of the Christian leaders throughout the world to-day.

No attempt can be made here to describe or to appraise them, but two points are of special concern for our purpose. First, they are a real and constructive force in student life to-day. For instance Mr. Brian Simon, whose own sympathies are remote from theirs, couples the largest of them, the Student Christian Movement, with the Socialist Society as being the most influential among the societies in the typical university to-day.[1] Secondly, the S.C.M. at least has recently devoted much attention to the structure and actual working of the university itself. In its own words it has set itself, for the time being, to be ' The University within the University.' This signifies that it is making some attempt to fill a gap and, being unhampered by inhibitions, to do the job which the university itself ought to be doing but is not yet doing, that is, to ask the fundamental questions about the university's task on the basis of its conception of man and the universe. No doubt other student bodies are raising the same question from a non-Christian point of view. The S.C.M., because its basis is Christian, seeks to do so in an atmosphere of prayer. In attempting the task it is, under present conditions, performing a service. But, as it is well aware, it is doing this with inadequate equipment, so long as it represents primarily only the junior members of the university. How can this effort effectively be reinforced by the wider experience of those who hold positions of more responsibility? For the ' community of Christians ' that is a practical question of immediate urgency.

## 2    THEOLOGY—THE ROLE OF A THEOLOGICAL FACULTY

On this subject there are two preliminary observations to be made. First, the contemporary university's approach to theology is timid and half-hearted. It admits theology, if at all, only in an ' un-principled ' way; that is, with a rather uneasy intellectual conscience and on grounds which it does not searchingly examine. Secondly, the Theological Faculty, where it does exist, has usually taken far too circumscribed a view of its own responsibility.

[1] *Op. cit.*, p. 89.

### a. Has a Theological Faculty a Legitimate Place in the University?

#### (1) Stages of Development

The first stage was that of ecclesiastical *monopoly*. In the Dark Ages and in the beginnings of the revival of learning, education was in the hands of the monastery and cathedral schools, and it was out of the latter that the first universities grew. It was an education exclusively of clerics by clerics. At that time no other class possessed or desired education.[1] So, at the outset, the universities were the great nursery of the Church, and to be so was their *raison d'être*. The education they provided was a strictly professional education, and all humane studies were subsidiary to this purpose. The student learned Latin in order to read his breviary, Mathematics to play his part in managing the finances of the great ecclesiastical corporations, Logic and Rhetoric to expound Christian doctrine effectively and to draw the correct conclusions from it, Music to understand the rules of plainsong. Further than was needful for such ecclesiastical purposes he did not seek to go. But, though his biblical and theological learning might be elementary, a rigorous orthodoxy was essential. Wherever the results of other sciences seemed to conflict with sound theology, they were sternly recalled to submission. The story of Abelard illustrates luridly the perils besetting any deviation from what was received. A similar atmosphere is found five hundred years later in some of the early post-reformation universities. For instance the first President of Harvard, though otherwise successful and popular, felt it incumbent on him to resign office as soon as he was no longer able to accept the rightfulness of infant baptism.[2]

The second stage is that of *primacy*. It is the glory of the great Schoolmen of the thirteenth century that, while making theological learning genuinely learned, they conceived it in no narrow or illiberal way. They recognized the intrinsic interest and relative autonomy of other studies. The civil lawyer and the physician, as well as the priest, received a university training. Yet Theology was still ' the queen of the sciences,' ' the architectonic science whose

[1] Rashdall, *op. cit.* I, p. 28.

[2] Morison, *op. cit.*, p. 19. See also Sir A. Grant, *The Story of the University of Edinburgh*, I, p. 131. ' In the then earnest mood of the national mind, personal religion, as well as a correct theology, would be thought of as primary requisites.'

office it was to receive the results of all other sciences and to combine them in an organic whole.'[1] Rightly understood all things in
the universe, all the realms of which the other sciences give us
information, sprang from God and pointed to God. Certainly there
need be no hurry to find a clash between any new scientific theory
and biblical authority. In the course of time and through free
discussion these things would find their level. This principle has
been expressed by Newman in a classical passage. 'The Catholic,' he
says, ' is sure, and nothing shall make him doubt, that if anything
seems to be proved by astronomer, or geologist, or chronologist, or
antiquarian, or ethnologist, in contradiction to the dogmas of faith,
that point will eventually turn out, first *not* to be proved, or,
secondly, *not* contradictory, or, thirdly, not contradictory to anything *really revealed*, but to something which has been confused
with revelation.'[2] But, in the last resort, if there were a clash, the
final word would rest with Theology, to which all other sciences
were conceived as subordinate though no longer as merely instrumental. It was the university's fundamental aim that, under God,
' true religion and sound learning may for ever flourish.'

The third stage, which is that of *equality,* may be said to have
prevailed in Oxford and Cambridge in the later part of the nineteenth century. The Faculty of Theology was one among a number
of Faculties, just as the Christian ministry is one among the common
callings for which the university gives a preparation. But it was no
longer regarded as the custodian of the university's unified world-
view.

The final stage, in which we are to-day, is that of *bare toleration,* though this takes a somewhat different form in ' Oxbridge '
and in ' Redbrick.' In the former the Faculty of Theology is still
formally the senior Faculty. That is, it enjoys a titular primacy
as does the House of Lords in the British Constitution. On ceremonial occasions, Doctors of Divinity precede other doctors. Just
as the Archbishop of Canterbury is, in formal precedence, the first
subject after the Royal Family, so the Regius Professor of Divinity
follows immediately behind the Vice-Chancellor and Proctors in
university processions. But this primacy is formal rather than substantial. So far from the Faculty's having any commanding
authority or special prestige, it is in a backwater rather than in the

[1] Rashdall, *op. cit.,* vol. III, p. 442.

[2] *Op. cit.,* pp. 466-467.

main stream of university life. The Honours School of Theology is a small school and attracts only a minute proportion of the abler undergraduates. In 'Redbrick,' theology was at first excluded altogether; and though this is no longer generally true, the 'Redbrick' tradition is secular, and theology is not naturally at home in it. For this exclusion we must recognise frankly that theologians have been largely to blame, owing to the use they made of their day of power, their contentiousness, intolerance and their internecine struggles. This generated a conviction among the promoters of modern universities, often not themselves irreligious men, that, however respectworthy theology might be in itself, the university was no place for it. It is true that the ban has now been lifted in three or four of the modern universities, and Departments or even Faculties of Theology have come into being. But they still are admitted on sufferance rather than on any clear and cogent principle, and with a good deal of doubt and hesitation. They are generally inconspicuous and isolated. They cater for the students of theological colleges or for older men, who are already ministers of religion and who take part-time courses at the university. They play little part in the life of the university as a whole. Thus to-day the older struggle for supremacy has given place to a struggle for existence.

(2)   What is Theology?

Here there is much confusion, and until that is removed, no discussion can be profitable.

Theology is *not* 'the science of religion.' It is not the study of religion as a human phenomenon, undertaken in the spirit of an observing naturalist, which is represented by such books at Frazer's *Golden Bough* and James's *Varieties of Religious Experience*. Its approach is quite unlike that of the psychologist or anthropologist, who studies the content of religious experience and the behaviour resulting from it, while reserving the question whether it is in fact, as it so generally purports to be, an experience of God and whether there really is a God to be experienced. Nor is it 'philosophy of religion,' which examines, as an open question, the existence of God, Freedom and Immortality. These are indeed entirely legitimate subjects for university study, but they are not the primary concern of a Theological Faculty. Any claim for its admission which confuses it with either of these is a claim on false pretences. For instance, it was felt in one university that there must be impartiality between different religions. The institution of a Faculty of Theology was allowed, but only on condition that there should be a Chair of Comparative Religion and that the subject should be compulsory for all theological students. But, in the event, practically all the students and all the teachers have been ministers or intending ministers of some Christian denomination; and the Professor of Comparative Religion has generally been a returned Christian missionary. If neutrality is indeed a necessary condition, any Faculty of Theology must be fraudulent. To admit it on such terms is either self-deception or else it is an intolerant attempt to mutilate theology and to prevent its being what theologians have always understood it to be. Any such demand must be met by the reply, ' Take it or leave it, but you cannot alter it.'

Theology *is* the study of the self-revelation of the living God; that is, of a corporate experience of God in which, from start to finish, He is the initiator. What are ultimate questions for Philosophy are primary assurances for Religion.[1] The theologian assumes that knowledge of God is both possible and actual; for him this is no longer an open question. ' God who at sundry times and in divers manners spake in time past unto the fathers by the prophets, hath in these last days spoken unto us by his Son.' That is the theologian's basic presupposition. If he should ever be driven to regard it as illusion, that for him would be the end of theology.

Thus theology implies commitment. For the theologian thinking is inextricably bound up with other mental functions, knowing God with serving and worshipping Him. Not an opinion about God, but a personal relationship with God, is his sheet-anchor. He is far removed from the attitude implied in an appeal for funds by the Corporation of Harvard in 1815, ' *not* to inculcate the peculiarities of any sect, but to place students of divinity under the most favourable circumstances for inquiring for themselves into the doctrines of revelation.'[2] In the words of William Temple, ' Religion finds its fullest expression in absolute surrender to the Object of its worship. But . . . it is not possible to surrender one's self to what is felt to be an unverified hypothesis; it is not possible to discuss impartially the existence of a Being to whom one is utterly self-

[1] See W. Temple, *Nature, Man and God*, p. 35.
[2] Morison, *op. cit.*, p. 242.

surrendered.' The theologian is not a detached observer, classifying and judging. He is a party to an encounter, the lesser party, conscious in judging of being judged. In a true sense, he must study on his knees.

This commitment is not only individual but communal; it is assumed in the reader as well as in the writer. The theologian, as such, is not an apologist. He is a member of the Christian community, and all his thinking is done within its context. Of course an agnostic—particularly if he happens to be a Scot—may read a theological book with a certain intellectual interest and may discuss the validity of any chains of reasoning which it contains. But he does not do so as a theologian, for he denies the major premise of theology. A believing theologian may think critically and may reject certain elements in the tradition; but he does so from within the tradition and not from outside it. His appeal is from faith to faith.

This, and nothing less intransigent, is the nature of that 'Theology' whose academic status is in question.

(3) Devil's Advocate—Case Against Admissibility of Theology

The original reason for the exclusion of Theology from the modern universities was not indifference or disrespect to religion. It was the division of the Christian Church into a number of 'jarring sects' such that to adopt the theology of any one of them was felt to be to repudiate the theology of all the others. It was just because it was felt that religion demanded to be treated with deadly seriousness that any compromise seemed impossible. 'Theology,' said the *Edinburgh Review* at the time of the foundation of University College, London, 'cannot possibly be taught except in one of two sorts of university—either where all are of one religious persuasion or where religious belief is a matter of perfect indifference to all.'[1]

But there is a far more formidable and fundamental objection, and it behoves us, as Christians, to face it frankly and to allow it full weight if we are to preserve our intellectual integrity. It runs as follows. On our own showing a Faculty of Theology has not an open mind; it does not ask, but begs, the ultimate questions. For it there are some issues which ought not to be raised or which, if raised, can only be settled in one way on pain of exclusion from office. But that is a confession of disqualifying bias. In the university, whose essential principle is to follow the argument whitherso-

[1] *Edinburgh Review*, 1825.

ever it leads, it is intellectual treason. In effect the Faculty says to the individual theological teacher, 'Enquire as pertinaciously, weigh evidence as meticulously, apply scientific canons as rigorously as you please so long as you do so within the prescribed limit. Transgress that limit, carry the same methods and the same caution in coming to conclusions beyond it, and you will be struck off the roll.' But, 'Thus far and no further' is an injunction intolerable in a university. As Mommsen declared in a notable protest, research without presuppositions and without a foregone conclusion, is the *Lebensnerv* of the university.[1] Can a thinker, for whom one set of conclusions entails official death, approach his subject with the objectivity and freedom from bias which is the condition of intellectual respect? Further is not the hollowness of the theologian's claim exposed by the fact that he is himself the first to protest against any bias other than his own? If the Central Labour College contends that education is to be treated as a weapon in the class-war, if Russian biologists are required to make their scientific conclusions square with dialectical materialism, if Fascist professors must be politically trustworthy, no one is quicker than the Christian to protest against tyranny and to denounce as worthless a 'rigged' conclusion. 'As long as my practical business is to teach philosophy,' wrote the youthful William Temple in 1906, 'I must refuse to close for the practical purposes of my life questions which are theoretically open, for the practical purpose of my life at present is to be theoretical.' But is not such an open mind a condition not only of philosophy but of any study at the academic level?

Further there is no parallel in other Faculties to the orthodoxy demanded of the theologian. With them no penalty or obloquy attaches to the most complete change of view. No British university would think of accepting a Chair for the propagation of Marxist economics, of Logical Positivism, of Whig history or of Mendelian biology. If, as we fully admitted (Chapter IV) the modern university cannot as a whole be officially Christian, how can one Faculty within it be so?

Again there is the difficulty of dual allegiance. A theological teacher is commonly an officer of his Church as well as of the university. That is, he is an officer of an institution which is essentially propagandist; it is a 'Will-organization' rather than, like the university, a 'Thought-organization.' It is noteworthy that, though Unitarians are free from dogmatic commitment beyond all

---

[1] Quoted in Stirk's *German Universities through English Eyes*, p. 47.

other professedly Christian bodies, Grote regarded the fact that Martineau was a Unitarian minister as disqualifying him for a Chair of Philosophy in the University of London.[1]

These are 'liberal' criticisms from which the Neo-Marxist is debarred, since he has no objection to commitment as such provided it is commitment to the true faith. But he regards Christianity as Christians themselves regard Astrology, that is as a pseudoscience based on illusion and, worse still, as actively harmful and corrupting owing to the admixture of elements other than purely intellectual; as having in it something morbidly fascinating and mentally debauching, on a par with 'exploring the womb or the tomb or dreams,' something which evokes credulity and wishful thinking and benumbs even the desire for objectivity.

Lastly it must be recognized that some damage has accrued to the academic reputation of Theology through a reason not intrinsic to it. Owing to special historical circumstances there has come to be, at some of our older universities, a generous number of theological chairs out of proportion to the number of students in the Faculty or to the establishment of other Faculties. Not unnaturally this causes, in academic circles, some uneasiness and raising of eyebrows. It is questioned whether, in the Theological Faculty, the title 'Professor' can imply quite so high a standard of intellectual and scholarly distinction as is normal. To afford any ground for such misgivings must be not only a stumbling-block to the university but damaging to the Church and to the Christian cause.

### (4) The Reply

The denominational difficulty *solvitur ambulando* since the possibility of an inter-denominational Faculty has been demonstrated in practice. This has been due, first and foremost, to the growth among the non-Roman Christian bodies of an 'ecumenical' spirit and of a sense of proportion. The atmosphere has changed decisively since the early days of London and of the 'Redbrick' Universities. In face of secularism, the common foe, there has been a closing of the ranks. Indeed the major divergences in theology to-day do not follow confessional lines. Theologians of different communions read and profit by one another's books and have common standards of scholarship. In common allegiance to the same Master, they are even able to explore thoroughly the questions that divide them; discussion carried on in that spirit does not estrange but draws

---

[1] Bellot, *History of University College*, pp. 339 ff.

the parties together. St. Paul withstood St. Peter, but they were one in the eyes of Nero and they are one in the eyes of the Church.

It has been due, secondly, to the presence in the university neighbourhood of a variety of theological colleges and to the working out of a technique of collaboration between the denominational college and the undenominational university. It is the college which undertakes the liturgical training of the ordinand, his technical preparation for the ministry of his own Church. It is the college again which undertakes his devotional training, and in which it is possible, as it is not in the modern 'mixed' university, to produce 'an atmosphere filled by Christ, an environment imbued with prayer.' But the major part of the biblical, historical and doctrinal teaching can be given in the university by teachers in whose university appointment denominational affiliations have played no part. In the older universities, it is true, both in England and in Scotland, there are some denominational chairs, attached perhaps to canonries or other ecclesiastical offices. But these are survivals; the universities in question have still some degree of prescriptive association with the Established Churches of either country. In the modern universities such limitations would be quite unacceptable and ought not to be proposed.

But the more formidable difficulty, the reproach of disqualifying bias, still remains to be considered, though first perhaps one possible misunderstanding should be removed. For the theological student there is not and cannot be any credal condition of a degree or of the highest honours. His examinations are in no sense a test of his orthodoxy or piety, but only of his knowledge and intellectual grasp. Secondly, to regard all commitment or acknowledgement of presuppositions as a disqualification is impossibly naïve.[1] It rests on the unfounded assumption that it is possible to dispense entirely with presuppositions; and this in turn rests on a complacent ignoring of the whole field of unconscious presuppositions. A truer doctrine was laid down many years ago in the Report of the Adult Education Committee of the Ministry of Reconstruction, of which Dr. A. L. Smith was chairman. The form of bias with which that Committee was concerned was political rather than religious, but the same principle holds good. 'The basis of discrimination between education and propaganda is not the particular opinions held by the teacher or the students, but the intellectual competence and quality of the former and the seriousness and continuity of study

[1] See Chapter III above.

of the latter . . . In actual fact most adults start with some fairly definite point of view and find in that a motive for study.'[1] A teacher or a body of teachers are not to be rejected by the university simply because they have already arrived at definite convictions on controversial questions, but only because they are dishonest or incompetent.

Whoever rules the theologian out of court as an academic thinker or teacher, simply on the ground that he is a committed man, should first scrutinize his own position and mark the unproved assumption which he himself is making. His position would be reasonable only if any claim that there has been a self-revelation of God in history could be dismissed dogmatically as inherently incredible, before examination of the evidence. But that would be to beg the whole question at issue between the Christian and the unbeliever. But if the claim can be admitted as a hypothesis to be examined, then, on that hypothesis, the humble, receptive and ' committed ' attitude of the theologian would be reasonable. In any case commitment one way or other is unavoidable. Suspense of judgment is an illusion, since it is impossible to suspend living. Throughout his thinking, the student of theological questions is actually living either a godward or a godless life. There is no third alternative. The true obscurantist then, as we have already urged, is the man who claims to be without presuppositions and therefore never criticizes those which he has. Therein very possibly he fools his neighbours, and certainly he fools himself.

As to intellectual integrity the effect of the financial sanction can easily be overrated. The theologian is not peculiar in that a complete reversal of his convictions might be incompatible with his retaining his job. A medical professor who became a homœopathist or osteopathist or Christian Scientist, a historian who came to believe with Henry Ford that ' History is bunk ' must, as honest men, resign. Apart from financial considerations the theologian no doubt is liable to shrink unduly from the emotional wrench of abandoning a lifetime's convictions and repudiating a position with which he has been publicly identified. But so is everyone else. A rare degree of intellectual energy and courage is required for such conversions. But the theologian shares with his academic colleagues common standards of intellectual probity.

On this issue we are bound to challenge many of our colleagues in the university who demur on academic grounds to the inclusion

---

[1] *Op. cit.*, para. 215.

of theology. We invite them to examine themselves and to make sure that the apparently neutral and academic reasons for rejection which they adduce are not merely a cloak for anti-Christian prejudice. We have admitted that, here and there, theological titles may be somewhat too easily achieved. But, apart from possible local and temporary aberrations, to deny the intellectual competence of theologians as such is not really plausible. Unless Christian belief is to be regarded as, in itself, conclusive evidence of intellectual incapacity—and that would be to beg the largest of questions—to deny intellectual equality to theologians as a class is mere ' Hubris.' By any ordinary standard of academic eminence Lightfoot, Westcott and Hort, or Driver and Sanday, or Hoskyns and Dodd, or overseas such men as Barth and Brunner, Dibelius and Berdyaev, Maritain and Niebuhr can challenge comparison with any. Also to the main point at issue, which is the credibility of the Christian faith, they have devoted a considerably higher quantity and quality of attention than have most of their critics.

We conclude that Theology is a legitimate subject of university study. And, if legitimate, it is also imperative unless the Christian hypothesis is to be ruled out of court *ab initio*. But, having been under suspicion, the theologian is under a special obligation to be vigilant in guarding his intellectual integrity.

### b.   The Job of a Theological Faculty

#### (1)   The Advancement of Sacred Learning

The first duty of the staff of this Faculty is to contribute towards the systematic understanding of the Christian faith. For this purpose there is required, to say the least, scholarship as finished, thinking as far-reaching and penetrating, erudition as massive, as in any other academic study. Naturally this contribution has mainly taken the form of biblical exegesis or of the study of Christian doctrine or of church history. But if this is to be relevant and genuinely effective there is required in addition some theological estimate and appraisement of life in the modern world, its institutions and occupations. Here the responsibility of the theologian is inescapable, and, as yet, it has been far too little fulfilled. But it requires very careful statement, for it is easily misunderstood. Ecclesiastics have oscillated between a timid avoidance of commitment on all social and political questions and a proneness to make rash pronouncements on issues on which their technical competence is inadequate. Certainly the theologian cannot, unaided, deliver an authoritative judgment on the theology of engineering or of medicine; he needs the co-operation of the Christian engineer or doctor. But neither can these dispense with the theologian. If they are to solve their practical problems on Christian lines they need a much fuller understanding of the central Christian verities and their implications than, as amateurs in theology, they can hope to possess, and they are entitled to look for help from the professional.

## (2) The Basic Intellectual Training of Clergy and Ministers

The preliminary professional training of clergy and ministers has at most times been one of the functions, and often the chief function, of universities. At many times it has been scandalously inadequate. For the mass of the clergy in the Middle Ages it included little theology proper.[1] But after the Reformation the demand for a learned clergy was a leading motive in the foundation of new universities.[2] To-day the university cannot undertake, what it once professed but never really performed, namely the devotional training of the minister; that must be the affair of the theological colleges. But it has no more reason to be ashamed of giving their basic intellectual training to clerics than to lawyers or to doctors.

The great advantage of a university training for parsons is that it is not seminarist. It gives the opportunity of intimate contact with those engaged in preparing for quite different callings. Notoriously one of the greatest hindrances to the work of the ministry to-day is its apparent mental remoteness from the ordinary layman. A certain moral and spiritual apartness is inevitable and right; it is challenging and we want more and not less of it. But the remoteness resulting from a sheltered life and a restricted experience is wholly bad. Since the minister, on one side at least of his office, is essentially the representative man, it is well that as an ordinand he should plunge into the intellectual world of the day. He should not only do this in the spirit of an advocate who studies in advance his opponent's case in order to be able to make the most telling rejoinders; he should genuinely stand alongside his fellow-men and personally experience the characteristic strains and stresses of the time. Only so can he acquire an imaginative understanding of all

[1] See Rashdall, *op. cit.* III, pp. 449 ff.
[2] This is true for instance both of Harvard (Morison, *op. cit.,* pp. 3 and 4) and of Edinburgh (Grant), pp. 157-8.

T

sorts and conditions of men. But this need to enter into and to share the standpoint of others is only one side of his task. He must not be the mere creature of his environment, absorbing and mentally shaped by the existing atmosphere of the modern university. He must also react vigorously on his environment in the light of his faith. He must be awake to, and critical of, current presuppositions. It is the business of his teachers to augment his power to do this.[1]

Unfortunately such a statement of the opportunity and of the task of a theological student in a university may seem merely ironical to many of those who are most familiar with the inside of universities to-day. So often the theological student mixes hardly at all with students of other Faculties, and even within his own Faculty he associates chiefly with those whose temperament and ecclesiastical colouring harmonize most easily with his own. Indeed much change of perspective and deliberate out-going is required both of staff and of students. Also it is highly desirable that the theological course should normally be post-graduate, as it already is in some universities. The theological student would then be relatively mature, and he would already have shared the life and have been steeped in the outlook of another Faculty.

### (3)   Its Duty to the Whole Body of Students

At present the Faculty (or Department) of Theology has a regrettably small impact on the university as a whole. It tends to be isolated and to be regarded as a sideshow, and it has been over-ready to accept that rôle. Its students mix little with others, and its teachers have little or no contact with the general body of students. Its appeal is highly esoteric. But it ought to be making its own contribution to the main university problem with which all our previous chapters have been concerned. It ought also to seek opportunities of expounding, to the ordinary non-theological student, the fundamental doctrines of the Christian faith in untechnical language which he can understand. The need is great, for such a student's grasp of theology, even if he comes from a Christian home, is commonly infinitesimal. Such students need to be provided with an intelligible alternative to secularism, a Christian map of the world however provisional. Failing that, they are left, at best, with a Christian top-dressing on a thoroughly secularized understanding of history, literature, or natural science,

[1] See Jenkins, *The Gift of Ministry* Ch. VII, for an illuminating discussion.

on the lines on which these are commonly studied in universities. They have an equally secularized view of business and politics, as these are commonly conducted and judged in the contemporary world. On such points the Christian student is just one of the crowd; no Christian teacher has enabled him to be anything else.

Here is a magnificent field for the Faculty of Theology, waiting to be tilled. Some enterprise may be necessary, but it is not true that there is no demand. Just before the war, the S.C.M. in Oxford addressed a striking appeal to the theological teachers to do this very thing; not to confine themselves to giving a technical training for the Ministry, but to expound the Christian faith to the ordinary undergraduate as a positive way, and practical philosophy, of life. Professsor Hodgson in Oxford and Dr. Whale in Cambridge responded to this appeal. They gave short courses of lectures on Christian doctrine, open to all undergraduates who cared to come, and each had an audience of five or six hundred. But in general ' The hungry sheep look up . . .' Here is a great call for experiment and initiative.

### (4) Its Duty to Other Faculties

The Faculty needs a deepened sense of responsibility to the university as a whole, that is, to the university as an institution in its own right and not merely an appanage of the Church. There is no going back to the Middle Ages. No cheap and easy re-integration of the university is possible by the restoration of Theology to her old place as ' the queen of sciences.' In this respect perhaps the theologian's first duty is to strive to understand and to enter into what the other Faculties are doing. Departmentalism is always sinful, but in the theologian it is inexcusable for it is an example of the primal sin of pride. Disdain is the product of laziness; it is only to be rooted out by prayer, and then incompletely. Far from involving himself in his own virtue, the theologian should be an interpreter and a reconciler between others, a breaker down of partition walls. Only when he has reached this point, can he do effectively what is equally necessary; that is, to exercise his prophetic function and to expose and to criticize the tacit assumptions of other Faculties, and so to reveal to them what they are doing and where they are going. At the same time he must endeavour to ascertain his own assumptions and prepossessions. He must expose these to the criticism of others and be prepared to learn from it. Finally, in view of the chronic tendency of academic persons to sit on the fence, the theologian should at all times stress the duty of decision and commitment. He should stress, too, the futility of all attempts to shirk commitment, since such attempts themselves involve a decision, unconscious, ungrounded and irresponsible.

# XI

## TAKING STOCK

This is a book about universities and their policies, but it is written from a definite standpoint. The argument rests on certain assumptions or 'postulates.' It can only be thoroughly convincing to those who accept these assumptions, and it is to them that it is primarily addressed.

(1) We are living in an age of exceptional crisis

To the Christian, it is true, all life is critical; from day to day it is an affair of fateful decisions which are subject to judgment. But, for the history of civilization, the years round 1950 are critical in a degree to which the years round 1850 or 1900 were not. The development of discovery and invention have been such that, within twenty-four hours, a decision in the Kremlin or the White House may revolutionize the lives of millions of peasants in Central Europe. Power has been doubled and quadrupled almost overnight. The technique of manipulating men has been developed quite disproportionately to any growth in real understanding of their nature or their good.

(2) The issue depends chiefly on the human factor

In the last resort economic and political orders—and revolutions —depend on the beliefs and sentiments of men; not necessarily on those which they profess and suppose themselves to hold, but on those which really move them.

(3) The beliefs which govern men's actions are in flux

The old communal convictions concerning good and evil have broken up. A deep uncertainty about goals and obligations pervades all classes and all levels of culture. Our society has lost direction.

(4)   The clue to reconstruction is to be found within our own tradition

For Western civilization at least, and notably for Great Britain, reconstruction is to be achieved, not by abandoning our tradition, but by rediscovering and reinvigorating it.

(5)   In that tradition the Christian element is vital

That the Christian element in our tradition is large in bulk is an obvious fact of history. That it is the vital element on which others depend is our postulate. Of course it is open to challenge, but here its truth is not argued but assumed.

(6)   Yet the tradition needs purging and enrichment

'The letter killeth, but the spirit giveth life.' Salvation is not to be found in revival of tradition, whether humanist or Christian, just as it stood. Our tradition includes flaws which must be corrected; and though Christ is the same yesterday, to-day and for ever, the social embodiment of Christianity in one age is not suitable for another. To-day we need to incorporate in it some things which are both new and true.

(7)   Thus our generation is confronted with a stupendous intellectual task

If our tradition is to save us, it must be related to, and expressed in terms of, a large-scale, mechanical civilization. In such intellectual reconstruction a heavy responsibility rests on the universities as the chief organs of the community for sifting and transmitting ideas.

How far are our universities able and willing to respond to this challenge? Just now they are in a state of rapid expansion and development. The numbers of their students and staff are being doubled, and there is an intellectual ferment within them which shows itself in keen discussion of plans and policies. But, as yet, the questions debated have not, for the most part, been those which are really fundamental, though there are signs of a change. From our perspective we have to ask what is the proper rôle of the universities, what is the worth of what they are now doing, and what is their real impact on their students and on the world. Of what inward and spiritual graces are the young graduate's gown and hood the outward and visible sign?

In rough, general terms the answer seems to be that in technical advances the universities are showing the way, witness their contribution to winning the war; but that only to a small extent are they protagonists in the transvaluation of values. Their traditional rôle was to train students for leadership in a stratified society, such as we are ceasing to have and no longer believe in. But no other accepted ideal has taken its place. Their failure ' to rise to the height of the times ' is due to certain deep-seated disabilities; and to diagnose these thoroughly is no sign of defeatism but a first step towards their reduction or removal. In the sphere of ultimate loyalties, universities share the confusion and unsettlement of the world at large. They have no agreed criteria by which to assess their policies, organization, teaching methods and the forms of their communal life; they have not even fruitful disagreement. They tacitly refuse to take cognizance of really contentious and difficult issues. They label them ' Dangerous, do not touch ' and thrust them out of sight. But that is a lazy and pusillanimous evasion of responsibility. They can give no light or guidance to a directionless world, so long as they are themselves directionless and are content to remain so.

Much of this confusion of purpose is due to the presence, side by side, of three different and partly discordant sets of assumption by which the pattern of the university has been shaped—the Classical-Christian, the Liberal, and the Technological-Democratic. Its consequences are disastrous and far-reaching. Worst of all is the exaggerated departmentalism which splits the university into sections, each inhabiting its own circumscribed mental world. Where there is little concerted attempt to see life whole, students are unconsciously conditioned to irresponsibility for its conduct. Few graduates will have shared, even in a rudimentary form, in an intellectual experience such as was the youthful John Stuart Mill's on reading Bentham:

' I felt taken up to an eminence from which I could survey a vast mental domain and see stretching out into the distance intellectual results beyond all computation . . . At every page he seemed to open up a clearer and broader conception of what human opinions and institutions ought to be, how they might be made what they ought to be, and how far from it they now are . . . The " principle of utility " . . . fell exactly into its place as the key-stone which held together the detached and fragmentary parts of my knowledge and beliefs. It gave unity to my conception of

things. I now had opinions, a creed, a doctrine, a philosophy; in one of the best senses of the word, a religion; the
inculcation and diffusion of which could be made the principal
purpose of life. And I had a grand conception laid before me of
changes to be effected in the condition of mankind through that
doctrine.'[1]

A large proportion of staff and students appear neither to have
found such a ' keystone ' nor to have received much stimulus to
seek it. Further the task is neglected of digging down to presuppositions and subjecting them to critical study, whether they are
those inherent in a particular science or a man's own basic attitudes
and springs of action. There is an unconfessed reluctance to
undertake the painful, dismaying, and divisive task of deep self-
examination. Lastly there is a morbidly exaggerated cult of
neutrality which tends to inhibit all intellectual commitment. Such
neutrality, if genuine, would be irresponsible; universities would
be content to watch what they ought to play a part in shaping.
When fictitious, it is a modern embodiment of the Platonic ' lie in
the soul ' and leads to that form of bias which is most insidious,
precisely because it pretends to be unbiassed.

The contrast between the need of the time and present
academic inhibitions and disabilities creates a ' crisis in the university,' and teachers and administrators ought to be more awake to
this, and more concerned about it, than most of them yet are. In
face of it, every group within the university which has a positive
faith must feel a challenge to play the part of ' creative minority.'

But none of the groups already in the field can satisfy enquirers
who accept our postulates. ' Scientific humanists,' for instance,
have high merits. They have been more responsibly awake than
the rest of us to the significance of changes in the modern world,
to revolutionary possibilities of human control of events, and to the
relation of what goes on in the university to what goes on outside it.
But they offer no adequate ethic for the planner. They throw
much new light on the question *how* to plan, but little on the
question *to what end* to plan. They offer no adequate safeguard
to ordinary people against the inordinate power of planners. In
the main they ignore the most crucial of all questions—' Has God
indeed made us for Himself, and is our heart unquiet until it rests
in Him?'

On the other hand, no defensive return to old ways, whether

---

[1] J. S. Mill, *Autobiography*, pp. 65-7.

classical or Christian, will meet the needs of our time. Classical standards emanate from a small and tidy world, not yet industria-lized, in which change and turmoil, however violent, are surface phenomena, while, underneath, life is an affair of use and wont and persists substantially unchanged. But the world and the men with whom we have to deal are far more complex and intractable than the classical picture allows. Even in its own time that picture had what, to us looking back, are radical defects. Its temper was authoritarian where our own age is democratic, hierarchical where ours is equalitarian, complacent where ours is iconoclastic.

Similarly the Christian university (old style) was made possible by conditions which no longer exist and was defaced by faults which we can no longer tolerate. In the Middle Ages ' Europe was bound together by a common social system, a common religion, language, art, architecture, philosophy, law, common institutions of all kinds. It was a hierarchical society in the sense that it was like a great pyramid, and at the top was God transcendent over the world, man's maker and judge and redeemer, with whom you knew in your bones, whether you were a sinner or a saint, a feudal lord or a serf, that you had got to reckon in the end.'[1]

Such a society is remote from ours. Universities to-day cannot have a pattern of life and work implying such a background except by forcible imposition. Even if that were possible, it would be a betrayal of the Christian cause on which nemesis would soon follow, for the real paganism of the majority would absorb their masters; the ' Christianity' could be no more than a top-dressing. But in their own day Christian Universities, as well as the Holy Roman Empire or the Most Christian King, were in some respects radically unchristian. They were narrow, self-satisfied, unteachable. Their loyalty was too much to their own past and too little to the living God. They failed to recognize that God in Christ is always more and other than any Christian tradition or institution designed to embody Him, and that He is for ever breaking in from outside and wrenching us out of our comfortable certainties and anchorages. So any Christian revival, in our universities as in the world, must comprise not only *recovery* but also some element of *discovery*.

After these rejections, we come to the heads of the positive policy here commended. They are as follows :—

[1] Vidler, *Secular Despair and the Christian Faith*, p. 11.

(1) All inhibition of discussion of the burning questions of the day must be removed, for any attitude towards them is preferable to apathy and drift.  If it could be nothing more, the university must at least be a battle ground where the real intellectual issues of our time are fought out and their protagonists are confronted with one another.  In these wrestlings it must stimulate the characteristic academic excellences of precision, comprehensiveness and candour, and the penetration which discerns the principles underlying practical disagreements.

(2) If such confrontation is to be genuine, communications must be restored between the isolated mental worlds which different groups have come to inhabit.  Our debates must not be 'merely academic,' they must be conducted at the level at which our several basic acceptances begin to diverge.  For groups and individuals this entails, on the one hand bringing to light the hidden urges, inhibitions and aspirations which really determine our attitudes; on the other hand a resolute and sustained effort of imagination to enter into the mind of other groups and to discover, not only what they think, but why they think it.[1]

(3) There is a limit to neutrality.  There are issues so fundamental that ostensible neutrality is illegitimate and real neutrality is impossible.  In these respects the university in its corporate capacity cannot be content to be simply an arena in which special groups fight out their battles.  Admittedly this is an age of transition, and no imposing intellectual structure can to-day find general acceptance.  Yet there are a few basic values for which, irrespective of internal differences, the university as a whole must stand.  Without some such final frame of reference no coherent university policy would be possible.  What Cavour said of statesmen is true also of universities.  'A statesman to be worthy of the name ought to have certain fixed points or, so to speak, a polar star to guide him on his path, reserving to himself the choice of means and the right of changing them if necessary, but always keeping his eye fixed on the point at which he aims.'[2]

Some of these basic values are academic; a passion for truth, thoroughness in pursuing it to the bitter end, a delicate precision in

---

[1] Any wide adoption of these first two principles would transform the scene, even if the university in its corporate capacity remained strictly neutral.

[2] Whyte, *Political Life and Letters of Cavour*, p. 432.

analysis, a judicial temper, a willingness to learn from all quarters, an uncompromising insistence on freedom of utterance. In the first instance they are working assumptions of the guild, rules which experience has shown to be essential to good craftsmanship. But they have also wider implications; the university man who has assimilated them will have predetermined his stand on a number of political and moral questions, far beyond the confines of the university. Other values basic for the university are those common to the whole community in which it is set. For British universities they include recognition of some absolute moral obligation (the ' Tao ') an ingrained respect for law and order, and an unshakeable conviction that ' people matter.'

Whether these values are correctly stated in detail or not, probably the great majority of university teachers would give general assent to the first three points in our ' platform.' The crux lies in two further points which are undoubtedly more controversial. But it is to assert and maintain them that this book has been written.

(4) In the university it is not enough merely to recognize that, beneath our differences, we hold in common some values rather vaguely adumbrated. It is necessary constantly to explore and probe them and to discover how far they are genuine and coherent. They can only be a trustworthy basis for action if held with a firm intellectual grasp.

This is often disputed. It is suggested that such insistence on a common doctrine is over-strained, and rather febrile, and that, south of the Tweed at any rate, it is contrary to the national genius, Englishmen being notoriously ' hard to be worked up to the dogmatic level.' In practice, it is urged, our differences on Senate and Council do not follow doctrinal lines. In the actual running of a university there is no reason to suppose in advance that Mr. C. S. Lewis and Professor Hogben will be opponents or that Sir Richard Livingstone and Sir Will Spens will be allies. It is urged further that, to insist on doctrinal agreement as a basis for educational policy is in any case a counsel of despair, since such agreement is obviously unattainable in our lifetime; whereas we can have agreement sufficient for common action about specific things which are valuable without any minute investigation of the principles on which we value them. ' Here and now we know that hatred, cruelty, intolerance, and indifference to human misery are bad, that love, kindliness, tolerance, forgiveness, and truth are good, so unquestionably good that we do not need God or heaven to assure us of their worth.'[1]

Such an attitude might have been reasonable in quiet and stable times, when throughout a whole society there is a spontaneous conformity in moral judgments. It is not so in revolutionary times when all our wonted certainties are violently called in question. For instance Professor Stebbing's axioms may be unquestioned in our own circles, but they are vehemently repudiated in much of the world to-day. Customary beliefs, unanalysed and uncriticized, which we have heard from our fathers, or which, by introspection, we simply find ourselves holding, will not maintain themselves against the violent negations and the daemonic new faiths which surround us; still less will they have any missionary power. Only a reasonable faith can do that, a faith which is congruous with our other beliefs, and which has been tested and grounded by being exposed to criticism. In any case it is the special vocation of the university to think things out and to trace particular truths back to the principles on which they rest. That 'the unexamined life is no life for man,' is, for it, an article of faith. To confine such examination to the choice of means and to leave the nature of the values by which we live shrouded in haze, would be a stultifying paradox.

(5) But there is yet a further step to take, and for our immediate purpose it is the most important of all. Here our argument is addressed primarily to our fellow-Christians in the university, and indeed to ourselves. This is its gist. We have now to choose between two policies, one of which must be adopted and acted upon with determination. Either we must regard ourselves as a small Christian enclave within a predominantly pagan university, like the early Christians in the Roman Empire, or a Christian group within a Chinese, Indian or Russian university to-day; in that case, we must decline responsibility for a machine which we cannot hope to control, we must separate ourselves more sharply, as dissenters, from the sub-Christian motives and practices of the majority, and we must devote ourselves to securing sufficient freedom of action to build up an intensive Christian life within the small circle of the faithful. Or, as is here strongly advocated, we should

[1] Quoted from the late Professor Susan Stebbing by Mr. Lionel Elvin, in an article "Can Educationists Agree while Philosophers Differ?" *Adult Education*, Vol. XX., No. 2. This article is a lucid and urbane statement of the view contrary to ours.

aim at exercising influence on the university as a whole. We should then seek to play the rôle of a 'creative minority,' from which the whole community may gradually take colour; as, for example, the Utilitarians in one generation and the Fabians in another permeated British public life and shaped both legislation and administration. No doubt it would be fanciful to expect that, in any near future, British universities will be filled by good Christians, but they may still in a significant sense be Christian-minded universities.

In university as in nation, such 'Christianization' is only a legitimate or practical aim if there is already some predisposition to it in the general body. But if Mr. Eliot's three main contentions are accepted, that condition must be regarded as fulfilled. First, our culture, so far as it is positive, is still Christian. Secondly, it cannot remain in its present state; it must soon become wholly secular, unless it becomes more Christian than it now is. Thirdly, if the majority of our people understood the issue in all its bearings they would choose Christianity. For ourselves, we accept this diagnosis as probable enough to act on. So, in effect, we are saying to our non-Christian colleagues, who do not yet accept all our postulates: 'Dig deeper into your own convictions and their grounds, into the values which in your hearts you respect and for which, in the last resort, you would give your lives, in short, into "the religion of the Englishman." You must do that if they are to survive, and still more if they are to be a basis on which our people can give any degree of moral leadership to the world. When you do, we believe you will find that much of what is most real and vital in them is Christian. You will find too that they are unlikely to make converts, or even to maintain themselves against assault, unless they become more fully and effectively Christian than they now are. Like us, you have a crucial choice to make. You can move towards complete secularism or you can move towards Christianity; what you cannot do is to "stay put." '

Such 'Christianization' will affect university policy in at least three ways. First it will emphasize the indefeasible value of the individual person. This valuation rests on faith in a reality underlying appearances which often seem to contradict it. It is independent of kinship, likeableness or intellectual ability. Whether he looks like it or not, every student (or potential student) and every teacher is made in the image of God, has been redeemed by Christ, and is in process of preparation for eternal life. Such a faith must radically affect the university's attitude on questions of admission, curriculum, teaching methods and the ordering of communal life. Secondly, a Christian outlook also includes a profound sense of the ubiquity and the humanly ineradicable character of sin. The Devil is hydra-headed; foiled here, he continually renews the battle there. At each moral level he devises new forms and new dimensions of evil : *corruptio optimi pessima.* Hence education is a much less simple matter than the secularist supposes, for it involves the re-making rather than the making of men. Worse still, not only is the educator an artist hampered by the refractoriness of his material, he is ' let and hindered ' by his own untrustworthiness. If Christian-minded, he will be conscious of his own mixed motives and recurrent self-deception, and he will indulge in no utopian expectations. He will know that no reform is an unmixed blessing, that it always brings with it some harm as well as good. Build he must, but semi-permanent buildings are the best he can hope to erect. Yet, thirdly, in the last resort the Christian outlook is unconquerably hopeful, because it is shot through with the sense of divine providence. All genuine effort is worth while, because the educator can trust to superhuman sources of power to make strength out of his weakness and to superhuman wisdom to shape his roughhewn ends. In that perspective, he can persevere with the often tedious and disappointing business of university reform in humble dutifulness and confidence.

The university then should not be colourless or merely neutral on major issues. Any rational ordering of its life and studies must be related to some scheme of values, and it is better that this should be conscious and honestly avowed. But while we contend that these values can, and should increasingly, be Christian values, we repudiate many of the deductions which Christians in authority have been accustomed to draw from this premise. The university for which we are working will differ from the older type of ' Christian university ' in being open and not closed. Though it can distinguish between orthodoxy and heresy, it will mark off no areas where discussion is taboo, and it will neither exclude nor silence heretics. It will demand no formal profession of faith as a condition of membership or of office. If it is not ' liberal,' still less is it ' totalitarian.'

There are various grounds for this. In the present confused state of opinion, any agreed basis can only be elementary, and there can be no academic equivalent for an Athanasian Creed. But even if some day this confusion were dissipated, the basis of agreement much extended and a good deal of ' christianization ' were achieved the case would not be altered, for toleration within the university is not only a tactical necessity but a matter of principle. We have learned, and cannot forget, that intellectual regimentation is fundamentally unchristian, since it can only result in ' the forced and outward union of cold, neutral and inwardly divided minds.' It is not the business of the university to impose on its members any readymade philosophy of life, but to give them material for a genuine personal choice. Also the difference between ' true believer' and ' heretic ' is a difference not between white and black, but between lighter and darker shades of grey; and the heretic has generally some positive contribution to make. Further, the university is unlike the Church, in that it is its function to facilitate the trying out of opinions. A bishop undertakes, at his consecration, to ' banish and drive away all erroneous and strange doctrine contrary to God's word,' but any such exclusiveness is emphatically not the business of university authorities. On the contrary, here too Milton is right: ' Where there is much desire to learn, there of necessity will be much arguing, much writing, many opinions; for opinion in good men is but knowledge in the making. . . . A little generous prudence, a little forbearance of one another, and some grain of charity might win all these diligences to join and unite in one brotherly search after Truth; could we but forgo this prelatical tradition of crowding free consciences and Christian liberties into canons and precepts of men.'

Yet when appointments to teaching or administrative posts are to be made, an applicant's working philosophy of life is not irrelevant, though it may not be decisive. The relevance varies in different cases and no clear rules can be laid down. But, on the one hand, the university should not attempt to exclude all who are not of its own colour, and in no event should it demand any declaration of conformity as a condition of membership. On the other hand, when a university bases its policy on any definite values, appointing bodies must bear in mind that the policy will be stultified unless, in practice, a large proportion of the university's officers respects and endorses those values.

This concludes our main argument which is one of principle. It seeks to establish a unity of aim with which practical reforms may be undertaken and of standard by which they may be judged. But, however valid in itself, it can be of small value until it is made

the basis of responsible decisions and is translated into action. Most
of the thinking and experimenting required for this has still to be
done. But the later chapters are a tentative effort to illustrate a few
of the ways in which adoption of these principles might gradually
modify the framework of university life.

In Chapter VII, on ' Studies,' the chief problem discussed has
been that posed by the Harvard Report— How can universities
to-day give an education in the art of living? By what curricula
can they train a student to choose ends and recognize values, and
so to live his life more purposefully and intelligently? How can
they correct the tendency to learn ' more and more about less and
less?' This cannot be done simply by reverting to older forms of
' liberal education '; the universities have once for all been opened
to students who must earn their living. Hence the problem is, how
to combine general with occupational education. It is from this
standpoint that various types of curriculum are here discussed.

The fulfilment of this purpose implies four conditions. (1) The
present isolation of ' subjects ' and of departments must be broken
down. More attention must be given to fields in which they overlap. Different disciplines must be brought to bear on the same
problem, as, for instance, jurist, doctor, psychologist, prison com-
missioner, social scientist and moralist, may combine to discuss the
proper treatment of delinquents. Teachers should explore ways of
bringing allied subjects into fruitful connection, perhaps by inter-
departmental discussions, and of combining, in the education of
the individual students, disciplines now remote from each other,
e.g. Arts and Science. (2) The overloading of curricula, which
begins far back in school days and leaves no time ' to stand and
stare ' or to explore by-ways, must no longer be mildly deplored;
it must be ruthlessly assailed as the monster that it is. (3) For
members of staff a new balance between teaching and research
must be found. A healthy insistence on discovery and original
thought must not be overstressed to the virtual exclusion of any
real intimacy between teachers and pupils. (4) Customary methods
of teaching and of testing must be reconsidered. All that savours
of mass-production must be discountenanced; all that entails genuine encounter of mind with mind must be fostered. On this basis
there is special need for experiment with the lecture and tutorial
systems in all their variations. The frequently unhealthy effects of
examinations must be recognized and ways must be found of
curtailing their disproportionate influence.

In ordering their corporate life as in ordering their studies, our universities have to maintain old values in new conditions and often in new forms, while rejecting their limitatons.  Through Oxford and Cambridge we inherit a rich, distinctive tradition, in which a stimulating communal life is itself the most potent instrument of education.  But, in its original form, this tradition was paternalist, and it was bound up with the existence of a privileged class and a feudal, rather than industrial, type of society.  The problem to-day is how to translate the ideal of the cultivated gentleman into democratic terms and to combine an intensive and relentless pursuit of excellence with a new sensitiveness to the demands of social justice.

This will take different forms in ' Oxbridge ' and in ' Redbrick.' In ' Oxbridge ' the need is to widen opportunities of access and to make the university more sensitive to the structural changes going on in the world and the new currents of thought by which the world is moved, so that it will in no degree seem to remain the preserve of the gentry or of the Established Church.  Communal life there is already strong and lively; it needs to be widened and varied. In the ' Redbrick ' universities on the other hand, communal life has often been meagre or non-existent, and they need to be humanized. In one way or another, whether by a vast increase of residential life, or by the development of Unions, Refectories and Staff Houses, they need to become genuine communities. Yet, that ' Redbrick ' should content itself with imitating ' Oxbridge ' is no more desirable than that the Glasgow or Manchester student should be urged to speak with an Oxford accent.

Any university situated in a large industrial city has positive opportunities and responsibilities of its own.  It should cultivate a somewhat greater austerity, and a closer touch with its environment, than is practicable for ' Oxbridge.'  It cannot, if it will, enjoy all the advantages of the cloister and it should make the most of those of the market place.

The relation between the university and the world is discussed specifically in Chapter IX.  When the world is in convulsion, mental as well as physical, it is unthinkable that the university should go on its way with objectives, standards and methods unchanged.  Yet it cannot be satisfied simply to reflect the world or to be ' a subordinate mechanism in the cultural organization of the State.'  It has its own values to maintain and its own standards

U

demanding allegiance. Its worth to the world depends on its maintaining the liberty of prophesying, if need be in the teeth of the world. Its peculiar virtue imperatively requires for it a high degree of autonomy.

In this country university autonomy depends, not on law, but on a tacit convention, that is, on a widely diffused sense of 'what is done' and 'what is not done.' The continuance of this convention will depend on the enlightenment, on the one hand, of ministers and civil servants, and, above all, of public opinion, and on the other hand of universities and their members. Guildsman and layman have each his rights and each his contribution to make. The only healthy relation between them is one of partnership. In a democratic community it is essential that public opinion should be educated to appreciate the function of universities and to understand that they can only perform it if given elbow-room. But to get elbow-room they must command public confidence; and such confidence has to be earned. Autonomy must be combined with responsibility. On their side, they must be reasonably quick to put their own house in order where it requires it, and to adjust themselves to a changing and explosive environment. It is in this perspective that we have discussed the relation of the universities and the State and of the civic universities with their regions.

Between the partners then a balance must be preserved; and, in this respect, our national habit of pressing no principle to its extreme consequences is useful, witness the constitution of the British commonwealth of nations. Yet there are some questions which should not be slurred over, but should be asked insistently and in trenchant terms. For instance, should universities persevere with the activities represented by their Education and Extra-Mural Departments? They have for some time engaged in these, but for the most part, they have done so rather half-heartedly. Here they should make a decisive choice. If these activities are really 'sub-university' in quality or are outside their proper function, they should gradually withdraw from them. Otherwise they should commit themselves to them more fully and energetically than they have yet done. We contend that, for both Departments, the second alternative is the right one.

Finally we come to the special concerns of Christians. For instance has Theology any legitimate place in our universities to-day? Once it was dominant, 'the queen of the sciences,' which gave the law to all others. It has long ceased to be so and clearly cannot be so again within any measurable period. But is there any other basis on which it is admissible at all? Must it not be dominant or nothing? Neither the framers of university constitutions nor the theologians themselves have so far put forward any clear principle on which a third alternative can be grounded.

One possible basis we have rejected. That is the reduction of theology to a neutral study of religion, designed to assimilate it to other academic studies. Theology is essentially the study of the implications of Revelation, within the context of the community which is founded on that Revelation; theological writings are addressed by committed men to other committed men. But theology, so conceived, is open to the charge of disqualifying bias. Such an approach, it is urged, is totally unfitted to a university. Is not theology then in ' Redbrick ' an interloper whose intrusion must be resisted, and in ' Oxbridge ' an anomalous survival, defensible if at all only on the ground of prescription?

We have tried to face this indictment candidly. But our reply is twofold. First, in this instance commitment is no disqualification, because it is inevitable and in no way peculiar to the theologian. On the main issue—whether there has been a revelation of God in Christ or not—neutrality is a figment. If genuine, such a revelation affects life at every point. Decision cannot be evaded. A detachment which affects to be non-committal is, in practice, denial. Secondly, intellectual integrity is possible for the contemporary theologian and is incumbent on him just as it is for any other university teacher. His attitude should be quite different from that of the totalitarian or of some earlier theologians. He is committed to the central fact of the Revelation and not to any precise formulation of it. Even as regards the central fact, there should be no refusal to re-examine or to give due weight to new objections or difficulties. For him there is no forbidden ground which he must not tread, no ark of the covenant which it is impious to touch, no censorship to which he must submit. But this does not impair his certainty and his commitment. In that, he is like a long and happily married husband who is sure of his wife's faithfulness. He will close his eyes to no evidence adduced; but he enters on any enquiry with a serene confidence, which is rational and not irrational.

But while Faculties of Theology can vindicate their right to a place in the university, they need to widen immensely the current conception of their function. The professional training of clergy and ministers for their future work and the furtherance of biblical scholarship are only a part of that function. They have also a responsibility to the whole body of university students and to the work of their colleagues in other Faculties which is, as yet, little fulfilled. To devise ways of discharging it is their urgent task.

But apart from the special case of the Faculty of Theology, our chief concern is with the practical duties and opportunities of Christian teachers or administrators. As such, we shall never be able to play any creative part unless we begin by realizing vividly the false position in which we now are. Clearly our Christian faith should be the unifying principle and the supreme motive force of all our main activities. But in most of our professional work it is not, and, as things are at the moment, perhaps it cannot be. That God the Father Almighty is maker of heaven and earth, that our Lord Jesus Christ came down from heaven for us men and for our salvation, that He was crucified and rose again and will come again with glory to judge the quick and the dead, that God the Holy Ghost is the lord and giver of life, and that we are to look for the life of the world to come; these may be sacred convictions in our private lives, but in the common life and study of the university in which we take part they are at most 'inert truths.' Its tacit assumptions and habitual practices are much what they would be if we were not Christians at all. In their daily work physicists, biologists, engineers, historians, philosophers, professors of language and literature or of medicine 'have no need of that hypothesis,' and, in Rome, we find ourselves automatically doing as Rome does. When the late Lord Birkenhead once attempted incongruously to champion the souls of Christian peoples, he was rudely greeted with 'Chuck it, Smith!' So long as we are involved in this double life, any commendation by us of a Christian outlook is open to a like, shattering, rejoinder.

To transform this secularist routine in which we are now enmeshed is a gigantic long-term task and no quick or spectacular success is to be expected. But the one thing needful is to make a beginning. If utopianism is a deadly heresy, fatalism is deadlier still. In this respect indeed, the university arena is only one particular sector in a battle front which is world-wide. Everywhere the large-scale activities of modern society are terribly curtailing the individual's sense of personal responsibility. This is probably the most sinister tendency of our time; unless it is checked, it must lead to what is, in effect, a servile society. That upshot can only be avoided, if there is developed in the individual a sense of responsibility of a new type, and if techniques can be found for making it effective. By that is meant a responsibility for the corporate activities of the large-scale society, or societies, of which he is a member and for its system of routines. These things, as we said earlier, are not mechanical but result from the interaction of myriads of wills. The utmost influence of any individual on the whole system is necessarily slight, but, to treat it as non-existent, is an example of the fatalistic fallacy in its most poisonous form. To emphasize and to act on this distinction, is a matter of life and death.

If these things are true, some of our immediate practical tasks become clear. The first is to identify one another and to get together. It is not creditable to us that, so often, we have little idea who our fellow Christians are. If we are to attempt any creative job, we must be 'in form,' and we must therefore deepen our discipleship. A more or less dutiful conformity with an inherited pattern of thinking, living and worshipping is a wretchedly inadequate equipment for any initiative in 'Christianizing' the university. We must also enlarge our understanding of our faith and make ourselves 'lay theologians.' But we cannot do these things effectively in isolation. There is a 'Student Christian Movement,' which does a great deal for students in just these ways. As yet, we have no 'Don's Christian Movement,' and it is for urgent consideration whether we do not need to create one, different as some of its techniques might need to be.

But the most immediate need is that Christian members of staff should come together in groups in every separate university or college, for it is there that effective action is possible. Every group should survey the working of its own *Alma Mater*. Its members should ask themselves what are the points at which the existing 'set-up' transgresses Christian values, and what clues to improvement Christian insight gives. They should do this as persons who will be responsible for trying to give practical effect to their conclusions. Their diagnosis should be only a preliminary to treatment.

But, by themselves, such groups could not do very much to change the character of their universities, and they should take the initiative in entering into communication with other groups, whose philosophies of life differ from theirs. They should do so, in the first

instance, with those to whom their affinity is closest, with a view
to common action. They should ascertain what is the greatest
measure of ' christianization ' which will commend itself to non-
Christian colleagues without whose genuine and unforced co-operation nothing can rightly be done. But they should also approach
those colleagues whose standpoint is remote, for full and frank discussion of their real differences. They should not do this in any
eristic temper, but in order to increase mutual understanding,
desiring to get as well as to give. If such discussions were carried
out on a deep level and with a view to action on the basis of the
highest common factor attained, much might be accomplished in a
few years.

In advocating such co-operation, we must face one last misgiving.
Some of our fellow-Christians may say to us, ' However unintentionally, you are in fact " selling the pass." You talk much of
" christianizing " but the actual reforms you suggest have little to
do even with theism. They are such as the humanist also often wants
and wants on precisely the same grounds as you. You advocate them
on grounds of natural reason and not of any distinctive, biblical
insight. They are possibly desirable in themselves, possibly even
compatible with Christianity, but Christianity is not their driving-
force, nor in your picture is God really the keystone of the arch.'

In such a charge there cannot but be substance. But, in spite of
faults of execution, we adhere to our principle. The relation of
Christians to such reforms is dual, and health depends on holding
firmly to both sides. On the one hand, the reforms in which we
combine with others are certainly sub-Christian. We must never
confuse the fifth-best with the best, and we must never lose sight of
the mixed motives which inspire improvements and the mixed consequences which will result from them. Sooner or later our best
planned schemes will ' gang agley.' It is our business to emphasize
this, to prophesy against them and to puncture all complacency in
ourselves and in others. On the other hand, in corporate action we
must adopt the principle of the half-loaf. Often the best course
practically possible, i.e. the best for which the genuine consent of a
sufficient number of people is obtainable is, in a Christian perspective, only the fifth-best conceivable. Yet it is our Christian duty
to fight for it passionately against an alternative which is only the
sixth-best; and often, in so doing, to co-operate with others who
see in it no flaw at all.

Such groups of Christian teachers in universities would be far

from being ' pressure-groups,' as ordinarily understood. Their aim
would be, not to manipulate nor to cajole others, but to appeal to
reason and will. On these lines they should contribute some new
reality and depth to the family life of the university. Only in this
spirit can they hope to give any constructive lead to the university
and respond to what, to-day, appears to be an authentic call of
God.

# INDEX